D1174646

THE
CUSTOMER
SUCCESS
ECONOMY

THE
CUSTOMER
SUCCESS
ECONOMY

WHY EVERY ASPECT OF
YOUR BUSINESS MODEL NEEDS
A **PARADIGM SHIFT**

N I C K
MEHTA

A L L I S O N
PICKENS

WILEY

Copyright © 2020 by Gainsight, Inc. All rights reserved.

Published by John Wiley & Sons, Inc., Hoboken, New Jersey.
Published simultaneously in Canada.

No part of this publication may be reproduced, stored in a retrieval system, or transmitted in any form or by any means, electronic, mechanical, photocopying, recording, scanning, or otherwise, except as permitted under Section 107 or 108 of the 1976 United States Copyright Act, without either the prior written permission of the Publisher, or authorization through payment of the appropriate per-copy fee to the Copyright Clearance Center, Inc., 222 Rosewood Drive, Danvers, MA 01923, (978) 750–8400, fax (978) 646–8600, or on the Web at www.copyright.com. Requests to the Publisher for permission should be addressed to the Permissions Department, John Wiley & Sons, Inc., 111 River Street, Hoboken, NJ 07030, (201) 748–6011, fax (201) 748–6008, or online at http://www.wiley.com/go/permissions.

Limit of Liability/Disclaimer of Warranty: While the publisher and author have used their best efforts in preparing this book, they make no representations or warranties with respect to the accuracy or completeness of the contents of this book and specifically disclaim any implied warranties of merchantability or fitness for a particular purpose. No warranty may be created or extended by sales representatives or written sales materials. The advice and strategies contained herein may not be suitable for your situation. You should consult with a professional where appropriate. Neither the publisher nor author shall be liable for any loss of profit or any other commercial damages, including but not limited to special, incidental, consequential, or other damages.

For general information on our other products and services or for technical support, please contact our Customer Care Department within the United States at (800) 762–2974, outside the United States at (317) 572–3993 or fax (317) 572–4002.

Wiley publishes in a variety of print and electronic formats and by print-on-demand. Some material included with standard print versions of this book may not be included in e-books or in print-on-demand. If this book refers to media such as a CD or DVD that is not included in the version you purchased, you may download this material at http://booksupport.wiley.com. For more information about Wiley products, visit www.wiley.com.

Library of Congress Cataloging-in-Publication Data is Available:
ISBN 9781119572763 (Hardcover)
ISBN 9781119572756 (ePDF)
ISBN 9781119572732 (ePub)

Cover Design: Hayley Cromwell
Cover Image: Carlo Nasisse | Hed Hi Media

Printed in the United States of America

10 9 8 7 6 5 4 3 2 1

Contents

Foreword

"The term *Customer Success* has become a buzzword in today's business world."

The statement that I wrote four years ago to begin the foreword of *Customer Success: How Innovative Companies Are Reducing Churn and Growing Recurring Revenue* now seems antiquated in 2020. After all, Customer Success is light years past buzzword status these days.

In 2016, most people in the business world, even those in cutting-edge, pure-play SaaS companies, were unfamiliar with the concept of Customer Success. It was crystal clear that the economy was rapidly changing. The old model of customer service—reactive, costly, bare-minimum customer service—was no longer going to work now that customers were holding all the cards.

Nick, Dan, and Lincoln's book was the perfect book at the perfect time. It gave forward-thinking leaders a blueprint to adapting to the changing market. It taught them the necessity of Customer Success as a strategy *and* an organizational function. It gave them the tools to create a Customer Success Management team from scratch and to lay a path to grow their careers in an emerging field.

Four years later, dog-eared copies of that book are on the desks of tens of thousands of leaders and practitioners of Customer Success around the globe. I've even seen it on several CEOs' shelves! It's been translated into four languages and has helped fuel a movement that's become one of the fastest-growing emerging jobs on the planet. There's a pretty simple reason for it: churn.

As the subtitle of the book suggests, *Customer Success* was focused on two deeply intertwined topics: "Reducing Churn and Growing Recurring

Revenue." It was about staving off the silent killer of subscription businesses and developing a defensive strategy.

In 2016, most people still didn't understand Customer Success beyond customer service. Where customer service is a necessary but reactive aspect of customers successfully using a product, Customer Success involves a more holistic understanding of a customer's business objectives. If you were in Customer Success four years ago, it's easy to imagine you spent a lot of time just explaining your job and its value.

Today, nobody needs to be convinced of the value the customers create for their business or the business imperative of proactively nurturing and deepening those relationships. But what's the next step? Why this new book? Why now?

It's become clear that too many businesses stopped reading after "Reducing Churn." The conversation ended with, "I'm not selling anything." In far too many cases, they stopped at Customer Success Management.

As Nick and Allison make the case in this book, Customer Success has a second phase of evolution that goes far beyond churn and far beyond CSM. In this new evolution, Customer Success is infused into every part of your company and is fulfilled in every interaction between every team member and customer—at every level.

Customer Success 2.0 isn't a defensive strategy. It's all about the offense—unlocking your customer's huge, hidden growth potential through people, processes, and technology built for 2020 and beyond.

There's a quote from Steve Jobs that I love: "You have to start with the customer experience and work backward to the technology. You can't start with the technology and figure out where you are going to try to sell it."

I think the same is true with books as well—you have to start with the reader and work backward to the book. In 2016, the reader was a Customer Success neophyte, likely learning about the need for a new way of business for the first time. But in 2020, the reader of Customer Success 2.0 already knows the imperative. They know how to run a CSM team. They know how to fight churn.

But they need to know how to scale Customer Success across the entire organization; how to go from Customer Success to customer growth; how to build Customer Success into the product itself; how to unify customer data; and most importantly, how to bring humanity back into technology.

I look forward to seeing well-worn copies of this book on the shelves of the next generation of Customer Success innovators.

Maria Martinez

Executive vice president & chief customer experience officer at Cisco

PART I

Why Customer Success Became Standard

1

Customer Success: What It Is and Why It Affects Everything

When you are finished changing, you are finished.

—Benjamin Franklin

What really matters in business? Every day we receive hundreds of emails, calls, and meeting invitations; knowing what's important can be a challenge. And every 24 hours, the world around us changes in infinite ways. Dissecting the most important trends can be hard. If you're like us, picking out the signal from the noise is a huge chunk of the job of leading a business. And it can be overwhelming.

That quest for what matters most in business brought both of us to the field of Customer Success, from different starting points. We'll each tell the story of how a discovery of Customer Success pushed our own thinking on what mattered in business. And we think these stories will resonate with you. Let's start with Nick.

Making and Selling Aren't the Only Things That Matter Anymore, Dad

When I was 8 years old, I vividly remember a "take your child to work day" with my entrepreneur dad. The thing I recall best from that event is him saying, "Nick, there are just two jobs that matter in business: the jobs of the people who make the stuff you sell and the jobs of the people who sell the stuff you make; everything else is overhead."

As oversimplified as that may sound, my dad was accurately describing the business model of pretty much every major corporation from 1900 to 2000. Making stuff and selling stuff drove the global economy. The sale was a one-time activity, and anything "post-sale" was a cost to the company (customer service centers, repair people dealing with broken machines, fleets of company vehicles, etc.). My dad's advice fared well for me in my early career as a leader in enterprise software.

Then in 2008, during the depth of the financial crisis, I was hired to run a company where we sold our software "as a service" (SaaS). I was finally in the cloud! I remember my first day meeting the employees and recalling my dad's advice. I wanted to immediately talk to the leaders of Sales and Engineering, the people who "sold stuff" and "made stuff."

I also met Steve, the person responsible for making sure our existing customers were successful. I thought to myself at the time, "Great. Steve's got that covered so I don't have to worry about it."

But what I learned over the four years of running that company was that the SaaS business model had fundamentally shifted power to our customers. They weren't "buying" stuff anymore, they were renting it. This changed the way I needed to operate as a CEO. Making and selling still mattered a lot. But our customers now had the "power of the purse." If they weren't satisfied, they could leave us at any time. As the CEO of this customer-powered company, I ended up spending way more time with Steve than I did with his counterparts in Sales and Engineering.

And that shift that I observed toward customer-centricity is why I was excited to join Gainsight and help launch the company in 2013, with our mission being to enable businesses to embrace Customer Success as the leading strategic differentiator of the next phase of the economy. And if you follow me online, you know I am fired up about the Customer Success movement!

But, that's not just my story and my irrational enthusiasm. That's an industry story—actually, that's the entire economy's story. Up until now, the history of business can be condensed down to two phases: the making stuff phase (starting with the industrial revolution), followed by the selling stuff phase (the Internet has pushed this last phase by making it possible to market your stuff globally, instantly, constantly). Now we've moved into a third phase. We still need to make and sell, but that's not enough. Our customers in the modern economy are looking for success—for their goals to be achieved—not just for "stuff" to be purchased.

And if you're reading this, it's probably your story, too. You may be dealing with "vendors" that don't seem to have a clue about what you really want. You might be running a sales organization and realizing that the end-of-quarter heroics can't go on much longer. You may be in the Customer Success profession and trying to get your company to wake up to the movement.

But no matter who you are, you probably cringe at the tools and systems you use at work, only to hop into an Uber or Lyft and be magically whisked wherever you want once you step outside of the office.

In short, we all know the story needs to change.

The Business of Business Is Helping People

Here's how Allison found herself at the dawn of the Customer Success movement, which fundamentally changed her outlook on business.

When I was in college, I spent much of my day poring over ancient philosophical texts, searching for the secrets of "the good life" and for the pillars of a healthy society. Like my peers, I hoped to do good in the world in some way. When an internship on Capitol Hill proved to be more about mailing form responses to constituents—leveraging a mechanical contraption to replicate my Senator's signature—than creating innovation, I realized that my eagerness to build things that helped people might be better suited at that point for the private sector.

Two subsequent jobs in management consulting and private equity investing offered an incredible bootcamp in business knowledge and membership in a community of talented, inspiring people. But something nagged at me. How could I translate the skills I was learning into the positive societal impact that motivated me at my core? In an attempt to get back to my roots of trying to "do good," I recruited a friend to help build a tech product with the aspiration of helping industrial workers—often underdogs in our economy—showcase their skills to get jobs more easily. But the market wasn't ripe. I was back to the drawing board and told myself I was too naive to think that business could be anything but that—business.

Soon after, I met Nick after my old investment firm led an early funding round, when Gainsight had about 30 customers in a new market called Customer Success. As I learned about the industry, I soon realized that this was a new group of underdogs. Here was a fledgling community of people—many of them women—who knew they had greater value than their companies and investors recognized. Tectonic shifts in the market were in their favor. They just needed some support.

I soon joined their ranks as I took on the Customer Success team at Gainsight. We incubated ideas for how to make our own customers successful and shared the results of our experiments—the good and the bad—with the CS community in hundreds of blog posts and podcasts. (In one experiment, we accidentally sent a "welcome email" to all of our clients, even the tenured ones. Whoops.) We also learned a great deal from our clients and other friends in the field, who conducted their own experiments and gave feedback on our ideas as well.

The biggest learning—to my happy surprise—was that doing good didn't have to be at odds with building a great business. In fact, it could be a differentiator. Genuinely helping your clients propels stronger revenue growth, market leadership, profitability, consistency, employee retention, and valuation multiples—as we witnessed across the Customer Success community. Now the underdogs (CS professionals) were helping other historical underdogs (clients) and generating incredible business results.

So back to the question: What really matters in business? Doing good for the human beings who are your clients.

That might sound soft. But actually, it's the hard reality of business today. This book is about how to compete and win in an ever-more-challenging business environment. Notably, it's not about "making your clients happy." It's about making them successful so that you can succeed. Let's discuss what we mean by that.

Why Customer Success Is About More Than Happy Customers

Not surprisingly, the Internet is the reason for the change in the relationship between customers and businesses. Everyone knows the basics: whether we are at home as "consumers" or at work as "businesspeople," we demand a great customer experience. This concept is so commonly said that it's now trite.

But in some ways, talk of customer experience or "making customers happy" is missing the core point. The power of the Internet didn't just empower customers to be "satisfied." Customers in the modern world demand that their goals are achieved. The fancy management consulting term for this is *desired outcomes*.

What do we mean by outcomes? Well, whenever anyone, a consumer or a businessperson, looks at doing business with another company, they have a goal in mind. Maybe they are on a trip and trying to get from one part of a city to another. Maybe they are hoping to get in better shape. Or perhaps they are an executive looking to drive more engagement from their teammates.

Whether you consider B2C (business-to-consumer) or B2B (business-to-business), the trend toward outcomes is unstoppable. If you are on a trip in New York, Uber and Lyft turn a product (car) into an outcome (getting you from point A to point B). If you are on a health kick, Peloton turns a physical device (bike) into a subscription service (spinning training—with great music!). If you are the executive at work, Workday turns a category of "Human Resources Software" into an SaaS solution.

In all these cases, customers are no longer stuck with the vendors they bought (sorry, Dad!) because technology has transformed the category for customers. They have choice. They have mobility. They are now at the core of the business model. Just as Copernicus showed us that the Earth isn't the center of the universe, vendors are now realizing that clients are at the center of theirs. Figures 1.1 and 1.2 illustrate this change.

Customer expectations are higher, customer power is greater, and holding onto customers is harder because they have so much choice. That

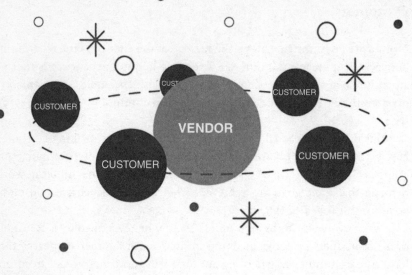

Figure 1.1

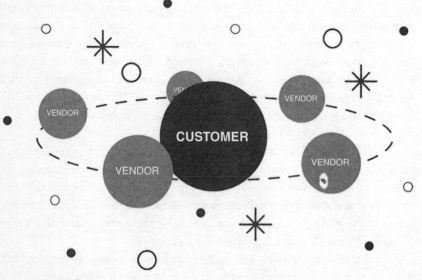

Figure 1.2

availability of options has changed the way customers think about vendors, and it has upended the way you have to act if you want to retain your customers. If you're not operating from a customer-centric playbook, you will lose. Your strategy should help you make sure your customers are actually using what they bought from you, that you are giving them the sort of customer service they demand, that you are expanding the relationship, and in the course of all of this, making your customers your advocates.

Do all this and you'll join the companies that are growing most rapidly through Customer Success. Shrug it off and we can guarantee you the market will pass you by.

So Why Do You Need This Book?

Our first book, *Customer Success: How Innovative Companies Are Reducing Churn and Growing Recurring Revenue*, laid out the basics of the Customer Success approach to business. If you read our first book, you're probably wondering why—or even if—you need another book on the same subject.

New fields change a lot. Remember how we thought about the Internet in 1999 versus now? Besides cat pictures, pretty much everything else is different.

In the same vein, Customer Success is evolving rapidly. Think of our first book, *Customer Success*, as the foundation of Customer Success practices. But what has fundamentally shifted is Customer Success has gone from a job function to a company-wide movement. We predicted this in the first book, and in this edition we'll share many examples of the idea becoming reality. And in this book we are going to argue that that movement is changing the nature of our economy overall.

Customer Success and the Economy

That's a pretty bold claim, we admit. But what's happening in this third wave of the economy is that the power is fundamentally shifting to customers. If you think about it, power is all about who has the upper hand. In the first phase of the economy ("making stuff"), products were novel. Think about Henry Ford coming to your town and driving by everyone else on horses and buggies. The product itself was novel.

But consider products today. If you want to buy marketing software for your office, you have thousands of solutions to choose from. Looking for meal delivery? Choose from Grubhub, Doordash, UberEats—the list goes on. Trying out a new subscription clothing service? Google the concept and find hundreds of alternatives. Want an intelligent speaker? Choose from Google, Amazon, Sonos, and many more. Remember when Fitbit was really novel? Now tracking is built into everything.

Then the economy shifted to "selling." With lots of choices, the challenge was finding what you wanted. One big innovation in this front was retail. Walmart made it so you could get the products you wanted in your neighborhood. Telesales allowed you to buy from a catalog through the magic of your phone (think about how dated that sounds now). Shipping companies like UPS and FedEx let you get packages to your door. And Amazon, of course, took all this to the next level.

But think again about the choices you have in how to buy. The number of options is almost intimidating. Amazon Prime Same Day? Instacart? Walmart delivery service? Maybe 3D print the object in your home? Do you want to buy via mobile or web, or maybe through your smart speaker? Selling stuff is no longer differentiated.

With infinite choice in products and infinite ways to buy, the scarce commodity is now the customer. So making sure the customer is successful isn't just a job or a strategy—it's truly the economy.

In this first chapter we'll take a quick look at Customer Success just to establish the basics.

A Little History Lesson: Customer Success vs. Customer Service vs. Account Management

Here's where the shift from old business thinking to current-day practices really comes into focus.

Customer Service has always been and continues to be an important part of business. When a customer needs assistance, how can you help them quickly, effectively, and empathetically? Similarly, Account Management in some businesses is required to help customers find more ways to do business with the vendor ("sell more stuff").

But Customer Service and Account Management aren't sufficient. The missing link in the new economy is that the customer makes their decisions about whether to stay with the vendor or spend more based on whether their outcome was achieved. So you need to get them to that outcome. However, in many companies, Customer Service is there to react to client needs, and Account Management is ready to sell, but no one is *proactively* getting the client to value. (You will hear the word "proactive" a great deal in Customer Success circles.) After the client has purchased and before they are ready to buy more, who is making sure the customer keeps moving forward? Customer Service is ready to pick up the phone when it rings, but who is taking the initiative to call the customer to help them achieve more? You might think that Account Management is the "outbound team," but their focus is different. Kevin Meeks, Vice President, Global CSM and Renewals, at publicly traded data software company Splunk, phrased the difference succinctly. "When I think of account management, I think of commercial selling. When I think of success management, I'm thinking about advocacy and things we're doing to make the customer successful, without a focus on short-term sales." Customer Success is the missing link that helps your clients achieve their desired outcomes.

A true, company-wide focus on Customer Success ensures that *your customers reach their goals through using your product while having a great experience.* In order for that to happen, you need three things: (1) an *organization* waking up every day and thinking about driving more value for customers, (2) a set of company-wide *programs* to help address issues across the company that impede Customer Success, and (3) a *culture* that reinforces that the customer is at the center of the company.

Why Customer Success Isn't Optional

Customer Success is a natural outcome of massive changes in the economy, including but not limited to the following facts:

- Globalization and technology have dropped the barrier to entry for businesses.
- Lowered barriers to entry allow new entrants to disrupt almost every established category.
- New entrants have created lower-friction business models, which makes it easier for customers to try and buy—especially with shorter-term pricing, granular consumption, and easier deployment.

- This lower friction makes it easier for try-and-buy customers to say "Bye!" and leave—which means customers have more power and choice than ever before. And they choose to stay with vendors who deliver the outcomes and success they want.

The only real question you have to address regarding implementing Customer Success–focused practices, then, is whether your business will react quickly enough to survive.

And if you're not motivated yet, let us try the carrot and the stick, because both apply in Customer Success.

On the positive side, Customer Success creates a big opportunity for businesses in four dimensions:

1. **Opportunity for Predictability:** Traditional "one-time sale" business models were great in one respect in that you got the client's money upfront. But on the other hand, you always had to find another client to win. The recurring nature of the Customer Success model means more stability in your business long-term. Because of that, shareholders love subscription and cloud financials and value them at higher levels than their comparable peers.
2. **Opportunity for Growth:** Companies today have more levers to pull for sales than prospecting cold leads. They can grow by actually delivering on the vision they pitched in the sales cycle, which allows them to expand their existing client relationships and attract new buyers through warm referrals from happy clients.
3. **Opportunity for Innovation:** Customer Success and the data you get from a deep client relationship allows you to grow your business like never before. Perhaps you offer software for small business management, and you then realize that your clients also have a challenge accepting payments. With the intimacy of the Customer Success model, you are able to more rapidly launch new offerings for your clients.
4. **Opportunity of Balance:** Finally, we'll argue throughout the book that companies that adopt the Customer Success model are just better. They balance the needs of all of their stakeholders—customers, teammates, community, shareholders—in a way that works for everyone.

But if you're not motivated by that, let's look at the other side of the coin—the four risks of not investing in Customer Success:

1. **Churn Risk:** Leaders of modern businesses are realizing their clients' fundamental expectations are changing. No longer do customers want a "product" or "service"—they want their problem to be solved. So your job has changed as a company. Moreover, in new business models like SaaS and cloud, customers have all the power. If they aren't achieving value or "success," they will move on.

2. **Capital Risk:** Investors expect you to invest in your clients, because they know that drives returns. Whether you're planning to raise money, go public, or run a successful board meeting, Customer Success becomes a corporate imperative.

3. **Competition Risk:** Whether you adopt the Customer Success model or not, your competition will. And that differentiation will start showing in terms of the leaders and laggards in categories.

4. **Employee Risk:** Employees increasingly want to join companies that truly deliver on a premise of bettering others' lives. The rise of purpose-driven organizations means that if you don't truly help your clients, your employees will go elsewhere.

What You Can Expect from This Book

The nature of the economy has changed drastically since Nick was a little kid proudly grasping a tiny, toy-filled briefcase with his dad, and even since Allison left the private equity world about a decade ago. Customers have more power than ever before. With the advent of cloud-based technologies, most customers can—and will—change vendors whenever they want. This is becoming as true in the B2B arena as it is in the B2C arena. Where does that leave you? You now have a clear mandate to make sure your customers succeed with your product or service. This new world compels you to put Customer Success at the top of your priority list.

Most of us over the course of our working lives have had a moment or two when we wondered why we're working so hard. We've certainly had plenty of those moments when crammed into an airplane seat, flying off for yet another round of meetings. We knew that work was about something more than making money, but we were told not to talk about those things.

Well, the business world is catching up. We're realizing that we can win in business while being "human-first." Customer Success is simply realizing that your company is made up of humans, and your customers are humans, and you're all just trying to win together.

This book will help you figure out how to win, together with your clients. Part I focuses on the evolution of the Customer Success economy: What does it look like now and how did it get to where it is today? Part II explores the kind of company that this CS economy requires: What is required from every function? And Part III discusses implementation: What steps should you take to roll out CS at your company?

You won't just hear our point of view. You'll hear from dozens of CEOs, investors, chief customer officers, and other thought leaders on these topics—hailing from the diverse worlds of the Fortune 500, private equity, venture capital, and Silicon Valley—who offered to be interviewed so that we could share their perspectives directly with you.

We hope that by the end we will have planted a few seeds and also offered you some fertilizer to help those seeds grow. In other words, perhaps while reading this book, you'll reframe your view of business, even a little bit, and be on your way toward implementing Customer Success at your company.

If you haven't read our first book (or want a refresher), take a look at the recap below of the Ten Laws of Customer Success, a primer for what CS is all about. Otherwise, we'll see you in Chapter 2, where we'll look at how the Customer Success mindset is showing up in all sorts of areas outside Silicon Valley.

The Ten Laws of Customer Success

Here's a brief overview of the Ten Laws of Customer Success. For the full explanation and practical examples, head over to our website at gainsight.com/resource/the-10-laws-of-customer-success and download the booklet.

Law #1: Customer Success Is a Top-Down, Company-Wide Commitment

We introduced this concept in 2016, and we believe it even more strongly today. Customer Success is a true business revolution, and it's here to stay. Done well, it drives real value to your business's bottom line. If you're not on board yet, you will be soon. The demands of today's customers and changes to the economy mean that your company literally cannot survive long-term without making a solid commitment to Customer Success. Getting started is fairly easy as long as you keep in mind that Customer Success starts at the top. For it to work, it must be a company-wide commitment. The days of CEOs being able to say that customers are their top priority and then acting in exactly the opposite manner are over. By the way, this first law is the inspiration for us writing this book.

Law #2: Sell to the Right Customer

As a growth company, your entire organization must focus on selling to the right customer and being completely aligned with your product market fit (PMF). If your customer isn't the right customer, the impact on your organization can be disastrous. The wrong customers can inhibit your organization and take you away from efforts that drive success, efficiency, and scale. (On the other hand, occasionally a wrong customer can become a critical design partner to help you extend your use case and PMF—but only if you have honest dialogue with them and act on the feedback they give you.)

Law #3: The Natural Tendency for Customers Is Toward Churn

Customers and vendors start off their relationship like two boats side by side in the middle of a lake. If both boats are unoccupied, they will begin to drift apart. Eventually, it's highly likely that the two boats will end up far apart, perhaps even bumping into opposite shores.

How could you change that natural tendency? Simple: Put a person in one of the boats and give them a pair of oars. Better yet, put people with oars into each boat. Change is the constant. People change in vendor and customer companies: Business models change. Products change. Leadership and direction change. And on it goes. Only well-designed, proactive interaction on the part of one or both companies will overcome the natural drift caused by constant change.

When your company makes a meaningful commitment to Customer Success, you also commit to counteracting that natural drift.

Law #4: Your Customers Expect You to Make Them Wildly Successful

Customers don't buy your solution just for its features and functions. They buy your offering (and buy into the relationship with you) because they want to achieve a business objective. They are assuming you will drive their success. And, by the time the sales cycle is complete, their expectations are *really* high. Don't waste time complaining about the fairness of this attitude; just acknowledge and work with it.

Delivering wild success requires you to ask three fundamental questions:

1. How does your customer measure success?
2. Is the customer achieving that value (or are they at least on a realistic path to achieving it)?
3. What's the customer's experience with you along the way?

Law #5: Relentlessly Monitor and Manage Customer Health

Customer Health is at the heart of Customer Success. It not only *informs* your actions, it actually *drives* appropriate action when used properly. Customer Health is to Customer Success what the sales pipeline is to a sales VP's planning info—the predictor of future customer behavior. So just as sales VPs manage through their pipeline, Customer Success teams must manage through customer health. Monitoring and managing customer health is a core activity for Customer Success teams. It must be done and done well—even relentlessly.

Law #6: You Can No Longer Build Loyalty through Personal Relationships

One of the values of modern technology is that it makes our products much easier to buy for our customers. This almost always leads to a "long tail" of lower-value customers who, in most companies, end up being ignored. The best companies will figure out how to effectively and efficiently manage this large base of customers.

Software-as-a-service vendors realize that they need to systematically create programs that allow for interaction between them and their customers. Most SaaS companies need to address how to service the largest portion of their customer base in a technically friendly way while at the same time reducing the need for labor-intensive ways of building relationships.

Depending on your product and service, you will decide how to create a customer experience that develops a connection with your company. Once outlined, that customer experience needs to be captured, driven, and continually refined by your Customer Success team. Keep in mind that customer experience must be a top company priority; it can't be delivered by individual relationships with your customers or even by a single department.

This reads like common business practice, yet most organizations do not have a cohesive plan (key word being *cohesive*) to deliver the optimal customer experience.

Law #7: Product Must Be Priority Number One

The key to customer retention, client satisfaction, and scaling the support and service organizations is a well-designed product that's combined with a best-in-class customer experience. Consumer technology has changed the way we work, as well as our customers' expectations. To ensure you have created a product that meets the needs and expectations of your customers, create a client experience team that focuses on building out programs in a client engagement framework—one that drives community among clients, encourages engagement at all levels and roles of the customer base, and provides clear feedback loops that inform product improvements. The data about product usage and adoption should be available to everyone—from the Product team to Marketing to Customer Success. In addition, increasingly Customer Success teams are using in-application messages and guidance in the product to scale their Customer Success operations.

It's also important to note that, in the new customer economy, we need to think very differently about how we build products. Gone are the days of big, monolithic applications. Today's world demands building blocks that enable the land-and-expand model. This is the only way to take advantage of the major investment we are all making in Customer Success.

Law #8: Obsessively Improve Time to Value

Why do people or companies buy? They think they'll get value from their purchase. If you're a consumer, this might mean spending a lot at a fine restaurant because you hope to get an outstanding meal. In that scenario, you find out pretty much right away if the expenditure was worth it: The food is either delicious or not. Based on that, you can decide whether you'll return.

But when you're selling business products and services, it's often tough to show value so close to the expenditure. Buyers know that, but they still expect to see value in a reasonable time frame. For SaaS vendors, that time frame is the length of the subscription: If the customer hasn't seen real value by the time renewal discussions begin, they're far less likely to renew. Working against the vendor is how long it might take to get the customer up and running with the solution. Obsessively improving time to value is the way to address this challenge.

And the time-to-value point is important throughout the customer lifecycle, not just in the initial onboarding phase. Every time a new release happens, for example, the process starts again in helping the customer derive value from the new features as quickly as possible. Obsessing over time-to-value needs to become a constant mindset for successful companies.

Law #9: Deeply Understand the Details of Churn and Retention

Successful subscription-based companies must understand the details of churn and retention in order to maintain and accelerate their revenue growth. Nothing slows your company's growth rate faster than having revenue from your installed base evaporate. As your installed base revenues grow, even a 1% increase in churn can make a huge difference in your company's velocity.

To sustain a subscription-based company for the long term, your company must grasp the concept of churn from the standpoint of understanding why and how often customers leave, and the concept of retention from the standpoint of why and how often customers stay. The earlier in your company's lifecycle churn and retention are addressed, the easier the problem is to solve.

Great companies will truly understand why customers churn ("It's just not working for us" or "We can't afford it" are not real reasons). They will also learn why customers churn individual products, which causes downsell (dollar churn).

Law #10: Customer Success Teams Must Become Metrics-Driven

As with any new business endeavor, maturity is required to ensure long-term viability. Well, that time has come for Customer Success, which is still relatively new as a formal organization within most enterprises. Repeatability, process definition, measurement, and optimization are the hallmarks of maturation. We see glimpses of these at more mature recurring revenue businesses, but there's still a long way to go for most.

Ultimately, the purpose of Customer Success, like any other part of a thriving company, is to achieve real business outcomes. Defining what success means both for you and for your customers, and then establishing clear metrics that will deliver that success, is a necessary part of accelerating the maturation process.

Remember: You can't improve what you don't measure. So establish your metrics, start measuring and responding to those measurements, and watch your Customer Success program deliver ever-increasing positive results.

2 | Customer Success: It's Not Just for Silicon Valley

In *The Third Wave*, Steve Case's bestselling 2016 book, the former CEO and chairman of America Online (AOL) predicted the rise of regions outside of Silicon Valley as technology became infused in more-established industries. The same trend that is pushing "digital transformation" everywhere is also creating the need for Customer Success.

As an example of Case's observation, consider Rockwell Automation. Founded in 1903 and headquartered in Milwaukee, Wisconsin, Rockwell originally produced motor controllers for industrial cranes. Today, over 22,000 employees work to achieve the company's mission to "bring the Connected Enterprise to life," according to its website, through products ranging from process controls, to sensors, to safety systems. Customer Success has been fundamental to Rockwell's transformation. In particular, it has helped Rockwell transform the "services" that they sell around equipment maintenance and management from a reactive model to a more proactive one.

Nicholas Goebel, director of Global Customer Success at Rockwell Automation, explains how that happened at their firm: "We realized as a services organization that our contracts and our annual recurring revenue are the keys to our future success. We needed to have a Customer Success organization in place to drive our renewal rates. So we made organizational changes," says Goebel. "We recognized that the real goal of the CS organization at Rockwell Automation is to make sure we help our customers adopt, in the most efficient possible manner, whatever service or software package they purchase from us. And we have to communicate to them the value that it's having on their operation. So we track whatever they deem most important along the life of that subscription or service contract, instead of waiting until the end to try to justify the value we bring to their business." Defining what counts as value to the client, delivering against that, and demonstrating that value has indeed been delivered are three core CS activities that keep Rockwell's recurring revenue humming.

GE Digital similarly found a need for Customer Success, despite not having Silicon Valley roots. The subsidiary of storied industrial giant General Electric produces software and machine learning technology for industries that range from aviation to manufacturing to power generation. Customer Success is fundamental to defending GE Digital's subscription business. VP of Customer Success David Kocher made it a priority to develop a customer journey map, no differently from the way a Silicon Valley SaaS company would.

> The journey map has five stages, from the buyer's journey into the customer's journey, all the way through to outcomes. It identifies the critical steps at each of those different stages—what the customer needs and what we need to provide. Those are the deliverables. We ended up with this 3D-looking spreadsheet that outlines what's happening, when, and who's responsible for it. It's so critical to have transparent communication and an internal agreement about the client journey. That way it would feel seamless to the client, even though there's underlying complexity.

Healthcare is another industry that has embraced Customer Success. Founded in 1997 and headquartered outside Boston, athenahealth has a network of more than 160,000 medical providers and 110 million patients and provides software and services to help providers manage their practices; athenahealth recognizes customer centricity as a business imperative. "We have two priorities: to demonstrate differentiated value to our clients and to deliver a good experience," says Bret Connor, SVP, chief customer officer at athenahealth. "And, we have to do that while the world is constantly evolving. It's not news that healthcare is becoming more complex in how care is provided and how people get paid. Those dynamics mean that you must keep up from a Customer Success perspective. We have to be constantly learning and evaluating our performance. And we change the things that we monitor over time as the things that matter change. It's a nonstop process of monitoring, learning, and adapting to the changes so we can help our clients get good outcomes and ensure that patients are seeing better care." Customer Success ensures that athenahealth as a company can continue to evolve as quickly as its clients.

Even the physical devices that keep us healthy can be transformed via Customer Success, as is the case at ResMed. Based in San Diego, ResMed offers cloud-connected devices that transform care for people with sleep apnea, COPD (chronic obstructive pulmonary disease), and other chronic diseases. In addition, ResMed offers a portfolio of comprehensive software solutions for providers caring for people in settings outside of the hospital.

For ResMed, Customer Success means supporting home medical equipment providers and other channel partners to help patients achieve better health outcomes, which is fundamental to the company's mission. ResMed's software remotely connects devices, enabling providers to better support their patients and ensure strong adherence to sleep and other respiratory therapies.

In 2016 the company launched a formalized Customer Success program to further support respiratory therapists with ResMed's software solutions, provide greater support for patients, and drive better therapy outcomes. Raj Sodhi, president of ResMed's SaaS business, points to the result: "Because of our approach, we've improved patient therapy adherence from a traditional 50 percent to as high as 87 percent. The patient and provider response is strong." Moreover, the success of these solutions fueled provider profitability, which has in turn resulted in positive growth for ResMed. "ResMed has grown its business to be #1 in CPAP [continuous positive airway pressure] devices and our Customer Success program has been a key enabler; it has allowed us to scale our digital health solutions to become the largest global medical device telemonitoring business."

As in healthcare, companies in the human capital industry embraced digital transformation and subsequently recognized the importance of driving outcomes for customers. ADP is one of these companies that is dancing to the Customer Success tune. The company was founded in 1949 and became a 58,000-person human capital management solutions provider. As they built more digital offerings over time, it became necessary for them to build a Customer Success initiative. Erin Siemens, SVP Client Success at ADP, was asked by her business unit president to design a CSM organization in 2018. At that point, Siemens and her team read the first *Customer Success* book that we published. They refer to it as "the bachelor's degree." She says,

> We all read it, and we said, let's make this the blueprint for our organization. As a starting point, I had a team of vice presidents from different parts of our organization, who had led several different relationship management organizations. There was a need for stronger guidance around what we expected from our relationship managers on a day-to-day basis. As we started to dig into Customer Success management, it really resonated with us.

Fascinatingly, Siemens was drawn to the same philosophy of CS that Silicon Valley SaaS companies have embraced. And the changes she made in her organization will sound familiar to any Silicon Valley readers. "We built playbooks. We built what we expected our client success executives to use as a success plan template, to identify what client outcomes a client was looking to achieve. We added a scorecard to help drive accountability on the client side for behaviors that we felt were needed in order for them to be successful."

Siemens identifies as a part of the Customer Success movement that's transforming many industries. "It's been really exciting to be given the opportunity to build an organization that's part of what is now a growing industry in Customer Success."

Charles Atkins, partner at strategy consulting firm McKinsey & Company, summarized the trend across industries:

> Customer Success has, of course, become popular for companies transitioning from up-front license to subscription business models. But truly, anywhere that technology enables businesses to engage with their customers is a place where Customer Success is taking off.

So far we've explored a few examples of Customer Success becoming infused in industries as far from Silicon Valley as industrial process automation, industrial field services, healthcare, and human capital management. These aren't one-off situations, but rather are data points along a trendline. Let's explore this trend further, first by looking at exactly how Customer Success tends to unfold at companies outside of Silicon Valley. Then we'll take a dive into one sector as an example—manufacturing—as it transforms with the Internet of Things.

Six Steps for Customer Success Adoption

Many storied companies with existing businesses have embraced Customer Success in a consistent pattern, based upon acquisition, integration, and innovation. We tend to see the Customer Success mindset penetrating older industries in six sequential steps.

1. Well-Known Brands Are Buying Cloud-Based Companies and Getting CSM Teams

Check out a news website and you'll see reports of established firms trying to reinvigorate themselves by getting into the cloud world. In 2013, the agricultural business Monsanto (which is now a part of Bayer) spent about a billion dollars to acquire Climate Corporation, a digital agriculture company that examined weather, soil, and field data to help farmers determine potential yield-limiting factors in their fields. In 2017 Caterpillar, the world's largest construction equipment manufacturer, bought Yard Club, which provided technology that helped construction professionals manage equipment transactions. ADP, the human resources services company that we discussed previously, expanded its digital offerings through many acquisitions.

There's a long list of traditional companies that have entered the cloud software space through acquisition. Many of these older firms have read Harvard Business School professor Clayton Christensen's *The Innovator's Dilemma* and realized that if they can't find innovation DNA inside their own companies, they'll have to look outside. If they sit on the sidelines, this integral part of business success will pass them by.

As businesses unpack the gift boxes that are these new startups, they find roles that they're familiar with (Sales, Marketing, Engineering) and also one that's brand new to them: Customer Success Management. *Huh*. What to do with *that*? they wonder.

Unless they get expert advice and understand how groundbreaking CSM is and will continue to be, many of the acquiring companies go through a predictable and ill-fated exercise of trying to shoehorn CSM into their Maintenance, Support, and Services organizations. However, eventually they're confronted with the truth that CSM is its own world—and that world is an inescapable part of cloud-based operations.

2. Corporate Customer Experience Groups Meet Acquired CSM Teams

Often, the assimilated CSM teams will try to network with other groups in the acquiring company and end up as part of the Customer Experience (CX) team. At a superficial level, these teams sound like good matches in terms of mission. But the CSM teams often find that corporate CX teams have brilliant people who lack power in terms of operations or a mandate to enforce change across the business.

Where does that leave the CSM teams? Up that proverbial creek without a paddle, usually. With no real platform for change in the new company and no financial clout to back up their programs, CSM teams are often frustrated and prevented from achieving their goals—which are to improve and stabilize the company's bottom line by enhancing customer outcomes with the product or service they've purchased.

3. Customer Success Fits Existing Business Models as Well

At the same time, the groups in the parent company that own maintenance, support, services, and in some cases consumables, often are thrilled to hear about Customer Success. This is the mantra they've been preaching for years! Their businesses that attach to core systems/device sales are fundamentally recurring and require a consistent customer engagement lifecycle. These groups get it and are ready to get behind supporting the new CSM team.

4. Customer Success Ties to Sales Reinvention

While Sales leaders might initially be worried about another group engaging with "their" clients, progressive executives look at the model and realize they can radically increase sales efficiency with the expertise and assistance of their new CSM group. By moving existing clients, renewals, and small expansions to a dedicated, scalable, and process-oriented organization, they can get the higher-cost Sales team more focused on true "hunting" and less concerned about how their clients will be treated after the sale.

5. Cloud Becomes the Gateway to Digital Transformation

In some cases, the leader of the acquired cloud-based entity becomes the larger entity's head of digital transformation or chief digital officer. This person is often charged with modernizing the entire operation and applying cloud playbooks to the business.

6. Through This, They Might Be (Digital) Giants

For many of these organizations, companies such as Amazon are the long-term disruptive threat—or inspiration. Amazon's use of technology to drive, as they call it, *customer obsession* can be copied to create a roadmap for each company's success and support their long-term vision to become the Amazon of their industry—hopefully with similar valuations.

★★★

Now that we've discussed the general pattern of how Customer Success thinking enters older industries, let's explore more deeply how Customer Success practices tend to unfold, using the manufacturing sector as an example.

The Internet of Things and the Six Layers of Customer Success

As in other industries, manufacturing companies have been acquiring cloud-based technologies, as described in the six steps above. These acquisitions helped them build an Internet of Things (IoT), meaning that manufacturers were now able to connect their devices through cloud-based communication. For the first time, manufacturers could gather data on how their devices were being used by customers. The new availability of enormous amounts of data created not only opportunities to help customers, but also an imperative to interpret and act on that data. It turns out that IoT has done for hardware companies exactly what SaaS enabled for software companies—making available the data about how/when/if our customers are using our products. And the best companies are already using that data to drive proactive actions, which lead to higher degrees of value (success) for their customers.

Our friends at PTC (a global software and services company) are leaders in this IoT-driven transformation, and we've spent a lot of time talking with them about it. Chief Customer Officer & Customer Success Operations DVP Paul Lenfest says:

> The pace of IoT innovation is accelerating. With IoT, you can leverage data to not only educate your customers on the new value they can capture, but also improve the customer experience and even increase the value they find in your product. Customer Success then becomes critical to smart-connected product manufacturers—a competitive must-have—to proactively and rapidly guide clients to value.

We find that as manufacturing companies become more sophisticated in Customer Success, they layer on new practices that benefit their customers. Figure 2.1 shows the six layers we're observing in Customer Success in the IoT world.

Layer #1: Individual Device

Vendors used to be in the dark about the client experience. They might have seen the results of Customer Satisfaction (CSAT) surveys after field service calls. They might have gathered qualitative insights about the client experience during a sales meeting. But overall, their ability to see and act on the data at their disposal was limited.

As vendors collect more data on how devices are used, they can use that data to expand their ability to improve the client experience. An easy way

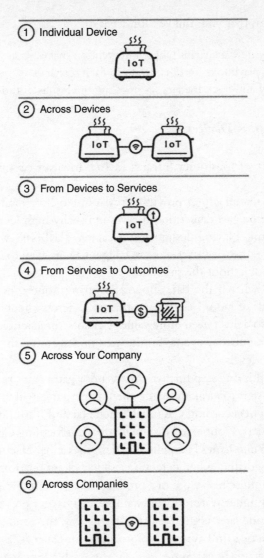

1. Individual Device
2. Across Devices
3. From Devices to Services
4. From Services to Outcomes
5. Across Your Company
6. Across Companies

Figure 2.1

to start? Be more responsive—follow up when the data signals that a device is malfunctioning. *Knowledge not only implies opportunity for the vendor, but also responsibility.* If clients know you're collecting data on them, they'll expect you to follow up in the right scenarios.

That means that you, the vendor, have to:

1. Identify new scenarios where intervention makes sense.
2. Design playbooks for what to do in each scenario.
3. Identify and track metrics for assessing the results of those playbooks.

Layer #2: Across Devices

The next layer of Customer Success in IoT involves capturing synergies across devices.

Let's say a manufacturer providing real-time in-home radon (a radioactive, carcinogenic gas) detection observes unusually high levels of radon in someone's home. Having designed the reactive playbooks we discussed in Layer #1 above, the manufacturer can trigger a technician to call the homeowner and troubleshoot the problem.

However, what if the data shows that many homes in the same area have high levels of radon? Capturing this trend across clients can allow the manufacturer to deliver even more value to clients, for example, by notifying the necessary regulatory agency in the area to determine the root cause of the high radon levels.

Let's take this one step further. As a vendor gathers more data across all devices, it can start to *predict* how the client experience will unfold and then support the client accordingly. A much-cited Harvard Business Review article,[1] "How Smart, Connected Products Are Transforming Companies," by Michael Porter and James Heppelmann, describes a manufacturer's ability to intervene immediately when detecting risk in a client relationship: "Knowing that a customer's heavy use of a product is likely to result in a premature failure covered under warranty, for example, can trigger preemptive service that may preclude later costly repairs." In this way, the vendor can progress from being reactive (in Layer #1) to proactive (in Layer #2).

Detecting patterns across devices can also enable longer-term improvements. If one device malfunctions, the vendor can provide a software update that fixes the problem across all devices.

Layer #3: From Devices to Services

Manufacturers have an opportunity not only to build devices, but also to drive tangible business results for clients through new types of services.

Current services might focus merely on product warranties. But future offerings can include "Insights as a Service." Providers can connect point-of-use information gathered from connected devices with external data sets to help their clients make more informed business decisions. In addition, preventative maintenance services can leverage data to prevent problems from escalating, and thus offer higher product performance guarantees or service level agreements.

As an example, before innovations in IoT, any warnings of in-flight airplane engine irregularity would require airlines to conduct a long, costly inspection of the entire engine. Today, Rolls Royce's IoT-enabled jet engines use in-flight data to generate real-time safety assessments and determine exactly which areas of the engine are in need of maintenance. This generates massive time and cost savings for the airline.

A plethora of other services that drive value for clients are emerging—including remote services ("Can you fix my problem without arranging a service visit?"), services involving augmented reality overlays ("Help me figure out how to fix this myself!"), comparative benchmarking ("Am I getting full value out of my devices?"), and education services ("How do I use these more complex devices?").

Beyond offering services as a supplement to devices, vendors may even forgo charging for their products and instead charge for their consumption. Big Belly once manufactured trash cans for sale, but now it provides trash pickup as a service—pricing its offering to more closely match the value that clients derive.

Layer #4: From Services to Outcomes

Vendors can go one step further by demonstrating to the client that they've driven strong outcomes. Clients don't just want to consume services—they want to achieve a real return-on-investment on their purchase.

Point-of-use data can help quantify the ROI and also showcase that value in executive meetings with the client or with monthly or quarterly email updates. Demonstrating ROI to the client preempts the question, "Why are we paying so much money for this service, and do we really need it?" It also paves the way for upsell or cross-sell, since clients are more likely to invest when they're convinced of the value they've already derived. eCompliance, a workplace safety company that offers a product called Field iD, tracks equipment on the job site and identifies potential risks to workers. They can track incidents that have been averted through use of its products—meaning they can report back to clients, "Here's the return on investment you've achieved by working with us." That information is invaluable to both vendor and client.

Once vendors recognize that they're in the business of driving outcomes for their clients (Customer Success in its most basic form), they realize that they don't merely have the responsibility to offer a device in a transaction—they must also shoulder the responsibility for change management. Clients of connected devices may have to change their own behaviors and operations.

None of this occurs without an empowered CSM team at the vendor. CSMs take responsibility for driving client outcomes and often quarterback on the client's behalf to mobilize resources at other departments within the vendor. In other words, CSM teams function as a client's advocate inside the vendor.

That cross-functional collaboration comprises the next layer of Customer Success.

Layer #5: Across Your Company

Data can help vendors fix a problem or drive an outcome. But even more importantly, the data collected by devices can help vendors improve their entire delivery model.

A vendor can dramatically improve its operations by marrying data from devices with data from other sources such as Support tickets, Net Promoter Score surveys, and Customer Relationship Management systems, or contract data. Vendors can now do analyses such as, "Is there an opportunity to sell more maintenance contracts among large clients with low Net Promoter Score survey ratings but high consumption of the devices and frequent Support interactions?" The results of such an analysis yield insights for departments across the company.

This feedback loop allows multiple departments to iterate together on the client journey. Feedback also allows your Research and Development (R&D) department to accelerate product improvements.

Arguably, R&D teams at device manufacturers should have the client in mind even more than their peers at software companies. When initially designing the product, they must consider *exactly* what sorts of outcomes they want clients to achieve, because changing physical products is much more challenging than releasing new software. They have to consider from the outset (1) what indicators define success? and (2) how can we gather data on those indicators by building the right sensors, microprocessors, controls, ports, and other components into the product? Those decisions on design typically can't be revisited later. Getting input early on from other departments—such as Support, Field Services, and Sales—will make a huge difference.

Layer #6: Across Companies

The opportunities to drive outcomes for clients multiply when manufacturers build devices that can communicate with each other through application program interfaces. For example, a Nest thermostat can share data with a Kevo smart lock so that the thermostat can adjust the temperature when the homeowner enters the house. If Nest and Kevo collaborated on additional use cases, they could expand the value that the client derives from the system of their devices—in other words, they'd examine the existing ecosystem and act on what they find there.

Settings such as hospitals, cities, factories, and work sites, which may purchase connected devices from multiple manufacturers, have multiple and expanding opportunities to drive synergies between devices.

Here's an example: PTC's customer Teel Plastics, a custom extruded plastic tubing and profiles company, leveraged an IoT solution to connect disparate machines on their Baraboo, Wisconsin, factory floor, by including programmable logic controllers from both Siemens and Allen-Bradley. In doing so, Teel Plastics improved factory efficiency (reducing setup times by 30%), reduced the risk of human error in shifting from manufacturing one recipe to the next, decreased asset downtime by leveraging predictive maintenance, and ultimately produced greater output at a much higher quality.

This example shows the value of creating systems across vendors. When vendors don't merely solve for Customer Success in the silo of their own products but instead work with each other (perhaps through the involvement of a third party), they can achieve much greater overarching outcomes for mutual customers.

Summary

The well-known venture capital investor Marc Andreessen once said, "Software is eating the world."[2] As companies outside of Silicon Valley acquire software companies and adopt cloud-based technologies, they also adopt practices that benefit their customers—which means that Customer Success is eating the world, too.

In Chapter 3, we'll discuss how the spread of Customer Success across industries has catalyzed growth in the Customer Success profession, making it one of the hottest job markets across the globe.

3 | The Customer Success Job Market Is Taking Off

Why is the Customer Success job market growing so rapidly?

Let's turn to Ruben Rabago, who leads Gainsight's CSM education and certification efforts, Pulse+, for answers. Rabago is responsible for creating programs to educate all these newcomers to the CS field—so he's got his finger on the pulse of the job market.

As we discussed in the previous chapter, Rabago observes that "CSM is infiltrating every industry, not just high-tech. In general, companies are realizing, 'Holy smokes, if I can implement a Customer Success practice, I will totally transform my business.' That opens up a huge job market."

How huge is it? As of November 2019, close to 70,000 Customer Success Manager jobs were listed on careers site LinkedIn. Since 2015, CSM positions at a global scale have grown at a rate of 176% year over year (see Figure 3.1). And although CSM positions are most abundant in the United States, jobs are trending upward worldwide, with Europe leading the way in increased CSM roles (nearly 235% year over year, 2015–18). Tech companies might have the largest number of people employed in Customer Success positions, but the industries adding CSM jobs at the fastest rate are

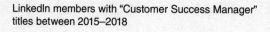

LinkedIn members with "Customer Success Manager"
titles between 2015–2018

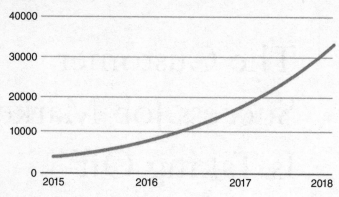

Figure 3.1

agriculture, real estate, and media and communications—none of which are traditional Silicon Valley industries.

Another sign of the field's rapid rise is the growth in Gainsight's Pulse conference, which brings together Customer Success people from around the world every spring. The first Pulse conference in 2013 had just 300 people in attendance. In 2019, that same conference attracted more than 5,000 attendees, growing by more than 15 times in 6 years.

Recruiting for CS executives has also taken off. Alexis Hennessy, a principal at search firm Heidrick & Struggles, concentrates heavily on Customer Success.

> The number of CS recruiting searches that we've seen in the last five years has skyrocketed. The first post-sales executive search that we did was in 2009. Around 2016 we hit 100 searches. Today we're probably close to 150. Most of the time, our client is recruiting for an entirely new role. If they're replacing someone, it usually means they're upleveling the role. They're growing and so they need someone who's had bigger scale or can own more functions. Or they may be about to go through a major transformation and need someone with relevant experience.

Rich Decembrele, managing director at staffing and recruiting firm Kindred Partners, has observed a similar trend: "We have seen an incredible uptick in the number of CS searches in the market." He observed that five years ago "it was a toss-up if you had a CS leader in your company or not." By contrast, today it's "abnormal" to see a company without one.

The intense growth in the CS job market means that hiring managers need to be savvy in recruiting and retaining team members, and candidates can be more ambitious. Next up, we discuss more deeply the implications for each side of the market.

The Demand Side: What Should Hiring Managers Expect?

Decembrele from Kindred Partners sees Customer Success becoming increasingly elevated by companies. "There's always been some sort of post-sales function inside of software companies, whether it was support, professional services, or account management. But it wasn't always top of mind at the exec and board level." But now "boards are calling us about CS specifically."

As companies seek to hire CSMs across the three profiles above, they invariably encounter obstacles. One challenge is that often companies are under significant pressure to hire quickly because the CSMs are needed for "plugging the leaky bucket"—preventing customers from churning. Sometimes they need to hire fast because they lost one of their CSMs (perhaps due to the hot job market for CSM), and that former CSMs' clients need help, right now. The risk of hiring the wrong person due to hasty recruiting is a real one.

A second challenge is the newness of the Customer Success profession means that companies sometimes have to recruit people who do not have Customer Success backgrounds, although the market has matured enough that this isn't as big of a problem as it used to be. "We are definitely getting better quality candidates, and we're getting candidates who understand the role a lot more," says Stephanie Berner, global head of Customer Success at LinkedIn. "Five years ago, most candidates were just looking for an entry point into tech, and they came from all kinds of backgrounds. Today, we're getting people who want to have a career in Customer Success, which is great."

Even with the rise of qualified applicants, the sheer number of jobs available makes hiring the right person a challenge. To help address these urgent, specific hiring needs, many existing recruiting agencies have developed Customer Success practices, and new firms have emerged as well.

One of those newer firms, Twin Oaks Recruiting in Atlanta, was founded by recruiting veteran Marianne Faloni in 2018 and was created to serve her tech clients in the Sales and Marketing verticals in the United States, with laser-focus on recruiting best practices. She quickly realized the need to expand into the Customer Success space as her clients repeatedly asked her to fill roles for this important organizational function. "The job market is continuing to expand by leaps and bounds, especially in the Customer Success area. As more companies look to strategically align Sales and Marketing, they are also including Customer Success in that equation to cultivate the ultimate organizational powerhouse."

This demand for CS professionals has made it harder for some companies to keep their employees. LinkedIn's Berner agrees. "We have to work harder to retain CSMs. It's so easy to jump companies for a bigger salary or maybe a fuller lunch bar here in the San Francisco Bay Area! But we're doing a better job of investing in people so they have a reason to stay and a reason to believe in a career trajectory in CS. LinkedIn and some of our peer companies are investing in programs and training curriculums to help build skills for Customer Success roles and beyond. It will help us retain the best talent." As Berner says, professional development has become incredibly important in this field, so we've dedicated a whole chapter on that topic later in the book.

Companies are also concerned with the retention of their CCOs. Hennessy from Heidrick and Struggles observes that turnover among CS executives is high. "They're so highly sought after. Very few of them bring experience in cloud technology and in managing a team of a couple hundred people globally, across all of the functions within the post-sales organization. People who do have that experience have many opportunities in front of them."

The Supply Side: What Should Candidates Expect?

The supply of CS professionals has grown quickly, but it hasn't kept pace with demand, so the job market still favors the applicant. Hennessy from Heidrick and Struggles says, "In general, it's a candidate's market. There are so many high-quality opportunities out there, and candidates really have their choice in terms of where they want to go next and what they want to do." The hot job market means that candidates not only have better luck finding great jobs; they also can have justifiably high expectations for their subsequent career growth. According to LinkedIn, the CSM role has the highest career advancement score possible, meaning that it ranks highest in terms of how quickly people advance once they're in a CS role.

Decembrele from Kindred Partners concurs. "CS has finally found its voice. This is a testament to the quality of the candidates, which is up markedly from five to seven years ago." Rich is seeing up-and-coming execs coming into CS from other backgrounds like business school and management consulting. "Five years ago, they would have gone into marketing—now, some are going into CS."

Rabago says that's because CSMs become more intimate with the customer base and the product or service than any other job function does. "As a CSM I have to become a product expert in order to translate how my product will bring value to you, the customer. And I have to become an expert in your business in order to know how to position my product." This means that CSMs can be strong candidates for roles in other functions within a company that demand knowledge of the product and clients; for example, Marketing or Product Management roles. Going into Customer Success can be a great foundation for the rest of your career.

The shortage of prior Customer Success experience has inspired people in other professions to enter the field. Even executives are moving into CS from other parts of the business. "I've seen a lot of executives move from other functions into a newly created Customer Success function within their company," says Hennessy, the executive recruiter. "Usually they're coming from support or services, but I'm also seeing people come over from product, marketing, operations, and other areas." As Berner from LinkedIn noted, CSM candidates increasingly have several years of CS experience already under their belts, but recruiters are staying open-minded about folks from other fields in order to bring qualified candidates into the market. Candidates are coming from areas such as:

- **Sales:** Salespeople who want to own a number but also want to drive value for clients more directly.
- **Account managers:** They're accustomed to managing existing client relationships and also have experienced challenges meeting their quota when the right things weren't done early in the account—which they can now take responsibility for as CSMs.

- **Sales development representatives:** Faloni from Twin Oaks Recruiting observes, "Some of the candidates entering the Customer Success function are Sales/Business Development reps who have realized they enjoy some aspects of Sales but not others. They see this new, shiny piece of the organization that's exciting and has endless possibilities to impact the customers and the business, and they want to get involved and make a sizable impact."
- **Project managers:** They know how to run structured engagements to reach a result, but like that the CSM role gives them the opportunity to build long-term relationships with clients.
- **Support representatives:** They have seen over and over again what happens when a client is neglected. Their technical and problem-solving skills make them attractive as CSM candidates, and they like the idea that they can proactively help their clients rather than merely react to crises.
- **Operations managers:** They have experience running internal cross-functional initiatives, which translates well to "herding cats" at the client and mobilizing internal resources to support them.
- **Management consultants:** Consultants from firms such as Accenture, Bain, BCG, Deloitte, McKinsey, and PwC have managed strategic, long-term engagements with some of the same clients that they may be working with in a CSM role.
- **MBAs:** They're often eager to join tech companies and have the multidisciplinary background that helps them think creatively about strategies in working with a client.
- **Recent college grads (including those right out of college):** They often are drawn to rotational programs where they can get exposure to different departments—including CS, Services, Support, and others—to help inform their choice of a permanent home.
- **Clients:** Finally, what better for a role to "walk in the client's shoes" than hiring people who have literally worn those shoes? Particularly for their larger customers, many vendors have started hiring people from their clients to become CSMs. For example, an HR software company could hire an HR manager at a client to be a Customer Success Manager. They'd have to train the person on the vendor's processes but know they'd hit the ground running immediately in terms of having empathy for the client.

The entry of people with varied backgrounds into the CSM role has coincided with the rise of programs to train people in the profession. Rabago provides several universities with curriculum guidance to add CSM to their business programs, although degree-granting programs are years away. Gainsight's Pulse+ program has grown into the world's largest education and certification program for Customer Success professionals, educating more than 10,000 of them so far.

What *Is* a Customer Success Manager, Exactly?

What do we mean when we say "Customer Success Manager"? It's a valid question, since the CSM role comes in all shapes and sizes. We tend to see three types of CSMs:

1. **CSM for Value Gaps:** This type of CSM is necessary when a product is in its early stages. There is a significant "gap" between the value that the client gets out of the box and the value that clients are expecting. The CSM is there to plug that gap, by proposing creating workarounds and other solutions for clients, to help them achieve their goals in using the product's features. Typically, this type of CSM is very technical, coming from more product-oriented roles such as Support or Services.
2. **CSM for Value Delivery:** Once a product and its associated paid services reach a certain critical level of maturity, a CSM can free up their time to focus more on guiding clients through the journey of achieving value. This CSM typically has strong communication skills, executive presence, and the business judgment that helps them serve as a strategic advisor to clients.
3. **CSM for Value Expansion:** Some products are so well-designed (or have associated services that are so well executed) that they can automate much of the process of value delivery. In that case, a CSM can free up their time to expand the relationship with the client, by expanding the deployment to more people at the client (including more business units) or by selling additional products. This type of CSM often has a sales or account management background. The CSM and Account Management roles may even be blended into one role in this scenario.

Roles along the CSM career ladder, however, aren't the only ones that have become more prominent as a result of the CS movement.

The Rise of Customer Success Operations

As CSMs have grown in number, operations roles to support them are also on the rise. By analogy, Sales Operations became a standard role for supporting Sales teams by enabling account executives with content and other training, defining territories and compensation structures, and running reports and conducting analyses for Sales leaders. Customer Success organizations need to perform similar functions, and as a result they have been hiring Customer Success Operations Managers. Figure 3.2 shows how their responsibilities compare with Sales Operations roles.

A few years ago, CS Operations roles were few and far between, and companies had trouble funding them. But today, they're standard for CS teams that have more than five or ten CSMs.

Summary

Customer Success is one of the fastest-growing jobs in the world. It's an employee's market, and the opportunities to grow careers and accelerate one's advancement within the company are unprecedented. The job creation pace will continue as more and more industries outside Silicon Valley add CSM teams.

In the next several chapters, we'll explore how companies justify the investments in Customer Success that have propelled this boom in the field. Companies are seeking four pillars of their return on investment:

1. Reduce churn
2. Drive growth
3. Exceed client expectations
4. Increase enterprise valuation

Next up, we'll explore how fear of churn—the silent killer of companies—motivates those firms to focus on Customer Success.

	Sales Operations	Customer Success Operations
People		
Team Structure	Segment the market, manage account executives' territories, and forecast hiring needs.	Segment existing customers, assign them to CSMs, redistribute workload as needed, and forecast hiring needs.
Compensation	Determine commission structure and quotas.	Determine the metrics on which bonuses are based and define targets.
Enablement	Provide materials and data that help account executives work more effectively.	Provide materials and data that help CSMs work more effectively.
Process		
Customer Engagement	Determine the steps in the sales process to optimize conversion of pipeline to closed deals.	Determine the customer journey, including touchpoints and methodology.
One-to-Many Communications	Coordinate with Marketing on email nurture activities for prospective customers.	Run one-to-many emails and in-app communications.
Cross-functional Coordination	Coordinate cross-functional processes that help meet sales targets and deliver on prospects' needs.	Coordinate cross-functional processes (with Product, Engineering, Support, Services, Marketing, and Sales) that help meet renewal and upsell targets and deliver on customers' needs.
Technology		
Systems	Implement and manage software that facilitates Sales Ops activities.	Implement and manage software that facilitates CSM Ops activities.
Reporting	Report regularly on past results and sales forecasts.	Report regularly on past results and forecasts for retention and expansion.
Prioritization	Identify top accounts and give executives visibility into deals that are at risk.	Identify top accounts for upsell and detect at-risk renewals.
Analysis	Track leading indicators of sales and analyze them to understand what's going well and what's not.	Track leading indicators of renewals and upsell and analyze them to understand what's going well and what's not.

Figure 3.2

4 | Reason #1: Customer Success Stops Churn—The Silent Business Killer

Basic math tells us that as your company grows and your base of recurring revenue increases, the dollars of churn against that base get larger every month (in raw numbers), even if the percentage of churn stays the same. So you need more new business every month to replace the churn, which slows your growth. The bigger you get, the more your growth is slowed by the drag of churn.

Churn is like a weird kind of business-world gravity—an irresistible force—that's constantly pulling on your customer base. It's the silent, perpetual energy dragging the base down. Customers are exercising their right to leave more often than ever, thanks to the low-commitment pricing models and next-to-nonexistent switching costs brought about by the new cloud-based economy.

Remember what it used to be like when your clients would stay with you through thick and thin—and maybe the occasional steak dinner or sporting event? Yeah, those days are gone. Now you're earning your client's continued loyalty every single day.

But the next-level implication is where it gets interesting. One of today's key questions for business leaders is, "Which of my clients are at risk?"

Here's the hard truth: Any one of your clients could leave you at any time. In the long run, all of your clients are "red." They're all at risk. Let's look at why that is:

- Your sponsor at the client will leave and the replacement may have experience with a competitor.
- Your client could have a bad experience with your team that changes everything.
- Your customer could switch business strategies and have less of a need for your offering.
- Your competitors could evolve faster than you are and be more compelling in a year or two.

Gainsight's Chief Evangelist (and co-author of *Customer Success*), Dan Steinman, likes to say, "The natural tendency of clients is toward churn." And while this happens at the micro-level (client by client), it happens at the macro-level as well. We meet CEOs frequently who pride themselves on their "ninety-something-percent retention rate." They like to say that churn doesn't affect them. They're out in space where gravity can't touch them.

Until it does: What we've found is changes in churn rate (like changes in velocity from gravity) accelerate over time. Then the cracks appear and alternatives improve. The early churns look insignificant. But then they snowball. All of a sudden, 95% retention is 50% or worse.

So what do you do? Fundamentally, leaders have been evolving their thinking from assuming that clients are "acquired" and committed for the long term to the idea that vendors re-earn their clients' business every day. In the long run, this means prioritizing and budgeting investments to ensure long-term client retention and success—instead of just assuming it will happen.

Churn is like gravity. If something goes up, you need to fight hard to prevent it from coming down.

CSMs are at the forefront of that fight against churn. As a result, improved gross retention is the first reason why companies tend to invest in Customer Success. Five years ago, companies would invest in building Customer Success teams once they realized that the churn they were experiencing was too high. It was a reactive measure to stem the tide, and the hired CSMs would enter what was effectively a firefighting role. Today, companies anticipate that churn will come unless it's proactively mitigated, so they design their organizations upfront to ensure strong gross retention rates.

What do we actually mean when we say "churn" and "retention"? Let's turn to more precise definitions.

Churn: How Do You Measure It?

Churn and Retention—which are inverses of each other—are not yet generally accepted accounting principles (GAAP) metrics. That said, the Customer Success industry has converged on a few calculations for Retention Rate. Your choice of calculation depends on whether your business has renewals (not all recurring revenue companies do) and your strategic focus.

Type 1: Gross Dollar Renewal Rate

This is how you calculate it:

Gross Dollar Renewal Rate = $ Renewed/$ Eligible for Renewal

The difference between $ Eligible for Renewal and $ Renewed is the amount of Churn plus Downsell. Downsell captures a reduction in contract size, for example, due to the client not renewing a particular product module or not renewing some of their licenses. (This calculation obviously assumes that you have renewals in your business.)

Type 2: Gross Dollar Retention Rate, Including Multi-Years

This calculation takes into account the beneficial impact of multi-year contracts by including the contracts that are experiencing an anniversary (i.e. essentially renewing by default) in the denominator.

Gross Dollar Retention Rate

    = ($ Renewed + $ Experiencing an Anniversary)/

      ($ Eligible for Renewal + $ Experiencing an Anniversary)

This is the calculation that we recommend reporting to your board. Multi-year contracts are an important strategy for bolstering your recurring revenue and should therefore be reflected in this top-level revenue metric. (You can see that anniversary dollars, because they "renew" at 100%, will make this retention rate greater than your renewal rate from Type 1.) That said, if you are relying too much on multi-years to bolster your retention, because the clients that are up for renewal are not actually renewing at high rates, you should also pay close attention to the Type 1 calculation above.

Type 3: Logo Retention Rate

Here we're capturing the logos that have renewed, rather than the dollars:

Logo Retention Rate

= (Logos Renewed + Logos Experiencing an Anniversary)/

(Logos Eligible for Renewal

+Logos Experiencing an Anniversary)

You likely won't be reporting this metric to your board, but your CS team should pay attention to it. Every logo, no matter how small, that churns your product represents another detractor on the market who can generate negative word of mouth and hamper future sales. (In fact, the smallest companies are often the most vocal about their poor experiences as clients.) Even if your Dollar Retention Rate is high, a low Logo Retention Rate can hinder your growth.

Type 4: Net Dollar Retention Rate

This is another dollar calculation, and it factors in the expansion of existing client contracts through upsell or cross-sell. Expansion can include the sale of new licenses or products, or the sale to new business units or teams within the client:

Net Dollar Retention Rate = (Beginning of Period ARR

+ Expansion—Downsell—Churn)/

Beginning of Period ARR

where Expansion, Downsell, and Churn are for the last 12 months.

Because Net Dollar Retention Rate allows a company to offset churn with expansion, it's by far the most popular metric reported in public SaaS company's filing documents.

Here's a related calculation:

Net Churn Rate = 100%—Net Dollar Retention Rate

In this calculation, Expansion can offset the impact of Churn and Downsell, potentially making your Net Churn Rate zero or negative, but it's still important to pay attention to churn on its own. We'll explore when to use Gross Retention and when to use Net Retention later in this book.

Type 5: No Renewals

This calculation is for businesses that do not have renewals. An example could be a diagnostics company that makes money when it sells tests, rather than at the time of a renewal:

Dollar Retention Rate = End of Period Revenue/

Beginning of Period Revenue

for customers that existed at the beginning of the period (that's important because you don't want to count revenue from new customers; focus on the existing customer cohort). The period is 12 months. The numerator should reflect revenue from the last 12 months and the denominator should reflect revenue from the 12 months ending at the start of the period.

Because Ending Revenue could exceed Starting Revenue, this calculation works like a Net Retention Rate, which includes expansion, as we discussed above. In the case of the diagnostics company, a client may purchase more tests in the current period versus the previous one, or they may reduce the volume of tests or churn altogether.

So far in this chapter, we've discussed why churn matters (a business that's a leaky bucket can't survive) and what churn actually is (the leakage of dollars or logos). By now it's probably clear to you why companies would want to invest in reducing churn. But why does churn even happen in the first place? And therefore, what can companies *do* about it?

Why Does Churn Happen?

Venture capitalist, former CEO, and tech legend Ben Horowitz has written that if you ask salespeople why they lose deals, they'll always say, "It was the price." Maybe they do it consciously, maybe they do it subconsciously, but by blaming price, they aren't blaming their product, their team, or themselves. Price is a safe, easy scapegoat.

In the CS world, we can lead ourselves into a similarly easy, non-blaming trap. Most of us have a "churn reason" field in our Customer Relationship Management (CRM) system and we attempt to code each churn so that we can report internally why the customer left. Having sat in on loads of churn reviews for dozens of companies, we've seen some other top reasons, besides price, for customer departures. They include:

- Sales expectations
- Competition
- Other
- Sponsor change

Seriously? What do you do with that info? Are all of those reasons equivalent? (Spoiler: No, they are not.) Is someone going to leave because of competition or sponsor change, but not both? Is sponsor change the reason they leave? Or is it a catalyst? Is sales expectations a convenient catchall? And how do we prevent future churns due to the "Other" reason?

We're not the only ones to think this way. Companies have been realizing they need to think more deeply about the *why* behind churn.

First, they are separating the root cause from the catalyst. You can do this with just about anything in life and it's good practice for applying this line of thinking to churn. Here's an example: Why did that soccer player blow out her knee? Was it because of the final fall you saw on TV? Or was it because of the 1,000 falls before that?

Similarly, CS teams are now breaking down their churn reasons into root issues and proximate issues. This is quite similar to marketing, where you might look at the last touch that caused a buyer to engage with you (maybe they filled out a form) and also previous touches (they watched a webinar). In Customer Success, root-cause issues might include:

- The product doesn't fit the customer need.
- The customer had a poor on-boarding experience.

- The product had a low adoption rate early on.
- The wrong people were at the client early on.

By contrast, proximate (final) issues might include:

- Sponsor change (which would have been fine if we'd had better adoption early on)
- M&A (which could have been fine if they were using the product actively)
- Competition (who wouldn't have been able to swoop in if the customer had been getting value)
- Price (which wouldn't have been an issue if the value were clear)

The proximate issue is often more readily apparent but outside of our control, whereas the root-cause issue is the real underlying problem and is typically within our control in some way. When companies start identifying root causes more consistently, they realize that they *can* reduce their churn. This feeling of empowerment propels companies to invest more in Customer Success—because it can result in a real revenue impact through churn reduction.

(As a side note, this is a wonderful example of how intellectual honesty makes more business sense.)

Nowadays, these root cause analyses almost always show that CSM execution isn't the only problem—and sometimes isn't the problem at all. Tomasz Tunguz, a partner at Redpoint Ventures, tends to see a few common root issues.

If an organization has high churn, there are typically three causes. It could be that the account executives oversell and then pass the account to the CS organization in a bad state. It could be the product doesn't work as advertised. Or it could be that the Customer Success Managers are ineffective. But the last one is rarest. It's uncommon to come across an organization that's running its Customer Success so poorly that you have massive customer churn.

That last point shows how far we've come in CS over the past five years, since earlier in this decade, massive churn due to execution issues was very common. Since then, companies have invested considerably in Customer

Success both in terms of headcount as well as the implementation of best practices. That said, don't take your foot off the gas in CS. If you haven't achieved maturity in your CS operation, the gravity-like force of churn will inevitably result in leakage. What a shame to lose customers because of an execution problem!

Still, Tunguz's observations reveal that investing in churn reduction requires changes in other departments besides CS, a topic to which we'll turn in Part II of this book.

Summary

Simple math dictates that as your company grows, your churn increases in raw numbers—which means you have to bring in more new business every month to cover that churn. And although we all like to think that at least some of our client relationships are rock-solid, the truth is that every client is at risk of leaving. Given that the force of churn is as certain as gravity, companies have learned to invest in the foundations of their "house" of Customer Success in the same way that early humankind learned to create structures from sturdy materials.

Next, we'll look at a second reason why companies are investing in Customer Success: not only to plug the leaky bucket, but also to accelerate the flow of water into that bucket. In other words, companies believe that CS can contribute not only to revenue retention, but also to revenue growth.

5

Reason #2: Customer Success Is a Growth Engine— If You Move from Defense to Offense

When Mark Roberge started teaching a class on sales at Harvard Business School, he was dumbfounded. "We did not have Customer Success in our syllabus—in a course focused on growth!"

For Roberge, the former chief revenue officer at HubSpot, it was inconceivable to not talk about Customer Success in the context of sales. Roberge helped take HubSpot public as a leading multi-product growth platform. Along that journey, he saw how important CS was for growth.

> The first year I was at HubSpot, we were very sales- and marketing-driven. We went from 100 to 1,000 customers and 1 million to 3 million in revenue in seven months. We had amazing growth. But churn went from an already terrible five percent a month to eight percent a month.
>
> So we became obsessed with Customer Success. We hired a leader who built the team. We studied the customer segments that we were retaining and churning. We stopped selling to segments that churned at

too high a rate. We started tracking early indicators of success. We knew that if clients used five of the 20 features in the first 60 days, then they'd be a customer for life. If they didn't, they'd churn.

From there, it was extremely easy to operationalize everything from the definition of Marketing Qualified Lead (MQL) on the marketing side, to how account executives were compensated on the sales side, to our goals for customers during onboarding, to how we evolve the roadmap and reduce friction in the product. We set up the entire company around the customer's adoption in the first 60 days.

Let's pause for a moment. Roberge was the *sales* leader who grew Hub-Spot from $0 to $100 million in revenue, before heading up HubSpot's *sales* division as CRO. His biography screams "sales!" But he believes as much as anyone in the power of Customer Success.

Why are revenue leaders like Roberge touting the benefits of customer-centricity? They're embracing a new framework for revenue growth that we like to call the Helix.

The New Framework: The Helix Model of Revenue Growth

Throughout the history of business, CEOs and heads of Sales have woken up every morning thinking about how to grow faster. That hasn't changed. But as their companies shift to recurring revenue business models, they're realizing that *the way they grow* must change.

Ten years ago, revenue leaders were thinking about the pipeline of hand-offs: how to manage hand-offs from Marketing to Sales, and transitions from Stage A to Stage B in the sales process. Today, the best revenue leaders know that strong revenue growth doesn't come from a straight-and-narrow pipe. It comes from the Helix (see Figure 5.1).

Let's step back. Where does revenue come from in a recurring revenue business model? Check out Figure 5.2.

What revenue leaders have realized is that in the modern business world, successful customers are the start *and* end of the pipe. When you make a customer successful, you've created at least three new leads:

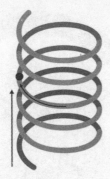

Figure 5.1

Figure 5.2

- **A lead for a renewal event:** This customer is prime to be renewed.
- **A lead for an expansion deal:** This customer will be amenable to get even more value from their partnership with you. In fact there may be *multiple* expansion opportunities.
- **A lead for a new logo:** This customer, depicted in Figure 5.3, will be happy to speak to a prospective customer about the value they've achieved. In fact, they'll be willing to speak to *multiple* prospects.

LEAD FOR RENEWAL
LEAD FOR EXPANSION
LEAD FOR NEW LOGO

Figure 5.3

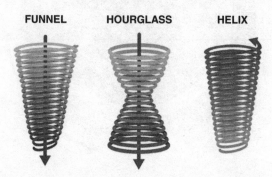

FUNNEL   HOURGLASS   HELIX

Figure 5.4

If you make your customers successful, you can turn one new lead into 3+ leads. And in turn those 3 incremental leads result in $3 \times 3 = 9+$ new leads. And those 9+ leads result in $9 \times 3 = 27+$ new leads. That's exponential growth.

You're not just looping around. You're looping around *and* moving on up, as shown in Figure 5.4.

The growth pattern of successful recurring revenue companies resembles an expanding helix: The successful customer brings you back to your starting point (leads), but your company is increasingly better off than it was before.

This phenomenon is causing revenue leaders to believe that their old framework of the "funnel" (representing a linear progression of leads to closed deals, without a view to the customer) is insufficient. That's why the Helix model is growing in popularity.

Whereas the Sales Funnel captured one lever for revenue growth (new logos), and the Land & Expand Hourglass model captured two levers (new logos + expansion), the Helix model captures all three (new logo, expansion, and renewal) and explains the causal relationship between successful customers and new logo growth.

In the previous chapter, we dove into the impact of Customer Success on one of those three growth levers, renewals. Now let's double-click into the impact of CS on each of the other two levers: expansion and then new logo growth through advocacy.

Double-Click #1: Customer Success Drives Expansion

In 2018 we surveyed chief customer officers at about 100 tech companies and asked them many questions to assess their "maturity" in Customer Success practices, as well as their Net Retention Rate. Then we grouped those companies into four stages of maturity (shown in Figure 5.5):

1. **Reactive:** These companies are in fire-fighting mode, managing escalations on a case-by-case basis.

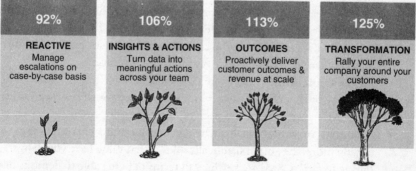

Figure 5.5

2. **Insights and Actions:** These companies are leveraging data to determine what actions to take to help those clients.
3. **Outcomes:** These companies are systematically delivering outcomes for their clients and revenue growth for their own companies.
4. **Transformation:** In these companies, every department is aligned around the success of clients. These companies are truly customer-centric.

We found that companies that had made it to the Transformation stage had Net Retention Rates that were on average 33 percentage points higher than those of their peers in the Reactive stage. (They also had 13 percentage points higher Gross Retention.) That's a huge difference, reinforcing the growing belief across industries that investing in Customer Success results in stronger revenue growth through expansion.

Why exactly does Net Retention increase when companies invest more in Customer Success? There are a few reasons:

- **Positive client outcomes and experiences:** When a company is further along on the maturity curve above, CSMs are guiding clients to achieve a return on investment from their purchase of your product or service, and ensuring that they have a positive experience along the way. Successful customers are more likely to buy more of your product or service.
- **More retained customers to expand:** When CSMs are effective in retaining clients (through the practices underlying the maturity curve above), they ensure that these clients are "still around" to be upsold or cross-sold.
- **Leads for expansion:** Many CSM teams are specifically chartered to generate leads from within existing customers. Those leads are often known as CSQLs, or Customer Success Qualified Leads. CSMs pass along those leads to Sales, who close them. An investment in Customer Success therefore implies an investment in expansion.
- **Faster expansion:** CSM is, in a sense, all about "time to value." Frequently, customers won't buy more until they have already seen value. So CSMs can accelerate the pace of expansion.
- **Evidence of value:** Finally, when an executive at a client is looking at buying more, they often skeptically ask, "What value have you delivered for me so far?" CSMs are key here in terms of being able to demonstrate the value delivered to-date.

Double-Click #2: Customer Success Drives New Logo Growth

It used to be that sales teams would bring in new business by cold-calling customers. Persistence was the name of the game, embodied in the mantra "ABC—Always Be Closing" by the character played by Alec Baldwin in the 1992 movie *Glengarry Glen Ross*. You can see this "hunting" mindset in the cold emails shown in Figures 5.6 and 5.7, which are real ones that we have received—and we're sure, not too different from the ones that you have received.

That second email cracks us up every time! We love the persistence that these sales development reps are demonstrating. But we want to point to a problem with this cold-emailing approach, which is that it doesn't meet the prospective client where they are.

In the modern business world, when your prospects are "in the market" for a product or service like the one that you offer, they're rarely a "cold" prospect in the traditional sense. They've already done an online search to learn more about their challenge and how to solve it. They've searched through the abundance of public reviews on websites such as TrustRadius or G2, and then read reports written by Gartner or Forrester. They've gone to a business conference where they asked another attendee, "How have

Meeting Request

Hi Alison, with ▓▓▓▓▓ a cloud based company with a holistic approach ▓▓▓▓▓▓▓▓
I would like the opportunity to schedule a time with you to go over your business proccessess and see if our solutions
are in line with any initiatives you have this year or next.

Gartner has us as the leader for the ▓▓▓▓▓▓▓▓▓▓▓ Solutions. I'm not too sure of your
business applications but we are ▓▓▓▓▓▓▓▓▓

As an overview:
We provide products ▓▓▓▓▓▓▓▓▓▓▓▓▓▓▓
Sr. Sales Developement Representative
▓▓▓▓▓

Figure 5.6

I Hope We Can Still Be Friends

Since you haven't responded to any of my cold prospecting emails, you know it's time for the dreaded "backup email" where I try to convince you of all the things you'll be missing.

Yeah.... right.... like you're going to fall for that!

Instead of breaking up, I figured I'd give you a present. Here's a 5 second trick that'll make cold emails more effective.

See you in another prospecting campaign a few months from now!

P.S. Or we could skip all the good stuff by hoping on a call. Spoiler alert: you're going to end the call loving ▮▮▮▮▮▮

P.S. If you don't want to hear from me anymore, just let me know

Figure 5.7

you solved this problem before?" "Have you used XYZ product? What was it like?" and "Which vendor would you recommend I work with to solve my problem?" So by the time this cold-calling sales representative gets this buyer on the phone, the buyer has already been educated about the product through word of mouth. The cold pitch doesn't land well.

In general, buyers trust word of mouth more than any other source when considering whether to buy a product. Analyst firm Forrester Research has reported that peers and colleagues are the number-one source for gathering information during the discovery stage of a purchase decision.[3] Researcher eMarketer found that referrals have the highest conversion rate from Lead to Deal compared to any other type of lead, about four times the rate for sales-generated leads.[4]

Companies realize that generating positive word of mouth about their products or services is crucial to their revenue growth. That goal to proactively create advocates—who will speak on stage at a conference, write positive testimonials online, serve as a reference for an uncertain prospective buyer, and speak positively at cocktail parties—has been a primary factor leading to companies increasing their investment in Customer Success.

And we're not the only ones talking about this. Marketing technology company HubSpot has advocated a similar analogy to our Helix—the "flywheel." Alison Elworthy is the SVP of Customer Success at the

Boston-based publicly traded SaaS company and shared her perspective on advocacy: "The whole idea is that a flywheel runs on its own momentum. When you attract new prospects, you want to engage them and convert them, but you also want to delight them. Our whole business has been focused on how to create a really great customer experience so we can generate that flywheel."

As a result, CS teams often track the number of advocacy activities that they generate. They sometimes use the metric, Customer Success Qualified Advocacy (CSQA). Examples of a CSQA include:

- A client collaborates on a case study that captures a new use case for your product or service.
- A client offers a written testimonial for use on your website or in your sales material.
- A client speaks at an event that your prospective customers attend.

In all three cases, the client shares the benefits of your product or service with prospects.

The CSM may have generated these advocacy activities by making the client so successful that they naturally volunteer to advocate for the company. Further, the CSM may have officially asked the client to participate in these advocacy activities.

Another type of advocacy is repeat repurchasing. Repeat purchasers involve a client of your product moving to a new company, where they choose to buy your product again, or otherwise advocate within their new company for the purchase. A CSM made the client so successful the first time that they wanted to come back to you.

For the more strategic segments of your customer base, your CSMs may be involved in a kind of "advocacy through surrogate." In this case, the CSM is directly engaged in the sales cycle, side by side with the sales representative, to share stories of successful customers. This is yet another way that CSMs can contribute to new logo growth.

★★★

Now that we've explored the impact of CS on expansion and new logo revenue—the two levers for growth that have been most broadly accepted among sales leaders and CEOs—let's return to growth lever #3, renewals. The fact is, companies have found that plugging the leaky bucket of churn *in itself* results in stronger revenue growth.

Double-Click #3: Gross Retention Drives Revenue Growth

In McKinsey's whitepaper, "Grow Fast or Die Slow: Focusing on Customer Success to Drive Growth" in October 2016, they gathered data from 200 high-growth SaaS companies with ARR between $100 and $200 million, then identified the "top-quartile" performers by quarterly revenue growth. They found that the top-quartile growers had gross retention rates of 88% on average, whereas the mean growers averaged 76%—a 12-percentage-point difference.

We think there are several reasons for this:

- **Churn results in a leaky bucket:** It's hard to grow fast when you have to compensate for a revenue leak, as we discussed in the previous chapter.
- **Lost renewals result in lost expansion opportunities:** If you're losing customers, there will be fewer customers to upsell or cross-sell, so your expansion revenue takes a hit.
- **More churn leads to more detractors:** If you're losing customers and they're talking to their friends and colleagues about their failed partnership with you, that negative word of mouth can impact your close rate for new business.
- **Companies with high churn rates raise less money:** It's harder to claim that your company is a great investment opportunity if you have a high churn rate. And if you raise less money, you can't invest as much in growth.
- **Companies with high churn rates are less profitable:** If your churn is high and you have to plug the gap with new business, you'll be less profitable, because it typically costs more to acquire a new customer than renew an existing one. Less profit means less to invest in the future growth of your business.
- **A "learning" organization:** Companies that succeed in generating high Gross Retention Rates have likely developed a culture and processes for learning from clients and their market. That learning mindset can help in all aspects of a company, including revenue growth.

Bottom line: Plugging the leaky bucket matters for your overall revenue growth. To amp up the velocity of your Helix, we recommend pulling all three levers: expansion, advocacy through new logo growth, and retention.

Summary

In this chapter we discussed a new concept for describing how B2B recurring revenue companies grow: the Helix. It's not enough to Always Be Closing. The businesses of the future have to Always Be Renewing, Always Be Expanding, and Always Be Advocating. Companies have realized that those three growth levers create a virtuous cycle of growth—the B2B version of viral growth that's well known in the B2C world—and that aspiration is motivating them to investing in Customer Success.

In the next chapter, we'll explore the third reason why companies are investing in CS: Their customers expect it.

6

Reason #3: Your Customers Want It

Think of your worst experience as a customer. Maybe it was with your (least) favorite airline or cable company, if we had to guess. Think of that feeling that you had as you were transferred for the 32nd time after being on hold for hours. What word would you use to describe the emotion you had then? If you're like us, it would be "powerless." In other words, we were frustrated not just at the company we were dealing with but also with our lack of ability to do anything about it. For evidence of this, check out Twitter to see the many complaints "into the wind" about airline delays that go unresponded to.

On the flipside, let's contemplate online shopping. You find a website through Google that's selling your favorite pair of shoes (or at least this is what Nick does regularly). Is the website slow? Go to another one. Is the pricing confusing? Click on further into Google and you'll find more options. Is the shipping policy not customer-friendly? Thank you—next!

If you're a B2B vendor, your customer is starting to look a lot more like an empowered online shoe shopper and much less like a helpless travel passenger delayed in Des Moines. Your clients have more power than they've ever had before. There are five reasons for that:

1. **The cloud enabled agile development:** You can develop products in an agile way and deliver instant updates, so customers expect you to make changes quickly.
2. **Clients dangle the carrot of subscription revenue:** Clients are increasingly paying you over time, as opposed to in a one-time upfront payment. They know you have to care about their success in order to guarantee your future revenue stream.
3. **Social media amplified voices:** Social media has amplified your detractors, but also the potential influence of your advocates. If a client is a detractor, they know they can take down your business. If a client is an advocate, they know they're valuable to you.
4. **Digital channels accustomed clients to instant responses:** You're interacting with customers through email, text message, Slack, and other digital channels. They expect instant responses.
5. **Commoditization of product features:** It's easier than ever to build a product. The second you think you have an edge with your new feature, a competitor catches up. You can no longer differentiate your company based on your product or roadmap; clients know you have to differentiate based on the success you generate for them.

These five trends mean that Customer Success is no longer an option; it's an existential imperative.

What do we mean when we say "Customer Success"? Well on one hand, as we've discussed, Customer Success is about driving more revenue from your customers in terms of renewals, expansion, and advocacy. But from the client's point of view, they don't care about that at all. What does Customer Success mean for a client? We were worried that this aspirational concept could end up like other marketing buzzwords—to paraphrase *Macbeth*, "full of sound and fury, signifying nothing." So we decided to take a more scientific point of view and propose an "equation" to quantify Customer Success from a client's point of view:

$$CS = CO + CX$$

where CS means Customer Success, CO means Customer Outcomes, and CX means Customer Experience.

An Outcome is the value that a client is receiving from your product or service. It's their return on investment (ROI) from their purchase. When clients buy from you, they expect they'll generate a meaningful outcome. They may be looking for improvement in a specific metric—for example, increase their sales bookings growth, cut costs, avoid future headcount expenses, or strengthen their Net Promoter Score. On the other hand, they may want to achieve a milestone—for example, unifying their company on a set of priorities, outsourcing a division, or completing another initiative. In either case, clients expect that you take responsibility for the outcome they achieve in using your product or service, not merely ensuring that your product or service "works." It doesn't matter if they failed to achieve their Outcome partially because they didn't attend meetings during the early stages of working with you, because they underwent a reorganization right as they bought your product, because their executive sponsor left the company, or because they didn't have the right skill set among the team members who were working on the implementation. In any of those cases, clients expect that you as the vendor (the expert, the thought leader, their partner) will guide them to do all the things they need to do to achieve the Outcome—and even when they're not following your direction, you still need to make it happen.

The Customer Experience is a summation of all the emotions they undergo along their journey with you, across all their touchpoints with different folks across your company. The Experience includes the client's interactions with your salesperson, their use of your product, their email exchange with your Support team, their phone call with your Customer Success Manager, and their attendance at the Customer Advisory Board meeting that your Marketing team scheduled—even their feelings reading and paying your bill, to name a few examples. Those interactions may leave them feeling all sorts of emotions about your company—ranging from angry and fearful to joyful and calm.

Your clients expect that you'll deliver Outcomes for them while also ensuring a wonderful Experience along the journey of getting to those Outcomes. Both are required. If you as the vendor don't fulfill one of those two expectations, bad things will happen. So we can create a two-by-two grid of the client's Outcome (positive or negative) and the client's Experience (positive or negative), as shown in Figure 6.1.

Let's look at the upper-left quadrant. The client has had a positive Experience with you ("We love your people. They're so friendly!"), but they

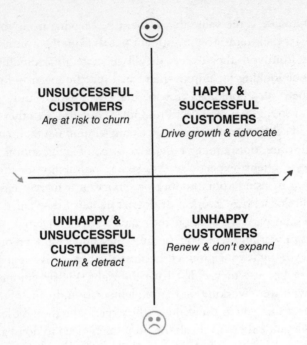

Figure 6.1

haven't achieved an Outcome ("We missed our goal"). It doesn't matter that your team was nice; this client is not going to renew, particularly if your key advocate leaves during the term of the contract. Many of us can think of clients who were "big fans" and even acted as references but didn't use our products or services effectively.

Conversely, if the client achieves a business Outcome ("We reached our bookings goal, thanks to you!") but doesn't have a great Experience ("It's so exhausting to work with your team"), they'll be able to justify continuing their relationship with you to their CFO and Procurement department, but when it comes time to finding a vendor for a new use case, they'll open up the door to your competitors. Clients expect you to be in the upper-right quadrant, delivering great Outcomes with a positive Experience. That's when they'll be truly loyal to you.

Your focus on Outcomes and Experiences may evolve as your company changes. Early on, customers may tolerate a bumpy Experience if the Outcomes you generate are unique and powerful. Conversely, as a larger company, poor Experiences can create a major drag on your growth.

Much has been written about customers' expectations for an effortless, delightful Experience, so we're not going to focus on that in this chapter. But knowledge of what it means to generate a strong Outcome has only emerged in the last few years. With respect to Outcomes, clients are expecting you to take three steps:

1. Set a *vision* for jointly owning their Outcomes.
2. Leverage a *methodology* for achieving that Outcome.
3. Adopt prescriptive *behaviors* that help them follow the methodology.

All three steps require real investment in Customer Success. Let's dig into what each one entails.

Step #1: Set a Vision for Joint Ownership of Client Outcomes

Bret Connor is chief customer officer at athenahealth, accountable for $1.7 billion in annual revenue across 10,000+ clients. According to its LinkedIn profile summary, athenahealth offers "medical record, revenue cycle, patient engagement, care coordination, and population health services" to "hospitals and ambulatory customers." But more than offering software products and services, athenahealth partners with its customers to drive clinical and financial results. In other words, athenahealth is looking to generate real Outcomes for the medical practices it serves.

Therefore, Connor's team is focused not merely on helping clients use their software, but on truly generating Outcomes for them. Here's how he describes his team's goals:

> What are the things that we measure? We start with the outcomes. We want to drive financial performance for the providers who are our clients, and also help them improve clinical outcomes for their patients.
>
> In terms of the financial performance of our clients, we look at whether they are growing the dollars that come in the door to their practices, and whether we are helping them with that. For example, are we helping them to maximize the yields on every single charge that they post? If a provider has a patient come into their office, we want to make sure they're paid fully what they should be paid. So we can measure in our system whether their yield on collections is going up or down over

time. And if the yield is going down, we look into what's causing it to go down and how we can help them get ahead of that. We also have the ability to help them target the right types of patients to serve, based upon what procedures they're good at doing and what they will actually get paid for. And we look at minimizing the patient no-show rate.

Beyond measuring the financial performance of our clients, we want to measure the outcomes to their patients and see how we can help with those. If patients haven't gotten the vaccines they need, then let's run outreach campaigns. Then let's measure whether we can actually get them in the door. Another example is we help Medicare patients get in the door for their annual wellness physicals with their care providers. The industry has about a 15% compliance rate for annual wellness visits. We can help clients get that above 60%. By doing that, you close key healthcare gaps for people on Medicare, they stay healthier, and that lowers the overall cost of healthcare for all of us.

You might think that athenahealth was literally a patient care provider—but rather, they're a vendor that has truly absorbed clients' outcomes as their own.

The workflow of athenahealth's CSMs is organized around these outcomes.

We have a playbook that guides our CSMs in working with the client to help them—and us—change behaviors so that we can drive those performance outcomes together. We run those plays and then look to see which CSMs have fully acted on them. Then we see which clients are taking the advice of those CSMs. And then we look to see whether those clients have actually seen performance improvement based on those actions. We test playbooks like these at a small scale initially. We see which ones work best and then we roll them out at a larger scale.

You can see the tight linkage between CSM activity at athenahealth and the Outcomes that clients achieve. The result? "Over the last two years, the Client Net Promoter Score has expanded by 35 points," says Connor, "and we've seen a huge impact on our actual financial results in terms of client retention." Connor is able to fuel athenahealth's growth through his team's focus on Outcomes. Sounds pretty good, huh?

Your clients expect you to lay out a vision where you jointly own the Outcome of their purchase—even the outcomes of their business, as Connor and athenahealth have done. From there, your clients expect you to offer a specific methodology for how they can achieve that Outcome.

Step #2: Create a Methodology

At Gainsight, we've given a lot of thought to how to generate Outcomes for our own clients. As you might imagine, our clients are companies that want to become more customer-centric. They have a vision in mind, even if it's not yet fully formed, of their company's end state. To help them picture how to get there, we designed a methodology that we call the Elements of Customer Success. The goal is to make it super-clear how to get from point A to point B.

This methodology involves four stages of Customer Success maturity (see Figure 6.2) based on our observations of thousands of companies, which we described in the previous chapter.

Our job at Gainsight is to help our clients progress from the early stages into the Transformational stage. To do that, we need to help clients achieve specific Outcomes along the way so they achieve progress step by step. Because we're complete geeks, we enumerated those Outcomes as a periodic table—like in chemistry—except in this case, it's a Table of Customer Success Elements. Each Element corresponds to an Outcome that the client wants to achieve: for example, getting better at Adoption Management (Am, Element #5) or Advocate Engagement (Ae, #12). Underlying each Outcome is a prescriptive, best-practice approach to combining people, process, and the Gainsight platform to drive success for our clients. As clients achieve more and more Outcomes by implementing the Elements, they progress further toward the Transformation stage, as you can see in Figure 6.3.

The Insights & Actions stage involves four Elements focused on gathering data about clients and taking actions based on that data. For example, in the Experience Health (Cx) Element, our client visualizes the health of their client interactions across their company, and then follows up on their knowledge of that health.

The Outcomes stage requires collaboration across multiple CS departments. For example, in the Renewal Management (Rm) Element, our client

REACTIVE
*Manage escalations on a
case-by-case basis*

INSIGHTS & ACTIONS
*Turn data into meaningful
actions across your team*

OUTCOMES
*Proactively deliver customer
outcomes at scale*

TRANSFORMATION
*Rally your entire company
around the mission of
customer success*

Figure 6.2

focuses on consistently executing on renewals and developing informed forecasts, leveraging a partnership between CSMs and account managers. In Risk Escalation (Re), our client gives executives and others at the company visibility into strategic customers that need their attention.

The Transform stage involves even broader collaboration across the company, in service of the client. In Services Experience (Se), for example, a Professional Services team aims to move beyond a focus on utilization and

Figure 6.3

73

P&L targets, to driving strong outcomes and experiences in client engagements. In Product Success (Pr), Customer Success and Product teams work together to prioritize clients' enhancement requests.

A client may not have to implement all Elements in the table—instead, we help the client prioritize them based on their objectives. For some teams, it may make sense to skip ahead to some elements in the Transform stage. But in general, we recommend starting on the left and moving toward the right.

We designed these Elements based on our experience working with many of you. But we also wanted empirical evidence that demonstrates the impact of these Elements. So at a recent Chief Customer Officer Summit, we gathered survey responses from 100 Customer Success leaders, from a range of companies.

We asked, What's your progress with each of the objectives represented by the Elements (options: Nonexistent, Manual, Semi-Automated, Optimized)? Then we grouped the respondents into the maturity stages and asked for their Gross Retention Rate and Net Retention Rate. As we shared in the previous chapter, the results showed a 13-percentage-point increase in Gross Retention and a 33-percentage-point increase in Net Retention as companies progress along the Customer Success maturity curve.

Those are the Outcomes that our clients want! So they can rely on the Elements as a methodology that can guide them from point A to point B.

We're sharing our Elements of Customer Success in this book as an example of the kind of methodology that clients expect you to provide. But that's not all clients expect. They also want you to communicate in a prescriptive way, so that they can reap the benefits of that methodology.

Step #3: Adopt Prescriptive Behaviors

Clients come to you dreaming of a home renovation—that sparkly beach home that you might see on Pinterest. They'd prefer not to think about the hammers, screwdrivers, or drills that were critical for making that home. They expect you—the vendor—to act as General Contractor and handle all the tools yourself. The client cares first and foremost about the Outcome, not the mechanics.

In other words, they want, expect, and need your expert guidance. If your team isn't proactive with proposing solutions, the client can flounder. After all, they're not the experts at building the home renovation. You are.

Wendy Pfeiffer has bought technology many times. She's currently the chief information officer (CIO) at Nutanix, the hyper-converged infrastructure company. She says,

> I want a CSM because they have a deep understanding of my business and the challenges that I'm trying to address, as well as a deep understanding of the technology. The last thing I need is one more person in the mix who knows less than I do. Don't just send me a CS person because there's this Customer Success thing now. We need someone who knows what will or will not work. If we're debating Choice A or Choice B, that person should tell us which one they recommend, based on what they know about our industry, our business, our competitors, the product itself, and what we already have in place. If they don't have that voice of authority, I'm not interested.

This means that clients often expect you to be a thought leader on *their* job, not merely an expert in yours.

Pfeiffer argues that CSMs should have enough clout within their company to go to bat for the client. "CSMs have to tell their Product team, for example, why it's important for a particular feature to be developed as part of the next release. Or to advise delaying the next release because it continues to have flaws or bugs or issues. That's super-important. If a vendor has an amazing CS organization but there are flaws in the product or in the operational model, a great CS team won't compensate for that."

The kind of CSM behaviors that Pfeiffer endorses—speaking with authority and advocating—are antithetical to the "helper" mindset that most CSMs had five years ago. Back then, we saw way too many CSMs trying to be "nice" to their clients. Their clients might have characterized them as:

- Good listener
- Attentive
- Receptive to feedback
- Contagiously positive

Let's take a look at the client journey that this kind of "niceness" produces. Imagine a hypothetical client getting on the phone with you to offer some feedback:

"I really like your team, so I bought your product. Then they asked me, What do you want to do in the product? I told them XYZ things. But to be honest with you, I had no idea if that was the right decision. Your team never pushed back. They kept asking me, 'What would you like to do next?' I felt like I was the one pushing the process. We still haven't gotten value. Truly what I wanted was for you to tell me what to do. You guys know best—I want to use the product the way your most successful clients use it. But we're starting from a blank slate, and this really just seems like a 'build' exercise, and IT says they can do it. My CFO is breathing down my neck about cutting costs, and I can't defend this expense if I'm not getting value. This isn't personal, though. You have great people."

You know what that is? That's the excruciating sound of a client churning—all because your team was too nice. That could easily be Wendy Pfeiffer canceling a contract with a vendor!

If you want to generate Outcomes for your clients, make sure your CSMs are prescriptive with their clients. That prescriptiveness will require bravery. We'll come back to this requirement in the chapter on professional development later in this book.

Anything to Add about the Client Experience?

While we're on the subject of CSM behaviors, we'll note that there are a few behaviors that we've found to be incredibly helpful for meeting clients' expectations for their *Experience*. While this chapter was focused on the newer trend of clients expecting to achieve Outcomes, we've written a Guide to Customer Etiquette that you may find helpful for educating your CSM team on behaviors that generate excellent Experiences: https://www .gainsight.com/blog/guide-etiquette-customer-interactions/.

Your Employees Care about Client Outcomes, Too

Today, employees want a sense of mission in serving their clients. Many, if not most of them, joined your company because they were enthralled with the idea of generating a certain type of Outcome for your customer base. They want to believe that they are "changing the world" in some material way by helping your clients.

As a result, just as clients are redefining what they want from vendors—especially the delivery of Outcomes—vendors are redefining their own raison d'être as *actually delivering on those Outcomes*. The rise of purpose-driven organizations has been a tailwind for the Customer Success movement, because more than ever, employees want to see their customers become successful.

JD Peterson is chief growth officer at Culture Amp. According to its LinkedIn profile, Culture Amp's aspiration is to "help companies become better places to work. Our goal is to build the platform that powers tens of thousands of culture-first companies to make better decisions about people and culture," using employee feedback and analytics solutions. You can tell this is the kind of organization that cares about generating meaning for employees.

We asked Peterson, How would you define a purpose-driven organization? His answer:

> A purpose-driven organization is one that first has a clear mission, which is linked to having a positive impact on the world beyond business results. We also see in a purpose-driven organization employees tend to be there for much more than just a paycheck or a notch on their resume. They believe in something bigger than themselves and they're aligned to that mission.

Why is this relevant to Customer Success? Typically the company's mission is intimately tied to helping clients. "If an organization truly is purpose-driven, they believe in the outcomes they're driving for their customers. They have to realize their purpose ultimately through their customers—the people who are adopting the product. And Customer Success is really on the front line of helping clients achieve those outcomes, by guiding that client on a new journey." So if a company is purpose-driven, they're going to invest in Customer Success—because CS is *the way* that they can deliver on their purpose.

Coco Brown is the founder and CEO of the Athena Alliance, which is dedicated to advancing diversity in the boardroom by preparing executive women for board service and facilitating board matches. She's given a great deal of thought to the nature of purpose-driven organizations, given her own desire to create good in the world through the Athena Alliance, and also given that many of her clients find purpose in making their boards more diverse.

Brown says that companies today are showing "a commitment to their ecosystem." She explains, "In today's world that means you have to be thinking about all the ways in which what you do touches the bigger world, the broader society that's impacted by you." Although Brown means "ecosystem" in a broader way—not just your clients but also the other stakeholders in your community who might be affected by what you sell—her point reinforces the need to avoid the kind of harm that used to result from when vendors sold products without regard for the impact they would have on clients. Today, companies need to be good corporate "citizens," and that requires being good to their clients.

Summary

In this chapter, we talked about how client expectations are the third driver of increased investment in CS. Clients expect vendors to generate both great Experiences and great Outcomes. The latter has been a major new trend during the last five years, requiring companies to define a vision for the client relationship that involves taking ownership of the client's Outcomes, developing a methodology for achieving those Outcomes, and adopting a more assertive communication style to ensure that both client and vendor execute in line with the methodology. The rise of purpose-driven organizations has made the achievement of those Outcomes an imperative not only from the client's perspective, but also from employees' perspectives.

As it turns out, investors, too, strongly believe in the value of those Client Outcomes. In the next chapter, we'll take a look at the fourth reason why companies have invested in Customer Success: Their investors believe in it.

7 | Reason #4: Even the Money People Are in Love with Customer Success

Picture a board meeting ten years ago for a typical B2B company. What would be on the agenda? Probably a smorgasbord of financial results and sales metrics. From time to time, you might have seen sprinkled in a discussion on product roadmap as well. Customer Success? That would only be a topic if there were a big issue.

Fast forward to today. Private company CEOs now know that when it's time to raise a new round of funding, they have to make sure that they have a strong Customer Success strategy in place. And public company CEOs are increasingly realizing that research analysts and fund managers understand how Customer Success fits into the SaaS business model. Far from looking at CS teams as just another flashy business fad, investors consider them to be critical to ensuring that revenue recurs predictably. That predictability gives investors peace of mind, when so many of the other variables they're analyzing in a business can change in a heartbeat.

Of course, most investors are data people. They take confidence in the numbers above all else. And we may have a soft spot for client emotions, but we love math as much as anyone! So, to understand why investors value CS so highly, let's turn to an example of Customer Success math.

Investors Are Doing the Math

Allyson White is a principal at Insight Partners, a leading global venture capital and private equity firm that invests in high-growth tech companies and has over $20 billion of assets under management. White has become a thought leader on how investors and their portfolio companies should approach Customer Success.

On the Insight blog,[5] White describes Sales as "the hare in the race to scale—new logos start the race and accelerate strongly out of the gate. But, retention is the tortoise, and, as we know from Aesop's fable, the tortoise wins the race." To illustrate the impact of higher retention on enterprise valuation—the total worth of a company—Allyson describes a hypothetical company. She explains:

> Fable Co is on track to achieve $20 million in Annual Recurring Revenue (ARR) in current year (i.e. Year 0):
>
> - $10 million is new customer ARR.
> - $10 million is existing customer ARR.
> - The company has a solid product and adoption with a 95% net dollar retention rate and 90% gross dollar retention rate.
> - Fable Co sells into a very large addressable market that is growing 10% annually.

Assume Fable Co's new logo business grows at the same market CAGR of 10% and net retention holds at 95%. The company will reach $77 million of ARR in 5 years (no small feat!).

However, if Fable Co can increase net retention by 5% from 95% to 100%, then ARR will hit $87 million.

Each 1% uplift in net retention yields an incremental ~$2 million in Year 5 revenue. At 5× revenue exit multiples, this 5-point retention uplift equates to more than $50 million in incremental enterprise value, a number sure to make Fable Co's employee and VC shareholders smile. (See Figures 7.1 and 7.2.)

Bear in mind that the 100% retention business is $10 million larger and growing faster (34% CAGR vs. 31%), and as a result will command a higher revenue exit multiple. The incremental EV from an increase in revenue exit multiple (from 5× to 6×) is >$135 million.

The second Retention Impact scenario to consider is what Insight calls the Opportunity Cost of Churn (OCC). What additional sales and

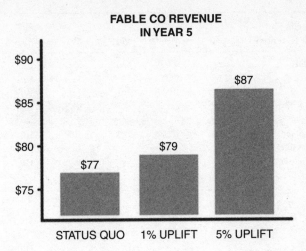

Figure 7.1

Incremental Revenue	–	$2	$10
EV @ 5x Multiple	$385	$395	$435
EV @ 6x Multiple	$462	$474	$522

Figure 7.2

marketing investment is required to make up for the revenue lost to churn—or to use a common SaaS phrase, to offset the "holes in the leaky bucket"?

To calculate: the Opportunity Cost of Churn (OCC) = (Churned Dollars + Downsell Dollars) × the Customer Acquisition Cost (CAC).

Let's take the same $20 million Fable SaaS Co with 90% gross retention and assume customer acquisition cost (CAC) is 1. In other words, Fable Co gets $1 of first year ARR for every $1 it spends on sales and marketing acquisition. What is the impact?

- In Year 0, Fable Co loses $2 million of starting ARR, which will cost $2 million to reacquire.
- In Year 5, churn loss is $6.4 million, which will cost $6.4 million to reacquire.
- Over the 5-year horizon, the Total OCC is ~$21M. (See Figure 7.3)

Hare Scenario (90% Gross Retention)	Year 1	Year 2	Year 3	Year 4	Year 5	Total
Starting ARR	$20.0	$30.0	$40.6	$51.9	$63.9	
Churn	$2.0	$3.0	$4.1	$5.2	$6.4	
CAC	1.0	1.0	1.0	1.0	1.0	
Opportunity Cost of Churn (OCC)	$2.0	$3.0	$4.1	$5.2	$6.4	$20.6
Margin Loss (as % of Starting ARR)	10%	10%	10%	10%	10%	
Margin Loss per 1% of Churn	1%	1%	1%	1%	1%	

Figure 7.3

To summarize: At a CAC of 1, each percentage point of retention equates to approximately 1% of margin.

Higher retention businesses can grow faster, grow more profitability, or most likely pursue a combination of both. . . . Companies need both the tortoise and the hare to win the race.

If we lost you in all that math, here's the bottom line: Investors like White know that even a 1 percentage point improvement in retention impacts enterprise valuation in three primary ways:

1. It preserves revenue.
2. It gives the company a higher valuation multiple of revenue.
3. It improves the profit margin.

Sounds good to us!

Now that we've gotten inside the brains of investors by doing the math that they're doing, let's dive deeper into the qualitative reasons why VCs look to CS metrics when they're evaluating investment opportunities.

Why VC Firms Love Customer Success

For a VC firm investing in early-stage companies, strong recurring revenue signals that the startup is a real business, delivering a product or service that people want. Poor retention can sometimes be an indicator that a company hasn't achieved product-market fit—in other words, their product isn't solving a customer problem. That can lead to a company going out of business or laying off much of its team to stem cash burn and buy enough time to develop a stronger product.

Alex Clayton, general partner at Meritech Capital and formerly at Spark Capital, echoed the gravity of this kind of existential problem in a post on Medium.com in January 2018: "Dollar retention is critical to the health of a SaaS company. . . . A SaaS company could be growing ARR over 100% each year, but if their annualized net dollar retention is less than 75%, there is likely a problem with the underlying business. . . . Poor net dollar retention will almost always catch up and slow a business's top line."

Therefore, VC firms consider retention when assessing whether a business's growth is going to continue well into the future. Bessemer Venture Partners (BVP), a leading VC firm with over $6 billion under management, has adopted that approach. The BVP team are thought leaders on subscription growth, having written the 10 Laws of Cloud Computing and launched the BVP Nasdaq Emerging Cloud Index, an industry index designed to track the performance of public companies providing cloud software and services. So they know a lot about the impact of Customer Success on both private- and public-market valuations.

"We care so much about CS at an early stage because it's a good predictor of whether the company's growth will continue at a high pace, which is otherwise very hard to know but also super-important to figure out as an investor," explains Byron Deeter, a partner at Bessemer Venture Partners.

If a company doesn't have strong retention and doesn't have the right CSM protocols in place, churn can be the death of an SaaS business. But if you have high retention, you can last for a very, very, very long time. And you get lots of opportunities to grow, to innovate on the product, to sell new product categories, and to sell in the new market.

We look at three top metrics before investing: growth, retention, and payback, or some measure of sales efficiency, and in my portfolio I'm particularly focused on retention. Because not only can it be as attractive as high customer growth, but if you have a positive net retention rate, you can sell even more to your existing customer base.

Tomasz Tunguz is also particularly interested in the potential of growing revenue from existing clients, not just retaining them. Tunguz, the managing director at Redpoint Ventures who appeared in Chapter 4, explains:

> One of the main differences between enterprise companies and consumer companies is that enterprise customers tend to expand on an annual basis. Best-in-class B2B companies might grow by thirty or forty or fifty percent per year. So a cohort of new customers last year who spent $1m last year would spend $1.5m this year.
>
> As a company grows and scales, the revenue managed by the CS team will outgrow new bookings by the sales team. Because of new sales and this compounding expansion, Customer Success becomes the single most important function of the go-to-market. CS manages the company's revenue base, which is laden with expansion potential.

VC firms see the value of Customer Success not merely as driving revenue growth, but also helping the company learn how to improve the product, aligned with our "Law #7" in Chapter 1. "I think the future of Customer Success is observations from the CSMs," says Tunguz. "If there's a tight coupling between Product Managers and CSMs, the products can get better and better. The companies with the highest net dollar retention combine a terrific product with in-depth analysis of the customer base through the CS organization." Deeter from BVP agrees on the value of CS-Product dialogue: "I think the best enduring companies are the ones who constantly get feedback from customers and act on that feedback through the entire life cycle of the company. Spend time talking to them, listen to them, and try to build a product that they want."

Whether VCs are looking for evidence of product-market fit, the longevity of the business, client expansion potential, or a strong long-term product strategy, they believe that CS is a primary indicator of the health of a business.

Private equity (PE) firms may be different from VCs on many dimensions—in particular, you may see more mahogany in their offices!—but they're drinking the same champagne.

Why Private Equity (PE) Firms Love Customer Success

If you follow trends in finance, you know that PE firms have had an expanded role in the technology market. Up until the past decade, many

PE firms were known for identifying companies with slower top-line growth, acquiring those companies with a combination of equity and debt, and then, once they became a controlling shareholder, they would trim operations in order to maximize cash flows, which allow them to pay down debt and increase equity value.

But increasingly, many of these same PE firms are more focused on the opportunity to drive top-line growth. Instead of just cutting operating costs at the firms they invest in, they are now getting involved in processes and technology to improve a company's recurring revenue. Recurring revenue means recurring cash, which makes it easier to pay interest on the debt, pay down the principal, and generate strong returns on equity. High retention rates were "made" for the PE model.

Consider the case of venture capital and private equity firm K1 Investment Management (K1). Neil Malik, founder and CEO of K1, sees Customer Success as core to the financial model—and mission—of K1. "K1 exclusively invests in enterprise software companies. We've invested in over 120 companies since the inception of the firm. Our mission is to help make people more productive, so they can accomplish more in less time. Our focus is realizing the value of technology through adoption. Customer Success measures that we look at include customer satisfaction, usage information, and ultimately these are reflected in client retention. We believe that growth combined with strong retention is one of the biggest drivers of valuation."

Consequently, it's very common—almost standard—for PE firms to create ways to infuse CS best practices in their portfolios. Many PE firms have annual summits to bring together CS executives; many have operating partners internally who work with their companies on CS; and many want to ensure that their companies are implementing CS technology.

As an example, K1 invests heavily in Customer Success best practices in their portfolio. Malik explains,

> We think about it as a multi-functional practice. K1 has a quarterly function-specific summit, including go-to-market, product and engineering, human capital and finance as well as a customer experience summit. All of these summits have components that focus on the customer experience. Our final summit of the year, customer experience, brings together professional services, support, and customer success professionals. They spend several days networking and learning from their peers across the portfolio. We bring in some renowned innovators

as keynotes, including Nick Mehta from Gainsight and Chris Bates from Tableau, talking about their customer experience journeys. This enables our companies to learn from each other as well as from industry experts and luminaries.

The end result is that PE-backed companies are some of the most innovative, in terms of Customer Success. Malik shared two examples from the K1 portfolio.

Emburse is a large player in the global travel and expense space. They've produced onboarding videos that help clients in a one-to-many experience, in advance of a more traditional white-glove implementation kick-off. This improves the scalability of our portfolio company by allowing clients to work asynchronously and absorb content and basic building blocks at their own pace, after which we can provide our resources in more synchronous and live formats.

Similarly, we have a portfolio company called Clarizen in the project management arena. In lieu of cookiecutter business reviews with a templatized deck, Clarizen came up with measures like usage, support, customer business, and adoption goals and uses those to design the agenda for the QBR, focused on our mission of realizing the value of technology through adoption.

At the same time, some PE-backed companies are newer to the CS movement and new to deploying technology to improve operational efficiency. At a recent conference that we attended among chief financial officers at PE-backed companies, those CFOs were vocal in describing the limitations in older systems for managing customer relationships. In particular:

- Modeling clients the way they experience you (by department, business unit, product, stakeholder), not just in the way you sell to/bill them.
- Blending a variety of data (telemetry, usage, analytics, surveys, support, CRM, billing) to holistically measure the customer experience.
- Analyzing this data in a scalable way to measure customer health in all dimensions.
- Driving proactive human and digital outreach along the customer journey.

Nearly every firm had experience trying to cobble together CRM, BI, spreadsheets, and the like—and the scalability limitations therein.

At the same time, many PE-backed companies are trailblazing for their peers. This is valuable for PE firms' portfolios, since the managing directors tend to want to see examples of success before rolling out a specific operational change to another portfolio company. They especially do not want to reinvent the wheel. Their companies are so efficient that they don't build internal tools when third-party vendors are available. In fact, PE firms often guide portfolio companies to standardize on a common stack of third-party business systems.

Why Research Analysts Are Scrutinizing Customer Success

Even in the public markets, Customer Success is becoming a hot topic. As Alex Clayton stated in the same post mentioned above, "Net dollar retention has a huge impact on the long-term success of a business; the companies that get public usually have net dollar retention rates of well over 100%, and in some cases 150%+. It's unfortunately at times overlooked, but increasingly becoming one of the most core KPIs for any SaaS company."

In nearly every SaaS research analyst report, retention is a topic of discussion. Analysts obviously cover the fundamentals of revenue growth, profit margins and the like. But they have shown a spotlight recently on retention metrics. Because most public companies only disclose Net Dollar Retention, churn is a bit more opaque to the stock market. But savvy analysts continue to dig in through primary research calls with end clients. As public investors understand Customer Success more, we expect it to be an increasingly hot topic on earnings calls.

Summary

Investors are now increasingly focused on CS metrics and strategy as indicators of a company's health. That's true when they're conducting due diligence on investment opportunities, and it's true when they're guiding their portfolio companies in the boardroom. As a result, the CS priority has reached the highest levels of the corporate structure.

That means that CEOs can't delegate CS—they have to own it. And they have to ensure that every function within their company makes meaningful changes from traditional models to adopt a customer-centric mindset.

In that vein, now that we've explored the *why* behind Customer Success—the four reasons behind the greater investment in CS—we'll move on to the *how*. Part II of this book is all about how to emulate the companies that have achieved great success for their clients. The question is, how can you bake CS into every single department of your company?

PART II

Baking Customer Success Into Every Aspect of Your Business Model

8 | It Can't Be Delegated

For Customer Success to be the driving force it needs to be, the CEO must own it. Why is that? Because without successful customers, your business will ultimately fail. It is your job as the head of your company to make sure that every part of your company is oriented around your customers. But how do CEOs cram one more responsibility onto their already-overloaded plates? Let's find out.

I'm Sorry, I Need to Own *What* Now?

That's right, if you're the CEO of your company, you need to own Customer Success—along with everything else you own. Granted, *ownership* is one of the most overused terms in the modern work world; it shows up in the business buzzword dictionary right next to *synergy* and "taking things offline." In a typical large company, you'll find at least a dozen people who "own" hot initiatives with buzzy names like "the cloud" or "our AI strategy."

If you're a CEO reading this, you're probably thinking, "Have you seen my schedule? How can I possibly own anything more?" You've already been told to own your product destiny, your growth plans, your capital strategy, your culture—heck, Nick even owns our "rap video offer letter strategy" (that's right: Nick occasionally sends rap videos to candidates).

But our challenge to you is, "How can you not own it?" The future of your company depends on it.

Truthfully, we don't know any CEOs who are eager to own more. Most are looking to recruit, delegate, and empower (more buzzword bingo). And in the early days of Customer Success, this tactic served companies well. Leading CEOs typically recruited a CS leader, delegated core functions to that leader, occasionally empowered the leader with resources and a seat at the table (more buzzwords), and maybe even doled out a C-level title such as "chief customer officer."

But what worked in the early days is no longer good enough. We've learned from working with literally hundreds of companies on CS strategy that Customer Success begins as a department and a function, but it only thrives as a company-wide transformation. This transformation *always* requires the CEO to personally own it.

When he joined Altify (later acquired by Upland Software) as its CEO, Anthony Reynolds was charged with driving the next phase of growth. He knew that Customer Success strategy would be critical, so he invested his own time in it. "As a CEO, you can't just give CS lip-service. The rest of the organization will watch your actions. So how you respond to customers and prioritize them is the most important thing to take care of when you walk in every single morning. You should personally spend time with your customers and truly listen to them."

Reynolds points to the importance of CEOs as role models in Customer Success. That sounds great in theory, but let's explore what it means in practice. We'll discuss three steps to becoming a more customer-oriented CEO—without losing sleep.

I Want to Be a Great Customer-centric CEO: What's Step #1?

Let's first make an honest statement that is really important: Most CEOs' natural tendencies are to lean toward Sales and/or Product. And that's because most CEOs grew into their role by coming up in Sales or Product. This means that leaning into customers is unnatural. And I don't mean just meeting customers. The CEO role in the new customer economy requires deep involvement in decisions made about the customer experience, journey, segmentation, and so on. No major Sales or Product decisions are made without the CEO's input. Neither should any major customer decisions be made without the same perspective. Specific activities that force this customer focus are included below.

Start by organizing to convey the importance of Customer Success. If you put Customer Success under Sales or Product or Support, it conveys one level of importance. If you make the leader of Customer Success a peer to your VP of Sales and VP of Product, it communicates something very different. Also, assign the retention number to that leader. You would never run a company without having one person owning the Sales number. You should not run a recurring revenue business without forcing the same accountability for retention, which over time will be a much larger number than the new business Sales number.

Now proceed to infuse discussions about customers into your conversations with each department. Some departments are by definition constructed around customers (Customer Success and Customer Support most obviously). Others are not intuitively aimed at customers. The trick is to define the jobs where there is natural orientation around CS and the roles where you need to inject CS into the existing way people work. Customer Success, when approached strategically, reimagines the way companies think about product development, marketing, sales, and other functions.

You can break it down with the following series of questions:

Product

- How can Product be instrumented to provide more data to inform Customer Success?
- How can Customer Success strategies get built into the product?

Marketing

- How can you take learnings from Customer Success to inform your "ideal customer" to market to?
- How can you use a lifecycle marketing approach to efficiently nurture existing clients toward adoption, expansion, and retention?

- How can you use Customer Success to identify customer advocates and indirectly drive new logo growth?

Sales

- How can Customer Success processes more seamlessly drive upsell and cross-sell for Sales?
- How can Customer Success increase perceived value to maximize renewal rates and pricing power?
- How can Customer Success insights help reps sell with more authenticity and to a more targeted customer set?

Channel

- What role does your channel play in Customer Success?
- How do you incent and enable partners to invest in this area?
- What data do you need to expose to partners? What do you need to get from them?

Services

- How can onboarding drive toward outcomes and value—not just project closure?
- What Customer Success capabilities can be offered "for fee" instead of "for free"?
- How can Customer Success identify opportunities for Services sales?

Support

- How can the support team help to scale Customer Success by taking the lead on issue resolution?
- How can the support team be aware of the larger context around a case?
- How can the support team use Customer Success insights to prioritize cases?

IT

- What data do you need to understand Customer Success?
- How can business processes come together around Customer Success?
- How do various systems align around your needs?

Now that you've started to infuse the topic of customers into your conversations with each department, let's explore how you can enable those departments to work together in service of your customers.

Step #2: Run a Success Briefing

We've done dozens of "Success Briefings" with CEOs and general managers where we get management teams together to talk about Customer Success cross-functionally. The goal is to get other departments up to speed on the business imperative and then introduce models for collaboration across functions. This cross-functional discussion covers how Customer Success changes every role.

From there, you can define tangible steps forward:

- **Charters:** Some execs focus on redefining charters (and related KPIs) in this new world of a shared ownership of the customer journey. (We'll cover each function in later chapters.)
- **Journey:** Many companies decide to collaborate across their departments around a codified and instrumented view of the ideal customer journey in this new model. (More on this later.)
- **Health score:** Similarly, teams often rally around defining a metrics-oriented view of what a healthy customer looks like. (You can check out Chapter 24 for more details.)

Even as you're empowering your management team to collaborate closely, you're not off the hook. You personally should be engaging with clients. Let's hear from Nick, in the first person, about how he does that.

Step #3: Ramp Up Your Client Meetings

We all have parts of our jobs we love more than other parts. My favorite thing is the diversity of people with whom I interact across all our stakeholders—teammates, their families, clients, partners, investors, and even folks in our community. Yes, I am definitely an "E" (for Extrovert) in the language of Meyers-Briggs personality types.

So when I saw a recent *Harvard Business Review* paper[6] that said the typical CEO spends 3% of their time with clients, I was shocked enough to ask an intern to determine, based on my calendar, what percentage of my time I spend with clients.

The final number was 17%. That averages out to roughly 11 clients a week, 45 clients a month, and over 500 client meetings a year. I love these meetings, but even for me, it takes a good process to make it work. Logistically, operationally, emotionally—it doesn't happen by accident. So, for all of you who are wondering how on earth you're going to truly own Customer Success, here's my process. (Note that we run a high-touch business, with our average client paying us more than six figures of Annual Recurring Revenue (ARR) per year, so this process may not apply to you. Even if your clients are smaller in spend, there's a way to scale this down.)

1. Meeting our prospective clients

I relish the chance to meet companies considering a Gainsight purchase. It gives me a vehicle to learn what the market is thinking, allows me to help set expectations with clients before they buy, and enables me to help our Sales team in a small way.

To make this happen, I have our Sales team identify specific client execs for me to reach out to. My assistant prepares a standard email draft for me and I personalize the message before sending.

2. Meeting stakeholders at our existing clients

Aligning with execs at our clients doesn't stop at the sales process. Many companies talk about "executive sponsor programs," but very few operationalize them. If you have "exec sponsors" on your top accounts, when was the last time the exec-to-exec connection happened for each account? Are you confident that you are "covered"?

When we close a new deal, we identify the exec sponsor on the relationship. If it's me, here's what happens:

The Customer Success Manager for the client will get a Stakeholder Alignment notification (in the Gainsight product) on a regular basis depending on the size of the customer. They send a sample email to me (based on a template) with a recommended "check-in" message for me to send to the client exec; it also includes some background for me. My assistant places the message in my email drafts. I can then personalize the message and send it out.

If I end up having a call with the client, I post my notes to our Timeline—the history of our client relationship within the Gainsight product—or simply BCC the email to the client to Timeline.

3. Meeting clients based upon survey feedback

As with most companies, we receive no shortage of feedback. We survey our client executives twice a year. When the response comes in, we auto-post it to our internal collaboration system (Slack). Since I'm kind of obsessed, I read every response. If I see a "promoter" (very happy) response from someone I know, I drop them an email of thanks. If I see a "detractor" (lower score), I drop them a note of thanks for the feedback and sometimes ask for a quick call to learn more.

4. Meeting clients based upon online reviews

Similarly, I read all the write-ups our clients post on third-party review sites like G2 or TrustRadius. We learn so much from our clients and our clients' users in this way. Sometimes, I'll even post my response to a review, thanking the client for the feedback. In other cases, if the client identified herself, I will sometimes email her to hear a more detailed account or to thank her personally.

5. Meeting our prospective and existing clients when I'm in a city

As painful as redeye flights are, I enjoy making sure that my business trips are full of meetings. When I go to a city, we do the following:

My Chief of Staff pulls a list of clients from Gainsight in the city and filters (1) clients that are healthy (where we could possibly get them to be an advocate or expansion) and (2) clients that need help.

We review the list with our CS team to make sure they agree with the targeted contacts. Similarly, our Sales team pulls a list of prospective clients to meet. My assistant drafts emails (which I personalize) from me to each potential meeting. After the meetings, I post our notes to our Timeline.

My personal record was ten in-person client meetings in one day in Manhattan. I'm particularly proud of that, given the number of Ubers, lobby sign-ins, metal detectors, and slow elevators I had to deal with!

6. Meeting clients in our advisory boards

Like most companies, we've identified a list of our top strategic clients for our advisory boards. We have one Strategic Advisory Board (SAB) that helps guide the company overall, and separate boards to advise us on new products, on our technology, and on our delivery.

We host our SABs in person when our clients are together. I've found that the strategic discussions are harder to hold remotely, no matter how great the video technology is. Our top client execs typically attend our Pulse event in San Francisco and our annual CXO Summit. In addition, many of them go to twice-a-year events hosted by the Technology Services Industry Association (TSIA), and we pick a lunch spot during these four events to bring people together.

7. Meeting clients in a monthly dinner series

To make sure I have a rhythm of feedback, one of my favorite traditions is a near-monthly dinner series that I hold for CS leaders in the San Francisco Bay Area. I have a few core rules for this:

- It's hosted by me and one or two other company members. We keep it small—10 to 12 total people.
- We always have a private room and one conversation.
- We keep it personal and vulnerable by starting with an icebreaker question ("What's your secret superpower?" was a recent one).

Logistically, we've made this pretty easy. My assistant keeps a list of client execs in the Bay Area. She books a private room. We then email the list and tell folks that (accurately) the dinner will book up fast. The takeaways from these dinners are invaluable as are the relationships that develop.

8. Meeting clients at our company events

We host a *ton* of events, from our annual Pulse event to CXO Summit to our Pulse World Tour to Pulse Europe. The event's cocktail party is a great opportunity to hear from clients in an ad hoc fashion. I always try to have some prepared questions to help get feedback:

> "What did you see or hear today that was the most valuable?"
> "What part of the product is driving the best outcomes for you right now?"
> "If you had a magic wand to make us do whatever you want, what part of the roadmap would you have us work on next?"

9. Meeting clients at third-party events

I attend a lot of third-party events, including some swanky CEO boondoggles. We make sure we are hyper-prepared for these. My Chief of Staff and I scour the list to identify clients and important prospective clients. If we decide to meet some, we draft emails in advance per the processes above. Then, when I'm on the spot at the event, I use our Gainsight Mobile App to look up the current health, sentiment, and financial relationship for a client that's walking toward me. (Yes, that was a shameless plug for one of our products.)

10. Meeting clients during job transitions

Obviously I love meeting clients, but what I enjoy the most about it has nothing to do with business goals or product roadmaps—it's connecting with them as human beings. As such, I relish the chance to talk to our clients during some of their most important and maybe even stressful times—such as when they're in transition between jobs.

I've spoken with hundreds of CS leaders one-on-one to help them navigate the job search process including:

- Understanding how to position themselves
- Giving them advice on their LinkedIn profile
- Introducing them to potential opportunities

- Giving them a backchannel or being a sounding board to compare various paths
- Acting as a reference for them

In these processes, I learn so much about the true motivations of our profession—and about how brave people in this new role are.

It's really a work in progress, this Customer Success phenomenon, and I always try to keep sight of the people blazing the trail. It's not easy to try to convince your board you need more budget, more people, more clout; it's not easy to carve out a place for yourself in a company that perhaps isn't sure what you're doing. I'm impressed by the CS professionals I meet every day.

Why Culture Isn't Enough

As we mentioned above, Nick meets a lot of customers. As such, he often finds himself waiting in many tech company lobbies. He's done his fair share of lobby sign-ins (he thinks he's signed every NDA in the world!) and has even resorted to eating office mints for the nutritional value. When you sit in a company's entrance, you get exposed to the business's culture. You notice the little things like how the front desk people treat guests—and how the employees treat the front desk people. You get to see the face they show to world, and more explicitly, you often see the values of the company. If you're like Nick, you've seen values on plaques. You've seen values on TVs. You've even seen values on poker chips! And you know what? Nearly every company Nick has seen has a value around "customer centricity" or "customer obsession" or "the customer is #1."

If "customer success is all about culture," and every company has a value around it, why do we still have such a long way to go in Customer Success? We don't want to turn this into yet another cheap denunciation of hypocrisy in business—we all know business can be better. We want to offer a solution.

In a recent meeting with a CEO, Nick heard that solution. This leader of a large software company told him that while a culture shift is clearly the beginning of a company transformation, it's not the end. Just because you have great people aligned around a mission doesn't mean your customers will consistently have great outcomes and experiences:

- What about the new teammate who has the company's values in their heart but hasn't been enabled and trained on how to implement the best practices the company espouses?
- What about the client who knows that the experience they get will vary based upon the person they deal with in your company?
- What about the issues between the seams in the company—where everyone is acting rightly in their silo, but collectively the client isn't getting the desired result?

That's starting to sound like a process issue—just improve your training, customer experience, and cross-functional cohesion. But as we have learned, it's much more than fine-tuning the problem areas where values are falling short.

The CEO went on to tell Nick that the next step is to "industrialize" customer success across the company—to move it from an art to a science. In the Industrial Revolution, new processes and technology enabled workers to specialize and allowed manufacturers to standardize, which powered companies to scale. It was much more than incremental improvement—it was transformative at a fundamental level.

This CEO was looking at customer success industrialization across three specific vectors, which we'll align to those three principles of the Industrial Revolution: specialization, standardization, and scale.

- **Specialization:** New teammates should ramp quickly to achieve best-practice competency.
- **Standardization:** Clients can trust in a consistently excellent experience across the company.
- **Scale:** Every teammate should have the full context of what's happening at the client at their fingertips.

In addition, the CEO wanted to be able to measure this process like other parts of the business that have been "industrialized." How effective is teammate onboarding? How quickly is it happening? What is the comprehensive customer experience and where are the gaps? How customer-centric is the company across functions?

Throughout the book, we'll talk about strategies to industrialize the theory of Customer Success.

Summary

To ensure a company's long-term survival and success, the CEO must own the CS process. Active involvement is a requirement! We've outlined how to make this happen without completely overloading your already-packed schedule. *Hint:* You start by leading through example. From there, you can take three steps: Ask questions about customers in your daily conversations with your execs, run a Success Briefing (we can help), and do a few more client meetings every week. We also discussed a long-term goal: that CEOs need to go beyond words on a wall and create processes, metrics, and systems to turn good intentions into success for clients.

In the next several chapters, we'll discuss how a CEO can guide each function to evolve in line with your overall CS transformation. In Chapter 9, we'll explore how to tweak your product design process from the start so that CS is at the forefront of the R&D team's mind whenever they're building for the next release.

9

Product: Design from the Start for Customer Success

The best way to make Customer Success happen is to "build it" into the product itself from the start. That means not just delivering an outstanding product, but building in the listening and follow-up methods that will allow your company to take customer feedback about problems with the product and act on that feedback quickly and successfully. We believe so strongly in the impact of baking CS into the product that we'll posit that the transformation of Product teams could be a solution to our societal challenges with technology.

Why Do Product Teams Need to Change?

Before we dive into how Product teams need to change, let's dig into the *why*. *Why* do Product teams need to change how they work to create better client experiences and outcomes? As someone who studied a lot of philosophy in college, Allison is constantly thinking about the deeper subjects in life, such as ethics and meaning. She believes that a liberal arts perspective can be useful in Product Management, where we can couple a humanist perspective with technology to create amazing outcomes and experiences for clients. Here's what she has to say on that topic:

As a COO, I'm always trying to figure out how to get a ton of things done in a short amount of time. I'm constantly thinking about how to do more with less. The danger for someone like me is that when you give them technology, the standard for what counts as "efficient" dramatically increases. Figure 9.1 shows what my typical workweek looks like.

Technology helps me pack my calendar to the brim: Any empty 30-minute time slot is immediately visible and available for me to book. In the two minutes I might have in between meetings, I flip through my inbox to see how quickly I can get back to inbox zero and how many text messages I can respond to. The busy-ness is such a good sign that our teammates want to collaborate, that clients want to meet, that there's opportunity. But the volume of communication is exorbitant. I'm playing a day-long game of whack-a-mole, as illustrated in Figure 9.2.

It takes its toll. By the time I'm at home, I am fried. My long-distance vision has declined because I spend most of my day staring at one or more screens, 12 inches from my face. I'm not as familiar with city neighborhoods, because when I'm in an Uber, I spend the time responding to emails. I am

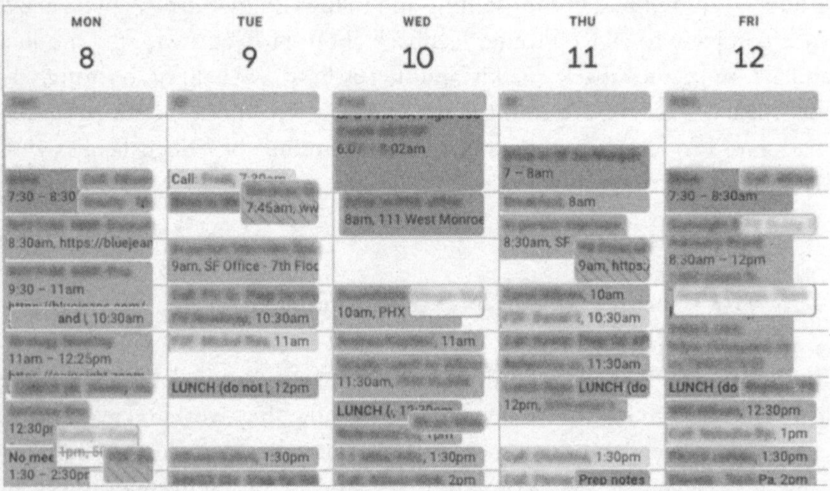

Figure 9.1

Figure 9.2

more forgetful than I used to be, because my brain operates in short-term memory as opposed to long-term storage.

I have my coping mechanisms. I don't check email in the morning until I've read a book for ten minutes, so my mind is in a more focused state. As a general rule, I don't check email after 7:30 p.m.; if someone needs to reach me, they know to text or call. I spend Saturdays completely outdoors, usually hiking in the Marin Headlands across the Golden Gate Bridge.

As much as I try to protect myself against technology, I'm struggling. The problem is that when I'm living this way, I don't feel completely human. I feel like I'm controlled by my technology. And I know that I'm not the only one who feels this way.

Today, the treadmill of technology has eliminated most autonomous moments we experience, so that we rarely exercise the muscle of reflection. When we do have a spare moment of space, we fear it. A friend of mine said to me once, "I don't want to pause and reflect, because it's terrifying to imagine what I'd think about."

Products today reinforce and take advantage of our basest emotions— especially feelings of inadequacy and fear of missing out or being left behind. They erode behaviors we once valued and that I would argue make us more human: independent thinking, deep consideration, and control over our actions. Products today don't speak to our highest human nature. Technology has become first; humanity, second.

In March, my husband, Scott, and I planned a trip to celebrate his birthday. We decided to go "glamping," which means glamorous camping. It involves sleeping outside in a tent, but with electricity. What's fascinating is that you forget entirely that the technology is there, because it's hidden in the background of nature (see Figure 9.3). Our humanity comes first; technology is here for us when we need it, but it's a servant to our higher interests.

Scott and I spent the day discussing the deeper things in life while wandering through the forested hills, shown in Figure 9.4. I even had a couple of breakthroughs about my work at Gainsight, which I never could have envisioned in the daily ritual of whack-a-mole. In this environment, humanity was first; technology, second.

Software products today don't fulfill this human-first standard. They don't recognize the humans they should be supporting as independent thinkers. They instead refer to humans as "users," as a large mass of units, perhaps distinguishing among them based on groupings such as "persona" or their company's size. These are users to be "activated"—like a machine—or "converted"—which sounds like religious conversion. The technology is supposedly the source of religious insight; the humans, mere recipients.

Products therefore come with a vision that says "people need to change," but the product doesn't facilitate that change. So a company

Figure 9.3

Figure 9.4

buys a new product, and they look to roll it out, and the team struggles. As a group of naturally independent thinkers, these users are dumbstruck by the thought that they have to conform their entropic thinking to the mostly inflexible interface of today's software—or else risk not performing in their jobs. They're smart, so they'll eventually figure out where to click and how this software might help them. But the act of conforming to software dehumanizes them. In a moment of independent thinking, one of these "users" might ask, "Why doesn't the software conform to us?"

Our industry is so far from this ideal that thinking about this might generate feelings of cynicism among us. One might say: "We're all trying to make money, after all—both the vendors and the buyers who want their teams to operate with greater efficiency." That's true, as we've discussed at length in this book! However, I believe that in the future, the ability for both sides to make money will depend on the degree to which technology conforms to and reinforces the most elevated of human behaviors. What will matter in the future is the degree to which a product is "human-first." And I believe that together, this community can help create a new era of human-first products.

What do I mean by a human-first product? I'd put forward five principles for how a product should view the humans it serves.

The Five Principles

A human-first product should treat each human as:

1. **Growing:** The product treats each human as having the raw material to improve their ways of working—but importantly, only if given time and coaching to master the new way, autonomy in how to do it, and clear alignment with a purpose. (I'm referring to the framework created by Dan Pink in *Drive: The Surprising Truth About What Motivates Us* (New York: Riverhead Books, 2009.)
2. **Special:** The product treats each human as unique, with distinct beliefs, preferences, and motivations, not as an undifferentiated user. The product is inclusive of that specific human.
3. **Vulnerable:** The product recognizes that a human can be abused by others who have their data on how they're using a product. It therefore assumes by default that any data gathered is owned by the human who generated it and offers meaningful ways to use the product without being forced to waive rights to privacy.
4. **Ends, not means:** The product holds the humans it serves as ends in themselves (with technology as a means to their goals), taking their feedback seriously and adapting its approach accordingly.
5. **Autonomous:** The product reinforces independent thinking and decision-making.

At Gainsight, we haven't totally fulfilled these five principles. You might think that this chapter is therefore hypocritical, but rather, it's an admission of guilt! That said, I honestly can't think of a single product that has fulfilled these principles. Our industry is not there yet. And it will probably take us a while—likely many years—to get there. To offer up a map to get us to that destination, I'd consider these five principles to be the five different stages of improving a product so that it becomes human-first.

The Path Forward

The five stages on the path forward are (see Figure 9.5):

Stage 1—Growing: Instead of expecting humans to adopt products instantaneously ("Go figure it out!"), let's design the product's UI itself

Figure 9.5

so that it coaches people over time on how they can take advantage of it and why it helps them. A simple first step is for Customer Success and Product teams to work together to create in-app guides to walk users through new releases.

Stage 2—Special: Product teams should design ways to learn about what makes a person unique, and help create a correspondingly unique experience for them. Customer Success teams should have tools to visualize clients as more than accounts, but rather as collections of unique individuals who need to work together. The goal is to be inclusive of every client.

Stage 3—Vulnerable: At the same time, gathering tons of data on people makes them vulnerable. So Product Managers need to create unique experiences while honoring people's need for privacy. And Customer Success Managers need to ensure that clients' sensitivities are communicated well.

Stage 4—Ends, not means: Since technology is a means to a human's ends, products should adapt to what that human needs. As a starting point, Product Managers need to create a 360-degree view of feedback from clients and also learn about what clients need based on their adoption of the product. And CSMs can contribute their observations to that 360-degree view.

Stage 5—Autonomous: Finally, products should be a "pull," not a "push." Products should help clients test their own hypotheses, not merely push recommendations. And CSMs should ensure that the configuration that's rolled out isn't overly rigid.

For the sake of a more humane software industry, Customer Success and Product Management can come together to help our industry honor these principles, and even to come up with new principles as well. But there's also a business reason for CS and Product to come together to design human-first products.

The Scaling Problem

We mentioned earlier in this book that last year we surveyed 100 Customer Success leaders about the maturity of their organization on a number of different capabilities. The most difficult pain point was *automating the customer journey* (see Figure 9.6).

And we've personally heard from many of you, "I need to scale my team." (We've also said this about Gainsight's Customer Success team in the past.) It's worth us asking, What's the root cause of that need to scale in CS?

Imagine a hypothetical conversation, where we ask ourselves *why* nine times:

Why do you need to scale?
"Because Customer Success isn't a priority at my company."
Why are you saying it's not a priority?
"Because my CFO won't give me more budget."
Why isn't your current budget sufficient for helping your clients?
"Because my CSMs have too many accounts."
Why is that account load too significant?
"Because my CSMs are already working nights and weekends in answering client emails, hosting best-practice calls, conducting trainings, running EBRs."
Why do they need to do those things?
"Well, because our clients need it."
But why do they need tons of email responses, calls, trainings, etc.?
"Well . . . because that's what it takes to enable adoption of our product."
Why is your product hard to adopt?
"Well, because . . . well, we released this new feature recently, and it was a version 1. So we had a slew of calls with clients about that. We also have a backlog of enhancement requests, and it means we have to do this workaround for our clients, which takes some time."
Why aren't you solving the product gaps?
"Ummm . . . well, that would be great. But it's not my responsibility. That's up to the Product team."
I thought you said your responsibility was to scale?
"Right. . . . Well, I guess it's a shared responsibility."
Sounds like you and your Product leader should set up a meeting.
"Good point."

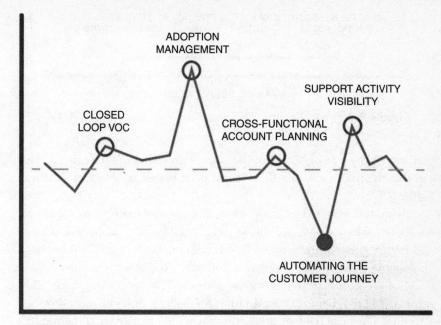

Figure 9.6

We have a massive scaling problem in our industry because we're not designing human-first products. This is an ethical problem. It's also a business problem.

We can break this scaling problem down into two related ones: a cost problem and a revenue problem.

The Cost Problem: "CSM of the Gaps"

Does the following situation sound familiar?

A new product is released. That product delivers a certain amount of value to the client "out of the box"—in other words, without human intervention to help the client. But the value that the client is hoping for—the Outcome that the client wants—is typically far greater than the "out-of-the-box" value. So the CSM spends their time plugging the gap between those two values: creating Band-Aid solutions or workarounds, running training sessions, and performing other activities that would not be necessary if the product delivered the requisite value in itself. The CSM is

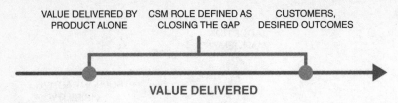

Figure 9.7

performing the role of "CSM of the Gaps," since they are plugging a value gap that the product would fill if it had been better designed, as shown in Figure 9.7.

As a result, your CS expenses grow, and your profitability is suppressed. Moreover, when CSMs are filling gaps, your Finance team will start to account for them in the Cost of Goods Sold bucket—since CSM becomes an essential team to deliver on what you sold. And that means investing in CSM of the gaps is terrible for gross margins. (On top of this, your CSM team isn't happy, because they'd rather focus their time on more strategic activities. They can tell that these efforts wouldn't be needed if the product were more effective.)

Besides the cost problem, you incur a revenue growth problem when your CSMs spend their days filling gaps.

The Revenue Problem

In the "CSM of the Gaps" model, you handicap your revenue in two ways. First, when CSMs are building Band-Aid solutions day in and out, they don't have time to do the things that could maximally drive growth in your recurring revenue. They don't align client stakeholders, propose a success plan, and enable change management. They don't facilitate faster expansion and convert clients to talkative advocates. Clients don't get as much value as they could. Your renewal, expansion, and advocacy rates suffer. You don't grow fast.

Second, in this model, you don't build the product that will maximally drive revenue growth. When CSMs are building workarounds, they paper-over the root causes that another team—Product Management—is better equipped to solve. They shield Product from the information they need to make better decisions. The only data point that the Product leader sees, likely in strategic planning sessions, is that the cost of CSM is too high (as discussed above)—which, to the untrained eye, looks more like an execution problem that a CS leader should solve with the CFO's active monitoring, rather than a problem that the Product team can help solve.

As a result, your product quality and value don't improve fast enough. Your competition catches up. Your customers churn at higher rates. They stop expanding with you. You can't get advocates to speak at your events anymore. Word spreads that your product isn't great. Sales cycles become longer. Over time, what seemed at first glance to be a CSM execution problem has turned into a growth problem. Because you're not growing fast enough, your board tells you to become more efficient—but that's hard, because your high CSM headcount is necessary to compensate for your suboptimal product.

You might get stuck as a low-growth, low-margin company unless you can transform the way your product makes customers successful—not just once, but continuously over time. For that, you need processes to consistently bake CS into the product. You need systematic alignment between CS and Product Management on how to solve the problem of scaling.

Now that we've discussed *why* that alignment is important—for both ethical and business reasons—let's discuss *how* to make it happen.

Product and CS: The New Sales and Marketing

Here's some conventional wisdom that's at least as old as the wheel: If you want to achieve growth, invest in Sales and Marketing; acquire new customers. Marketing would attract new leads and nurture them, then pass them along to Sales, who would close them.

As we've discussed, in the Age of the Customer, CS teams have joined the ranks of Sales and Marketing in driving business growth by focusing on customer retention and advocacy (see Figure 9.8). But as we've discussed, CS can't do this alone. Because the product itself generates so many invaluable customer insights and personalized interactions with clients, the Product Management team has become an invaluable partner to CS. Just as Sales and Marketing were once considered jointly responsible for top-of-funnel growth, so CS and Product Management are now the "two peas in a pod" for delivering experiences and outcomes, to keep and grow customers and turn them into advocates.

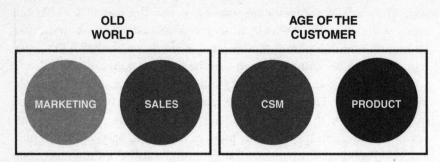

Figure 9.8

CSMs immediately grasp the idea that CS and Product are the new Sales and Marketing. CSMs are often, well, obsessed with the idea of sharing feedback with the Product team. "CSMs see how customers deal with the product post-sale, so they have the best view of what customers find valuable, and what they're trying to do with the product going forward," says John Sabino, customer success officer, SVP at publicly traded data software company Splunk.

> CSMs really live with the customer every day. So they feel it in a very personal way when the product doesn't work. They see how hard an upgrade is and what the client actually gets for that upgrade. They see how many support tickets are created and how many of those tickets have built up over time. They see the customer interact with the product and can usually advise better than anyone else on how easy it is to use and possible feature or usability enhancements. They are your key to ensuring new feature adoption and the value these investments create for your customers.
>
> CSMs are your number-one source of what's the next best thing to build, because they're your number-one source of info on how your product is being adopted and whether or not it's working as intended in the marketplace. And they know better than anyone how stable and scalable your product really is.

CSMs may be eager to provide feedback to Product teams. But how do we ensure that Product teams are happy receivers and that the partnership endures?

We propose nine solutions below.

Solution #1: Create One Common Data Set

Part of the solution lies in ensuring that CS and Product teams have the same data set. A while ago, our CS team launched revised Scorecards for Adoption. They called them Adoption-Breadth (capturing diversity of feature usage) and Adoption-Depth (capturing the degree to which individual users used the product). They presented them in an executive team meeting, only to hear from the Product team that *they* were already using their own, very different definitions of Breadth and Depth. The CS team had no idea! Each team was well-intentioned, trying to achieve similar goals. It wasn't the Product team's fault. It wasn't the CS team's fault, either. The problem was that we weren't all coordinated.

Make sure you have one set of data on clients across your company—a true "Customer 360." That data set should include adoption data, Support ticket data, survey responses, and Customer Health Scores. All of that data can help Product and CS teams develop a common point of view about how to prioritize enhancements on the roadmap. (We'll come back to how to build a Customer 360 and which metrics to prioritize later in this book.)

Solution #2: Bridge from Situations to Patterns

Let's turn to Steve Sloan, former chief product and marketing officer for SendGrid, a division of Twilio, and current CEO of Contentful. He has worked to build a tight connection between the Product Management and Customer Success teams.

> We assume that our entire company wants to consistently create products and experiences that our customers love and value, and each team works toward that goal. But for instance, in the case of Customer Success and product management, they're working from slightly different angles. I think of it as a two by two, with the x axis the number of customers you're focused on, and the y axis is impact. Both the CSMs and the product managers [PMs] are focused on high impact. PMs are usually focused on the impact across as many customers as possible, and CSMs are focused on the most impact on the subset of customers that they focus on. The trick in getting the groups together is how you bridge between the two.

We have a few ways to make this happen. For the PMs, we created something we call "listening posts"—ways in which the PMs are able to gain insights about customer problems. It establishes a regular rhythm where the PMs go to the CSMs and ask specifically for themes or trends to understand what they're seeing from customers.

The second thing we did was to have them focus on problems, not solutions. A team may get focused on the idea of "Let's go build X!," but it's possible that this solution won't ultimately yield what the customers want. But when we get everyone to focus on a really acute problem—again, that focus must occur across teams—we can have a fair amount of success. We can then go in and validate a range of potential solutions. But the problem always comes first.

Solution #3: Productize Those "Workarounds"

Remember those CSM workarounds we discussed earlier in this chapter? Product teams can turn those Band-Aids into enduring solutions. That's what Sloan's team has done.

We observed that CSMs were brilliantly and creatively coming up with their own little tools to handle the customer problems that they saw over and over again. We had a notion that we could create services offerings to do the work that CSMs were already doing out of the goodness of their hearts. Or we could actually productize those solutions—build them in as a new feature or a premium tier in our products.

To enable that productization, we assigned a PM and a product designer to work full-time with the Customer Success team. They noticed that time after time, CSMs had created a bunch of creative and insightful problem-solving templates, which were signals of a product opportunity. If the CSM had taken the time to create the template, it must mean that they saw that problem on a regular basis.

In 15 months, that pair of people in combination with the CS teams created a new set of products and services that went from nothing to about $7 million in revenue. That really showed us that we need to have people with the skills and the time to identify those problem patterns. Because we had both the product manager and the product designer, the team could come up with paper-based prototypes and share them both with the Customer Success managers and get their initial reactions. It works so well because the teams can sit down together, see what the other side is dealing with, and then work through the solutions literally side by side. The product folks sit behind people and just watch what they're doing. Then they reveal all these amazing insights.

One of the challenges for productizing these things is that CSMs do this work automatically. So they take for granted all the amazing little insights they have, and all the little tips and tricks they have for quickly getting a customer to a successful place. It's the exact same set of skills you have when you're doing customer research where you ask people questions, but then you need to go and watch them work and understand what they're doing. And then when you see something that looks interesting, you pause them in the middle of their work and get them to walk you through it. We're trying to get inside the brains of these awesome CSMs and figure out a way to generalize their insights.

Solution #4: Create a Product Risk Process

At Gainsight, we track Product Risk, which is when a client can't get sufficient value from the product unless an enhancement is made. When a CSM escalates a Product Risk through a Call to Action in our Gainsight software, it kicks off a formal process outlined in a Playbook, which the CS team and the Product Management team collaborate on. The Playbook often involves the Product Manager meeting with the client to understand why they're not getting enough value, and then closing the loop with the client once the Product team has made a decision on a change in the product roadmap.

Flagging Product Risks is a careful balancing act. Too many flags can result in a stretched Product team that handles a large volume of risks, but doesn't follow up any of them with sufficient effort, and/or a Product team that dedicates too little time to breakthrough innovation. That said, we usually see CS teams flagging too few risks to their Product teams, not too many.

Solution #5: Leverage Your Online Community

An online community allows you to gather feedback from your customers at scale. Customers post their ideas to the community forum, and Product teams can respond directly to their posts to learn more. CSMs can also post their own perspectives on the forum. Gathering product enhancement requests posted on the community forum allows you to track and analyze the requests that are common to many customers. Community participants can upvote product ideas; enhancement requests that appear most often or that have the most upvotes are prioritized on the product roadmap. Because both Product and CS have access to the community—including the upvoting data and the qualitative feedback—they can more easily align on the highest priority problems to solve.

Solution #6: Subject Matter Expert Program

CSMs are not the only client-facing team members who have a valuable perspective on the product. Members of the Support and Services teams should also have the opportunity to share feedback with the Product team. For example, while a CSM would lend an interesting perspective on the usability of a product for end users, a solutions architect might have a perspective specific to the configurability of a product for an admin.

At Gainsight, our Subject Matter Expert (SME) program connects our product sub-teams, each of which focuses on a different part of the product, with people across different roles in our CS organization. Each SME team meets once every two months, with the following agenda:

- **Product feature update:** Overview of trending usage stats, recently released enhancements/functionality and bug fixes.
- **SME examples:** Review of challenges faced by customers related to a feature, and proposed solutions.
- **Feedback on roadmap:** Review the upcoming roadmap and reprioritize, add, or remove proposed features based on SME feedback.

Sometimes, if we hit on a really juicy subject, we hold a follow-up meeting with the appropriate SMEs and Product Managers to deep-dive on specific issues.

Solution #7: Publish the Roadmap

In the same way that CSMs need to close the loop on feedback from clients, Product teams need to close the loop on feedback from CSMs. Product teams should share how the roadmap is changing as a result of the feedback: specifically, what is going to be built, when. "Eventually, we realized we needed to have a shared document that everybody could look at and know what was on the schedule and what wasn't," says Sloan. "Otherwise, the CSMs will assume the fix fell through the cracks, when what actually happened is that it was actively decided that the team isn't going to prioritize that build right now."

Solution #8: Develop In-app Messaging

It used to be that the only way for Product teams to make changes to the product experience was by altering the code through a new release. Today, in-app messaging tools allow Product teams—with close collaboration with their counterparts in CS and Marketing—to improve the product experience without touching the code. Product Managers can design walk-throughs for new customers, guiding them on what to do when they first log into the product. They can communicate with customers on how to get value from a new feature. They can surface knowledge base articles that may be relevant. They can even gather survey feedback from customers precisely where they get stuck—in the product itself—which generates response rates that are often three times as high as for emailed surveys.

Solution #9: Foster Mutual Empathy

All these processes are valuable. But they won't sustain their impact unless Product and CS demonstrate compassion for each other. "One missing piece in many of these conversations is a shared empathy," says Steve Sloan.

PMs need to understand that the CSM who they're talking with is explaining a customer problem. And the CSM probably had to deal with a tough conversation with that customer. Keeping that realization in mind helps to build empathy for that charged situation from the product management side. And from the CS side, it's important to understand that the product manager they're talking to has far more valid projects to pursue in any given week, month, quarter, year than they can actually deliver. There are good projects that won't make the prioritization list because there's a finite amount of engineering time. It's a painful reality of prioritization, not an excuse.

For all of us, there will be things that we'll be bummed out about because they're not happening. Without that shared empathy, cross-functional communication tends to go poorly.

Summary

What is the big takeaway from all of these best practices? Transforming the Product-CS couplet into the new Sales and Marketing requires an evolution in the data they share, the language they use to communicate, and the processes that systematize their collaboration. Your investment in these innovations will pay off in terms of reduced cost, improved revenue growth, and—more abstractly but equally importantly—the fulfillment of your ethical obligations toward your clients as human beings.

There is an enormous opportunity for Product leaders to build products that guide people through a journey from fear and confusion to success. There's also an opportunity for Customer Success leaders, who are staffing teams to break down the barriers between human and machine. The solution is for Customer Success and Product Management to join together to deliver technology that is human-first.

Let's come back to the feeling you have when you're walking through the woods. The clarity of thought. The freedom. The empowerment. What if every product experience could be like a wondrous hike through the woods?

In the next chapter, let's move on to how another department should evolve: Marketing. What's the new role for Marketing in this Customer Success symphony? *Hint:* It doesn't end with a hand-off to Sales.

10

Marketing: Your Job Doesn't End with the Lead

The weaving of Customer Success into a company's fabric calls into question: Who owns what when it comes to clients? Who handles which interactions with the customers? How do different departments get visibility into customer data to best drive Customer Success? The Marketing team is often a primary stakeholder in conversations on these topics.

To illustrate how the role of Marketing is evolving in the Customer Success economy, we'll turn to Chris Koehler, chief marketing officer at cloud content management software company Box, and a former Customer Success leader himself.

Marketing in the Helix

Koehler points out the importance of collaboration among customer-facing teams: "There are three legs to this stool and how we think about going to market. You have the CS organization, you have sales, and you have marketing. They all have to be aligned to make sure customers are successful."

In general, the rise of customer-centric thinking has inspired Marketing teams to reorient their focus toward existing clients. It used to be that Marketing teams could focus on warming up cold leads, then passing them along to Sales—essentially, the top of the "funnel." But in the Age of the Customer, Marketing teams need to help drive the full Helix—that new model of revenue growth that turns existing customers into lead generators.

"Marketing needs to play a role across the customer lifecycle," says Koehler. "In an SaaS world where recurring revenue is so critically important, and where you get a huge majority of your upsell revenue and cross-sell revenue from existing customers, marketing has to have a vested interest in thinking beyond just getting customers into the pipeline." Marketing teams have to consider how to leverage the existing customer base to drive revenue: how to encourage advocacy by existing clients, how to find leads for upsell and cross-sell in the installed base, and how to generate stronger brand awareness and loyalty among clients. This change in focus necessitates a total reframe of the Marketing team's charter.

Given that CS, Sales, and Marketing are together accountable for the three Helix outcomes of stronger retention, expansion, and new logo growth through advocacy, it's important to make sure they're aligned. Below we'll discuss four steps to generating that alignment.

Step #1: Align on the Customer Journey

Koehler says, "The first step is to have a shared vision of the customer journey. We often see this Marketing notion that their customer journey either stops at the qualified lead that gets passed on to Sales, or it stops with the sale. And then CS picks up on the onboarding, adoption, and retention. Well, they're not really two separate journeys. They're one long customer journey that both CS and Marketing have to facilitate in partnership with Sales. Having a common view of that customer experience is important."

Step #2: Adopt Shared Goals

"I carry both a growth goal and a retention goal for the Marketing organization," says Koehler. "So we're in lockstep with CS. We are aligned to drive both the right expectations for the client and the right experience for them."

Step #3: Share Data

Gal Biran is co-founder and CEO of Crowdvocate, a B2B customer marketing and advocacy automation solution. In an article published on Gainsight's blog, Biran says that CS teams are not trained as marketers, but they can share information that will elevate the marketing team's efforts. They know who might be a good bet for expansion. They can suggest clients who would be good advocates. "They can point out good technical references as well as leadership advocates who reference a managerial perspective. They might even have a good idea as to who is the best person within the customer organization to support an expansion campaign," writes Biran.

Inversely, insights from marketing data can empower CSMs as they work with their clients. What emails are customers reading? Are they contributors in the online community? By tracking these metrics, such as through automated Customer Health Scores, CS teams can keep tabs on the ebbs and flows of customer health.

Step #4: Collaborate on One-to-Many ("Tech Touch") Communications

"Customer Marketing" is currently a no-man's land. There isn't consensus on what it entails or who owns it.

When most people imagine Customer Marketing, truly what they're thinking about is one-to-many communications in the service of revenue generation. Figure 10.1 shows how we dissect it.

The ownership of the various activities listed in Figure 10.1 under Customer Marketing is often distributed across multiple teams. The Marketing team almost always owns (2c), the execution of the advocacy activity; that's standard Marketing stuff. They usually own (1b), which is cross-selling marketing. They don't always own (2b) and (3b), which are frequently run by a Customer Success Operations team (sometimes also called a Customer Marketing team) that reports into Customer Success.

	CSM	Customer Marketing
Expansion	Discuss new products during an Executive Business Review [1b].	Send one-to-many emails on the benefits of new products [1c].
Advocacy	Contact a client to encourage their participation in advocacy (e.g. an event or testimonial) [2b].	▪ Send Net Promoter Score survey to identify advocates. ▪ Work with the new client to execute the advocacy (e.g. plan their talk, write the testimonial) [2c].
Adoption	Discuss best practices for using a product to achieve the client's desired outcome [3b].	▪ Send one-to-many emails describing standard best practices for using a feature. ▪ Set up an in-app guide to onboard new users or explain how to use a new feature [3c].

Figure 10.1

The ownership of activity (3c) is contentious—Marketing, CS, *and* Product Management are vying for it.

That distributed ownership can work quite well. Just because all of the activities in the right-hand column above involve one-to-many communications doesn't mean that the same team has to own them. No one "owns" email within a company. Can you imagine if someone said that only one team could use a phone to call external people? Technology is valuable and shouldn't be restricted to certain people. But that technology does need to enable multiple teams to use it, without having them cross their wires. Specifically, email and in-app tools need to provide mechanisms for multiple teams to schedule communications (so as not to overwhelm the client) and approve each other's communications (so as to ensure consistent messaging).

In fact, collaboration between Marketing and CS in these activities can be mutually beneficial. "I've got a customer marketing organization that partners with the CS team," says Koehler. "We're experts at driving the messaging, the product aspect, but we don't know what the CS go-to-market is. We're not talking to our customers every day like the CS organization is. So you have to build these teams or pods where they can collaborate, work together, and collectively and cohesively build what those campaigns aimed at the existing base should look like."

There's a lot that Customer Success can learn from Marketing about how to craft messaging, notes Koehler. "Marketing has all the tools and all the experience. It's what they do every day. If a CS team tries to drive the marketing messaging, it's less effective because it's just not their core competency. CS is really good at engaging with customers, talking about business outcomes, value, understanding product capabilities. But leave marketing to the marketers. Just make sure you have a marketing organization that thinks about the entire customer lifecycle."

Not every marketing organization is as forward-leaning on Customer Success as Koehler's is at Box. So we typically see the Marketing-CS transformation occurring in three phases:

- **Phase 1:** Marketing is only focused on "net new" acquisition. The CS team ends up having to hire marketing skills into their organization (e.g. for one-to-many Customer Success).
- **Phase 2:** Marketing expresses interest in collaborating with CS but doesn't have significant resources. Therefore, Marketing starts helping in key areas like content design, email optimization, webinars, and other scalable programs.
- **Phase 3:** Marketing officially expands the charter to include supporting Customer Success. In this phase, "cross-pollination" often happens. People with CS backgrounds often end up in Marketing, as was the case in Koehler's personal experience. And people with Marketing expertise end up in CS.

Now that we've discussed how Marketing and CS can in fact coexist in a customer-centric environment, let's discuss a new aspect of the Marketing team's charter: Voice of the Customer.

Voice of the Customer

For a real-world example from Nick of the problems you run into when you silo CS and Marketing, let's consider a company we worked with that was getting Net Promoter Score responses of nine or higher from an executive buyer. Meanwhile, almost no one was logging into the tool. Another company had a customer that never responded to surveys or outreach. Meanwhile, they were logging support tickets regularly.

Nick, who tends to relate everything to subatomic physics, points out that in the absence of a tool or system that merges those data points into one picture, the customer is in essence both healthy and churning at once, kind of like a Schroedinger's cat from physics class, except without the box or the cat. But the basic premise—that the state of the customer is multifaceted—holds true, and informs the need to share information, pull out the right conclusions, and act on it regularly.

Our point of view at Gainsight is that any successful customer-focused program—many call it a Voice of the Customer program (VOC)—rolls up to a broader Customer Success strategy. Earlier in this book, we talked about how CS = CO + CX, or Customer Success equals Customer Outcomes plus Customer Experience. In plain terms, it means that the overall success of every customer isn't just whether they get their desired outcome from the product; it's also how they feel about it. It's possible to get the ROI you paid for while having a terrible time interacting with the vendor. We know the opposite is also true!

Therefore, you need a strong focus on Customer Outcomes. It's the single greatest indicator of renewal. Likewise, no Customer Success strategy is complete without a solid VoC component. It gives you insight into your customers' experiences as well as whether they're achieving their goals. Let's look quickly at what differentiates CS from VoC:

Customer Success

- Critical business philosophy, practice, and function
- Governs all customer-facing decisions
- Benchmarks customers based on data from many sources (including VoC)
- Takes action based on data to ensure successful customer behavior

Voice of the Customer

- Operational program (may be tied to a specific function)
- Proactively solicits feedback from customers
- Finds and collects unsolicited feedback from customers
- Closes feedback loop with manual and automated communications

The voice of the customer is an integral data source—potentially the most important to your overall CS strategy. These are your surveys, your one-to-many outreach, your social engagement, CSAT metrics, and CX data. Without actively pursuing and engaging with your customer's direct feedback, you don't have a complete CS strategy.

But what about a standalone VoC program that doesn't include traditional CS actions and principles? Why not spin up an independent, single-function survey tool that lives in your Marketing team or maybe even your CX team if you have one? We see three main reasons why a VoC program is fundamentally incomplete without being tied to CS:

First, VoC has blind spots. It's possible to score solid survey results without having healthy customers. It's possible (even likely) that the voice of the customer won't match the behavior of the customer. That doesn't invalidate either data source; it just means one is incomplete without the other. We'll give you an example of how this could play out: You get a glowing Net Promoter Score from a C-level champion at a client. You reach out for advocacy, and produce a high-value, co-branded webinar. Finally, you operationalize a glowing online review from your champion. It's a pretty successful VoC campaign, right? Meanwhile, usage is completely in the tank. The end users have gone dark and unresolved tickets have been waiting for weeks. The executive leaves the customer, the customer churns, and your valuable advocacy and content are liabilities.

Second, VoC must be mapped to specific customer outcomes. When you think about any business action or program, do so with goals in mind and metrics to track. That's not radical—it's typical. The question is whether your VoC program correlates to your customer's lifecycle and is mapped to a specific outcome. For example, a prototypical customer lifecycle might look something like this:

Closed Won → Onboarding → First Value → Executive Business Review

→ Renewal

VoC is most effective when feedback is associated with those transitions. We know that mistakes in onboarding are a major driver of unsuccessful customers and, therefore, churn. A survey outreach timed to coincide with the completion of onboarding can spot those mistakes and correct them. VoC done in a vacuum doesn't correspond to the lifecycle and it doesn't map to customer outcomes.

Finally, VoC should drive value across functions. VoC has the potential to inform and transform every team with an external touchpoint, starting with Marketing, then Sales, then CS, CX, Support, and so on. No matter where your VoC program rolls up, whoever owns it must be responsible for surfacing data relevant to Support, for example, to improve Support. They must surface Product feedback to the Product team, Sales feedback to Sales. You get the idea. That's starting to sound a lot like Customer Success, isn't it? CS is the only truly cross-functional team responsible for owning customer feedback and surfacing those insights to other organizations in the company. That survey that identifies a botched sales-handoff as a pain point needs to get into the hands of the Sales team. That tweet praising a first-class Support ticket resolution needs to get back to Support. Unless your VoC program is equipped to close that feedback loop, it's not making the impact it should.

For a quick takeaway, just remember: The three broad parts of a successful VoC program are Listen, Act, and Analyze.

Listen: Ask and listen to what customers think and then respond.
Act: Proactively improve the customer lifecycle based on that feedback.
Analyze: Correlate what the customer says with what the customer does.

Obviously technology is a critical part of each step. You need the capability to reach out, collect feedback, transform it into insight, and drive business actions. Without action and analysis, listening is a dead end. If your VoC solution doesn't have an action result or analysis capability, it's only one-third of a solution.

Summary

In this chapter, we laid out the basics of bringing Marketing and CS into alignment—why it's vital and how to make it happen on an ongoing basis. We also discussed the importance of a Voice of the Customer initiative as critical to ensuring strong Customer Experiences, one of the two pillars of Customer Success in the equation CS = CO + CX.

In Chapter 11, we'll discuss the evolution of another department—Sales—in the Age of the Customer. We'll explore why an outstanding CS organization is your differentiator in a world where CS programs are rapidly becoming the norm, not the exception.

11 | Sales: Customer Success Is Your Differentiator

If we had a company genie, one of the things we'd wish for is an extra month between the end of our current fiscal year and the start of the next. It feels like every year we go from the stress of closing strong to the new stress of starting from zero again. Many of us stare at the $0 bookings amount on the first day of the new fiscal year and say, "How the heck are we going to make our numbers?"

It's easy to feel nostalgic for the "old days" before SaaS. Making the number was still hard then (and dramatic) but the playbook was pretty simple:

- Hire reps.
- Ramp reps.
- Push reps.
- If things fail, blame Marketing!

All jokes aside, as bizarre as the licensed software world was in some respects, the model was well-understood and translated from company to company. Even though we're now 20 years into the SaaS/cloud transition, most companies still run sales with an on-premises/license software mindset. Every bookings goal is about more "rep capacity." But companies will miss their sales targets if they only use the old playbook.

The new playbook for sales is in fact Customer Success, in the sense that the SaaS/cloud businesses that grow quickly do so on the back of a business process that drives consistent and strong outcomes for clients. The four principal reasons for this are as follows:

1. Focused Markets Mean Rep Capacity Models Alone Don't Work

Remember when you could start a company that sold to everyone? Build a database. Sell CRM. Create HR software. Nowadays, starting a company is so easy to the point that every big market is carved up into focused markets—verticalized, regionalized, segmentized. You can no longer build a growth model that is based solely upon hiring more reps—there aren't enough clients to sell to.

2. Focused Markets Enable Advocacy

But hope isn't lost. With these smaller, fractured markets, you can have above-average economics by leveraging a sales force that is ten times your size and more than ten times less expensive—namely your clients. Why hire ten reps when you can "hire" 10,000 happy customers to sell for you? And in focused markets, everyone knows everyone. So make a client happy and when they switch jobs, they bring you along. Screw something up and they will kill ten new deals for you.

Advocacy isn't merely nice to have, it's essential, and it can be operationalized through:

- Clients doing references for you
- Clients doing reviews for you
- Clients switching jobs and bringing you in
- Lower-level users that used you coming into a company and saying, "That's a good vendor."

and the biggest one:

- The backchannel checks people do through LinkedIn.

3. The Renewals Eventually Get Big

Every CEO and CFO have that moment at some point. They look at the next year's financial model, they look at each other, then back to the model and say, "Wow. Our renewal number is bigger than our new number." Unfortunately, too many companies try to make a diving save on Customer Success at that point. It's usually too late. It's funny, because that moment is eminently predictable. New sales don't grow forever, and at some point, customers > prospects. If you don't have Customer Success dialed in at that critical moment, you will miss your renewal number and have no hope of hitting your plan.

4. Expansion Is the Only Way to Make the SaaS Model Work

The SaaS financial model is fundamentally brutal. You incur costs upfront and get paid over time. It's the opposite of the license model, where customers paid you upfront whether or not they used your stuff. *Ah*—the good ole' days!

Every SaaS business eventually has to grow up and become profitable. Mathematically, it's almost impossible to do it solely through new customer acquisition. You need a high renewal rate to be profitable, but you also need to have cheap growth in the form of expansion. It's no surprise that nearly every highly valued public SaaS company has net retention of 110%, 120%, or more.

If you don't have Customer Success dialed in, good luck asking those clients for more money. Our recommendation: As we've been saying throughout this book, you should get started now and take it very, very seriously. This is your company's success we're talking about. People's livelihoods are at stake.

Now that we've discussed how the entire framing of Sales needs to change, let's discuss what Sales stands to gain from this. We've already discussed the impact of Customer Success on the growth drivers of a business—renewals, expansion, and advocacy that propels new logos—in Chapter 5. But there's more. The actual *program* of Customer Success can help you sell.

How to Make Customer Success an Asset to Sales

One simple test of whether you are establishing Customer Success as a differentiator is this: If Customer Success is not a slide in your Sales deck, you're not doing it well enough. In an ideal world, Sales is asking for this, not waiting for it.

During Sue Barsamian's 37-year career as an enterprise software and hardware executive and board director at companies such as legendary technology maker Hewlett Packard Enterprise, security software company Symantec, and cloud content management provider Box, she watched the tech industry's focus on Customer Success sharpen. After implementing Customer Success programs in two firms and working in conjunction with CS teams as a sales exec for several other companies, she's passionate about the need for strong Customer Success departments and believes in the measurable results they bring.

In particular, Sue sees the value of having a Customer Success program that's *distinctive*. Earlier in this book, we talked about the fact that it's much easier to build a product than it used to be, which means that your competitors can more easily catch up with your supposedly distinctive roadmap changes. That means that companies can't differentiate themselves based on their products alone; rather, they have to differentiate based on the success they're able to generate for clients.

But it's not differentiated enough to simply staff up a Customer Success team. "The simplest way is to dedicate your teams to the phones day in and out. Their priority is the customer—ensuring they get onboarded and optimizing their engagement and utilization level. That is table stakes," says Barsamian. "There are countless 'templates' to spin up a Customer Success organization. So you often see a team dropped into place without customizing a playbook that truly suits the company, its values, and its customers." That reluctance to dig deeper, to personalize your Customer

Success program, means you'll be less differentiated in your market, and it will inevitably hurt sales, even if not immediately. To meet its bookings targets, the Sales team needs a differentiated Customer Success program.

So what does that differentiated program look like?

The advanced degree of Customer Success is when you do the work to define your customer journey. How does the customer get successfully onboarded? How do you get them to target utilization? What should happen then? And what are the indicators that can be automatically tracked and triggered to indicate where a customer is on the journey and whether they are progressing through the journey at the right pace that would indicate they're a healthy customer? That's a lot of work. That involves sales, marketing, Customer Success, the product team, the services team, literally everyone to be thoughtful and structured about the definition of the customer journey, and then to implement tracking the health of the customer base through that journey.

Tying Barsamian's point of view back to the language we used in Chapter 6, a distinctive CS program leverages a thoughtful *methodology* and ensures that all functions are working together within that framework to help the client achieve their *outcomes* over time.

That's great for the client, great for net retention and advocacy, and—more relevant to this section of the book—great for actually selling the prospect on working with you in the first place.

If you've really sold them on this notion that, "Hey, here's our model for what our journey together should look like, and the value proposition, and the significant outcomes that it should deliver for you," that helps create an ongoing relationship that all parties are happy to commit to. And when you do that, it's a completely different game.

The game of *selling* totally changes, because you're presenting your company as a strategic partner to the client in driving their business outcomes. You're not just selling a product.

Being able to pitch a differentiated customer journey to your prospects sounds great to a sales rep. But the worry that this journey can help resolve—"Will I be able to win this prospect?"—can easily be replaced by a new concern—"Will I have control over this account post-sale?" As we discussed during the previous chapter on Marketing, the process of defining that journey and the many functions that are involved can create headaches about who owns what. Specifically, "Who owns the customer?"

Who Owns the Customer?

When Allison thinks of this question, she thinks of a spat that she had with her younger brother when they were little kids: "I had a security blanket that I was very fond of. When my brother reached the age of two, and I was five, he would sometimes try to take my blankie. I would pull it back and say 'This is mine!' Andy interpreted that to mean that the word for blanket was 'mine.' So we'd have conversations that went like this: 'Give me back *my mine!*' 'No, it's *my* mine!' It's cute when toddlers have squabbles like this, but it's absurd when businesspeople do."

Allison believes that the way some sales and Customer Success teams talk about "who owns the customer" resembles two toddlers having a territorial fit. In modern businesses, *no one* owns the customer. If anything, the *company* owns the customer—but we're sure the customer doesn't see it that way. Better questions are:

1. What activities should each department conduct in order to benefit the customer along their journey?
2. How can those departments stay informed of each other's activities?

Both Sales and Customer Success need to engage with the customer. The question is, What's the division of labor for renewals and upsell?, a topic to which we've dedicated an entire chapter later in this book.

(As a side note, Allison and her brother made up after their fight and are on good terms now. He also has no recollection of their argument.)

Customer ownership becomes even more complex when you're selling indirectly through partners. Throughout this chapter, we've equated selling with a Sales team. But Customer Success isn't just for companies that have a direct selling model. It can be revolutionary for companies that sell through a channel as well. How can you share responsibilities with your partners to deliver success for your clients?

Collaborate with Your Partners to Boost Revenue Even Further

The key to rolling out Customer Success with channel partners is alignment—specifically, alignment on the customer's intended outcomes, on the touchpoints along the customer journey, and on incentives for the customer, vendor, and partner. When alignment happens, everyone wins. Customers get up to full speed more quickly, vendors earn more because they're not spending so much time hand-holding customers, and partners increase their margins and retention rates, home in on additional selling opportunities, and boost their competitiveness.

We're noticing a major paradigm shift in vendor–partner relationships, which leads directly to an ecosystem aligned around the customer's success. A world is unfolding where vendors and partners have:

- A shared responsibility for positive customer outcomes
- A shared toolset and 360-degree view of the customer along their journey
- Shared, trusted barometers for Customer Health (including Net Promoter Score, adoption, advocacy, and other metrics)
- Better alignment on prescribed customer journeys and the playbooks that make them happen

Let's reflect on that for a moment. The entire fabric of the vendor–partner relationship is changing as a result of the Customer Success movement. Going forward, vendors will include their channel partners alongside internal functional stakeholders (support, sales, marketing, product, CSMs, etc.) as another primary contributor in the journey toward Customer Success. In addition, vendors will be expecting their channel to contribute to customer outcomes.

This direction is a radical shift. It's not happening overnight. We know that many partners simply cannot invest in proactive, nurture-oriented team members without seeing proof of reward. So it has become the vendor's responsibility to prove the value of the new paradigm with a few progressive partners and then extend it broadly.

Based on what we've seen from successful initiatives in the industry, here's our recommended six-step playbook for working with partners to drive Customer Success, which we designed together with Chris Doell, head of Global Customer Success, Cloud Security at Cisco.

1. Profile your partners.
2. Define the ROI to the partner.
3. Share customer insights.
4. Provide enablement.
5. Define the division of labor.
6. Measure partner effectiveness.

Step #1: Profile Your Partners

As vendors encourage their partners to roll out CS programs, they must prioritize their time effectively across their partner ecosystem. Start with a small group of two to four people. Prioritize your partners based on these considerations:

1. Are services a core part of their business model?
2. Do they have a lifecycle or adoption practice?
3. Do we expect that the partner would derive a strong ROI from investing in CS?
4. Are there several people whose roles are focused on Customer Success or training?
5. For larger partners:
   - Is there an executive at the partner committed to CS?
   - Is there specifically a CS executive, or just CSMs reporting to a sales/support/operations executive?

Once you've got your small group, start a pilot. See what works well and what doesn't. Then expand your list.

Step #2: Define the ROI to the Partner

Work with your prioritized partners to help them demonstrate that expanding their CS program is worth it. Most partners won't do this on their own. It's your job as the vendor to show the ROI. To that end, get a handful of partners to actually demonstrate ROI from rolling out a CS program. Help establish a small set of "early adopters" among partners to showcase the value to everyone else.

There are four sources of ROI to a partner: (1) growth in product revenue, (2) growth in services revenue, (3) new revenue from CS as a service, and (4) point of differentiation in attracting new customers.

Step #3: Share Customer Insights

If you're like most vendors, you're going digital by building 360-degree views of your clients, across usage data, Net Promoter Score data, support ticket data, community portal data, and other types. It's time to expose that data to your partners. Information-sharing should be a two-way street. Vendors are eager to hear partners' insights into their customers and can create systems to share that information. Vendors also want to hear their partners' feedback on the playbooks above and on the product itself.

Step #4: Provide Enablement

Besides receiving enablement in the form of ROI models and customer health data, partners need three additional types of support from you (the vendor): training on playbooks, certification, and partner success managers. Some partners in particular need to raise their game because their paid adoption services may not be as robust as the free CS that the vendor offers. This can result in channel conflict, with customers abandoning the partner.

Be thoughtful in rolling out these enablement programs. Make sure that partners perceive them as a source of empowerment (bolstering the partner's ownership of the client relationship) rather than an intrusion.

Step #5: Define the Division of Labor

Partners can extend your reach among smaller customers. When a vendor forms a CS program, they'll typically start by assigning CSMs to their enterprise clients. They often also assign CSMs to the midmarket segment, but may not have the budget to assign CSMs to the SMB segment. For many businesses, however, partners play within every tier of the customer pyramid.

Regardless of where vendor or partner resources are applied, it's always important to understand who is doing what. For each segment, what do you expect your team to do? What do you expect partners to do? Be specific! The key here is to protect your brand across the lifecycle. Make sure your partners use messaging that's consistent with and leaves a positive imprint on your brand.

Step #6: Measure Partner Effectiveness

Vendors want to hold partners accountable. They want visibility into their partners' compliance with the recommended playbooks. They also want to see partners generate real value for customers. In fact, many vendors plan to pay partners based on their success in driving outcomes and growth in the installed base. Some vendors start simple, by paying partners based on renewals—not just new logos. Others are more advanced, paying their partners based on leading indicators of renewal and expansion, such as license utilization, active users, or client health score. The proof is in the pudding. Whatever metrics you use, the effectiveness of the CS investment must be measured.

This evolved payment model makes Step #3 (sharing customer data) even more important. Vendors and partners need a common system that's a source of truth for the data that informs payments. Furthermore, these KPIs should be mutually agreed upon in advance, reviewed together at regular intervals, and objectively measured and documented. Write everything down! While these steps require some effort and investment in a shared toolset, they're critical to aligning the vendor, partner, and positive customer outcomes.

How Can Sales Help Customer Success?

We've spoken in this chapter about how a differentiated Customer Success program can be useful to Sales. But we also know that Sales has a new role to play in helping Customer Success generate outcomes for clients.

Karthik Chakkarapani knows a thing or two about digital transformations. At Salesforce.com, Karthik helped customers with their CX reinventions. And as VP, head of CX Digital Transformation and Technology Strategy at technology giant Cisco, Karthik is helping the company reimagine its customer experience. Karthik sees Sales as having a big role in Customer Success and Experience.

At a tactical level, CSMs need a lot from their sales counterparts. "We want the sales team to capture the use cases and business priorities the customer is looking for as outcomes. In addition, we need them to track the contacts at a use case level so we know with whom we are working." If the CSM doesn't know who bought and why, they don't know where to start.

From a strategic lens, CS is a lot more than just CSMs; actually, it includes Sales. "Everyone at Cisco is in Customer Experience—sales, support, delivery. That's the vision."

Summary

Customer success is becoming more of a revenue driver than ever before, and that trend shows no sign of stopping. If you don't have a strong Customer Success program, you'll struggle to stand out, to get new customers, and to keep the ones you have. We laid out a plan for increasing your upsell and detailed why collaborating with your partners can (and should) drive your revenue upwards.

In Chapter 12, we'll examine why you'll be more successful as you focus on customer outcomes as a critical parameter for your CS team.

12 | Services: Go from Hours to Outcomes

Every service should increase my gross margin.

—Old-world services leader

Every service should be automated.

—Product-oriented startup founder

The rise of recurring revenue business models is causing an existential crisis for PS teams as they confront challenges from divergent, extreme points of view represented by both quotes above. Older companies are questioning long-held beliefs about the charter of their PS organizations. Newer companies, often led by founders who believe that their product should automate services, are questioning the value of PS teams, period. PS teams can be a critical part of the story for driving subscription growth, but they're undergoing massive changes in order to deliver on that promise.

The Old World of Services

Let's bring back Anthony Reynolds, the CEO of Altify who showed up in Chapter 8:

> The traditional world of software would say, you buy an on-premises license and then you implement in your own datacenter. And you buy a maintenance contract so you can perpetually have access to that software that you hope returns you benefit. That's the old world. The new modern world is you buy a subscription, and you buy that on the belief that it's going to provide you value. But if it doesn't start providing you value within months or after the first year, then you turn it off. From a vendor perspective, your interest is in making sure that the promise of the sale is followed through so that the customer is actually getting the benefits. And if you can't demonstrate those benefits, then the customer is simply going to turn you off and move on to another vendor that can provide them that value. So it's in all our best interests to figure out what are those benefits that the customer is looking to realize, and help them make sure they realize that value. Now, there are steps along the way. You don't automatically get to a value realization. You've got to spend some time implementing. There's usually a change management approach. You've got to drive adoption of the solution.

And that's the new role of Professional Services—helping the client realize those benefits that they're seeking.

Prior to the rise of the subscription model, the definition of success for most Professional Services teams came from an internal perspective—finishing a project on-time and under-budget was considered a success. While this worked in a legacy transaction model, where implementation was a large up-front investment by the customer, those operating within a recurring revenue landscape are finding that this definition no longer applies to Services that support subscription products. "The unremitting, industry-wide transformation toward new technology consumption models is generally undermining PS's traditional, core cash cows and competencies (product-led, project-based, deployment-oriented services) and forcing them to explore and deliver on new ways of being relevant in a B4B context," shared TSIA in their State of Professional Services 2017 Report.

As we discussed in Chapter 6, clients now expect that their vendors will deliver outstanding Outcomes and Experiences for them, and that expectation holds for PS teams, too. As a result, PS teams have begun to define success in their clients' terms:

- **Outcomes:** Has the project delivered a strong initial value for the client that aligns with the client's long-term goals? Has the vendor given tangible (often measurable) proof of achieving those goals?
- **Experiences:** Has the vendor coordinated seamlessly across the various client-facing people—project managers, solutions architects, Customer Success managers, salespeople, and product managers—to ensure a smooth experience for the client?

Instead of asking, "What's the quickest, least-expensive way I can onboard this customer?," PS teams are changing the question to, "How can I provide services to this customer so they achieve exactly what they wanted from our product/service?" By connecting their own definition of success to each client's definition of success, PS teams start to cultivate client relationships that can become a source of exponential revenue.

Reconciling Services with Product-Led Growth

The top SaaS companies these days are growing faster than their predecessors. Sometimes, such as in the case of the videoconferencing company Zoom that recently went public, they build a product that's so easy to use that they're able to grow through a bottom-up adoption model, with limited effort invested by client-facing team members. Success stories like these have set a new expectation for some startup CEOs, that a "self-serve" go-to-market model is not only the best way, but also the only way, to grow into a big company. As a result, CEOs are sometimes skeptical of the value of professional services. They may ask themselves, "Why would I want to charge my clients for lower-margin services, when that may cannibalize higher-margin subscription revenue?" or "Why would I want to hire people to onboard our clients, when I can automate an onboarding process in the product itself?"

These are important questions to ask. Certainly Zoom and other companies that have grown through a primarily self-serve model are terrific success stories. The reality is that not all markets are like videoconferencing. CEOs need to ask: What does my client need from my company? Can the product truly provide those terrific Outcomes and Experiences on its own, or will human intervention help? If human intervention will help, then can I provide enough of that intervention through a Customer Success manager (which is essentially a free service to the client), or will I need to cover the cost by charging the client? If the latter, then the company should make Professional Services a fundamental part of its go-to-market model.

That said, even when a PS team is an important growth lever within the company, the Product Management team should constantly be seeking to automate the PS team's work, particularly more manual activities. This will ensure that the PS team can meet its gross margin goals while also generating strong outcomes and positive experiences for clients.

Whether you're a large company transitioning to a subscription business model or a new startup that wants to embrace both automation and services, there are several processes that you'll want to get right when designing your services organization:

- Nailing the hand-off
- Generating strong "Time to Value"
- Capturing data
- Driving services sales

Nailing the Hand-off

The most contentious topic in conversations between Sales and PS teams is typically the hand-off of the client between them after the client signs the contract. During the period before signature, the Sales team learns a great deal about the client's objectives and expectations. If the PS team subsequently kicks off the project without reflecting a strong understanding of what the client shared to the Sales team (often only a few days earlier), the client is likely to be frustrated—meaning that you've started your partnership with an escalation. When PS and Sales teams are functioning well together, they create a process for documenting the client's desired Outcomes in pre-sales and sharing that information systematically with the PS team.

Once the contract signature happens, clients expect to get started right away. That means that clunky PS organizations just won't cut it. PS teams need to forecast their staffing needs more accurately than ever before, because under-forecasting may generate delays in kicking off projects. In general, enterprise clients won't wait for longer than a couple of weeks to get started, and SMB clients want to start immediately. PS teams also need to staff for agility. For example, if four highly specialized team members, who are not fungible for each other, are required for a project, then if one of those team members is unavailable, the entire project could be delayed. Agile PS teams are embracing less specialization, and when specialization is required, they adopt a thoughtful sequencing of activities so that the project keeps moving.

Generating Strong "Time to Value"

One of the most common root causes of churn is a poor onboarding. When clients struggle during onboarding, they often don't recover. Therefore, onboarding is arguably the most important part of a client's journey, and that onboarding is often run by a PS team. As a result, PS teams have become increasingly thoughtful about how to measure whether onboarding is successful—not by internally valuable definitions such a project margin, but by definitions that are valuable to the client.

A PS team may set a threshold for adoption of the product that they expect a client to achieve by the end of onboarding: for example, a certain percentage of users performing a certain action within the product with a certain frequency. That adoption metric should be a proxy for whether the client is getting initial value, or in other words, that the client is on track to achieve their outcomes. PS teams often have a standard metric that they use to measure the success of all onboardings so that they can benchmark projects against each other, but they'll couple that with a parallel assessment of whether this specific client is on track to achieve its unique goals. If the client hasn't achieved the standard adoption metric as well as its own unique goals, the vendor may decide that it would be justified to invest in extending the project, or it may find an opportunity to sell an additional services engagement to get the client to a higher level of value. Often, the hand-off of a client from the PS team that's managing the onboarding to the Customer Success Manager may be contingent on the achievement of these initial Outcomes.

You'll need a strong methodology in order to help clients predictably achieve Outcomes. We discussed our own methodology at Gainsight, the Elements of Customer Success, in Chapter 6. There's a standard way of implementing each Element using our Gainsight products. When a client says that they want to focus on certain Elements (in other words, that those Elements match their desired Outcomes), our PS team follows the standardized configuration for each Element, adapting the default to suit the client's unique needs. By the end of an onboarding, we're looking to make sure not only that the Element has been implemented properly, but also that the client is adopting the processes within each Element and thereby achieving value from the product.

When a client achieves its initial value by the end of onboarding, that tends to be the perfect time to ask the client if they'll serve as a reference for prospective clients or otherwise participate in an advocacy activity. At Gainsight we refer to the client's participation in advocacy following the onboarding as a PSQA, or Professional Services Qualified Advocacy event, and we measure the number of PSQAs as a primary metric for our PS team.

Capturing Data

Great PS teams are capturing many different data sources to ensure that the engagement is going well. Andrea Lagan, the former COO at professional services automation company FinancialForce and current chief customer officer at HR software company BetterWorks, has led that effort for her team and has also seen her PS clients do this as well. "If a consulting team that's implementing a solution doesn't know the peripheral activities that are happening for the client, they're missing half the picture. Customer centricity needs to be core for a PS team, so naturally you have to design systems to ensure you have the full context about your client."

We find that the most advanced PS teams track Customer Health Scores to assess the success of the engagement on multiple dimensions:

- **Adoption:** Per the discussion above, is the client starting to change their adoption behaviors in a way that signals they are achieving value?
- **Timeline:** Are we on track to achieve the client's objectives by the deadline? The goal isn't to close out the project by the deadline no

matter what, since what's paramount is the achievement of the Outcome, not simply checking the box on the project. That said, meeting the client's timeline is critical to their own Experience and to the achievement of the Outcome, which is inevitably time-bound.

- **Sentiment:** What have been the client's responses to Net Promoter Score surveys at critical junctures in the engagement? PS teams will use this information to circle back on clients' responses to gather more qualitative feedback.
- **Scope:** Is the project remaining within scope, or is there scope creep? In a world where client expectations have risen, PS teams need to manage to those expectations but also ensure that the engagement doesn't break the bank. A health score reflecting scope creep can help the PS team navigate thoughtfully through a conversation with the client about staying on track, or formally expanding the scope of the engagement if desired.
- **Engagement:** Is the client dedicating sufficient internal resources to the project and engaging with your team in the right way? If not, sharing this health score with the client can be a good way to initiate a conversation about the need for the client's team to dedicate certain efforts to guarantee their success.
- **Executive sponsorship:** Has an executive from the vendor touched based with a senior person at the client recently? Even if a project seems to be going well, executives often find that if they wait to talk to the client until their team asks them to, it's typically too late—a bad situation is already underway. Frequent executive check-ins ensure continuous alignment between vendor and client on the client's objectives and the status of the project with respect to those.
- **Support:** Is there an urgent ticket outstanding, or a high number of outstanding tickets? This health score helps PS teams make sure escalations are being resolved.

Driving Services Sales

For companies that are optimizing their Helix to drive fast growth, selling services is a way to drive value for the client, so that the client renews, expands, and advocates to other prospective clients. In other words, great companies view services as a strategic lever for growing the business. As a result, they don't just look to sell services for onboarding; they look to sell services throughout the client journey, driving both value and revenue along the way.

Some companies find it valuable to sell services in a subscription, matching the subscription nature of the software. They may sell the client access to a technical account manager who can prescriptively guide the client over time on optimizing the technical configuration of the software (especially when there's a heavy data component), keeping up with new feature releases, and doing some work that would otherwise have to be handled by a team member at the client.

Other companies find they're able to elevate their relationships with their clients to be more strategic—thereby ensuring stronger renewal rates and faster, larger expansion—by selling advisory services. An advisory engagement may not even relate directly to the company's product, but it may address questions that ultimately allow the client to derive more benefit from the product: for example, how to design processes, how to structure teams, and how to incentivize team members. Sometimes companies sell these advisory services even before they sell their product to the client, because they find that they will be able to sell the product faster once the client resolves some of the big questions that they feel are precursors to a product purchase. When a client trusts the vendor as a source of thought leadership, they are more likely to believe that the vendor's product reflects their expertise and is therefore more likely to help the client achieve its desired outcomes. Like advisory services, education services tend to deepen the partnership between vendor and client for the same reason.

Given the benefits of selling services to clients—driving faster value, faster sales cycles, higher renewal likelihood, and faster expansion—the companies that are most advanced in Customer Success design systems for various departments to help sell more services. The most important type of collaboration is between Services and Sales. Salespeople may earn a commission on services, but even if they don't, they have strong processes for working together with the Services team: they're aligned on what services should be sold to what type of client, what's the right approximate attach rate (dollars of services sold per dollar of product sold), how services team members will be involved in the sales cycle, and when should we involve a partner instead of our own internal services team. Larger organizations often build specialized Services Sales teams to own a services bookings quota and work hand-in-hand with the subscription sales team.

Other teams also tend to be crucial participants in the selling of services. Product Marketing creates collateral not just about products but also about services, and helps determine the pricing and packaging. CSMs have targets for services leads that they generate by discussing the value that services could bring during key meetings (such as Executive Business Reviews) with the client and at other major milestones. Support teams identify situations where services (such as education) could help a client avoid future issues. When everyone at your company is aligned around the value of services, selling them becomes a repeatable motion, and your clients achieve far more value than they otherwise would.

Summary

In this chapter, we discussed the trend that older services organizations have had to adjust to subscription business models, and the trend that newer startups are realizing the value of services even in a world where products can help automate learning and onboarding. We'll discuss in the next chapter another client-facing organization that's undergone significant change as a result of the Customer Success movement: Support.

13 | Support: Go from Reactive to Proactive

You might be staring at this chapter title with skepticism. In fact, if you're like us, you may immediately be thinking of your least favorite support experience with your least favorite consumer brand. And you probably would come up with a number of words to describe that scenario before you suggested the term *proactive*. Historically, that poor perception of customer support has been appropriate.

In the age before recurring revenue business models, Support teams were often the only ones thinking about the client after the purchase. The client would be sold a multimillion-dollar contract and an implementation package, only later to escalate to the Support team because they weren't getting value. That escalation would be leveraged as an opportunity to sell the client a lucrative support maintenance contract, which was essentially a way for the vendor to get the client to pay for when they escalated.

In the new Age of the Customer, as we've discussed, vendors have become much more proactive in ensuring that clients get value. Many of the people who grew up in those reactive Support organizations are now excited to build and lead Customer Success teams in order to solve the root causes behind the flurry of escalations that once defined their working lives. The question becomes, What happens to the Support team in a world where proactivity is paramount?

The first CSM teams were often Support teams that were reconfigured in two ways: (1) the reps were assigned to specific clients, instead of giving each client to whichever Support person was available or had the requisite product expertise, and (2) the reps were assigned in perpetuity, instead of for the duration of the ticket. The result was "firefighting in perpetuity." The teams continued to be reactive to client needs—except now, they didn't have the queue and clear conclusion of an issue to help them streamline their work. Many of these folks burned out, and their clients often burned out, too.

As CSM teams realized the need to be more proactive in guiding clients in the right direction, to preclude a crisis, they realized that their old friends in Support could be helpful partners to them. Support would continue to operate in "reactive" mode, handling inbound technical issues, and CSMs would free up time to be more proactive.

The Division of Labor between Support and CSM

This division of labor sounds easier than it is, however. Marlene Lee Summers is the VP of Global Product Support at Vlocity and previously was VP Customer Support Services & Community at Zuora, so she has first-hand experience in creating collaborative relationships and processes between Support and CSM teams, in both a startup environment and a publicly traded company. Here's how she explains the challenge:

When a client works with Support, they're not always going to talk to the same person. That's by design, because we have people working around the world to maintain continuity of communication. By contrast, clients are assigned a specific CSM, so they tend to feel a personal connection to them. As a result, clients often start asking their CSMs questions about how to use the product or fix it. Since CSMs are often friendly, customer-oriented individuals, they try to be helpful and respond to the client's questions. But this can sidetrack the CSM from achieving their primary goals. You really want the CSMs to be focused on building their relationship with the executive clients, driving more feature adoption and upsell, and generating referenceability, which helps Sales drive new logo revenue growth. So you don't want your CSMs to be explaining how to use or fix your products. This presents a challenge and opportunity. How can you get the client to trust Support in the same way that they trust their CSM?

Moreover, how do you get the *CSM* to trust Support enough to feel comfortable sending their clients to Support when they have an issue? Summers recommends limiting the number of times a client is rerouted within Support. You can do this by creating specialized Subject Matter Expert teams, so that "you're not going to go through five different people to just to be able to get to the one person who could actually answer your issue." Summers adds, "Highly tiered Support models are the equivalent of the dreaded phone tree hell in my mind. No one wants to deal with a phone tree—you want to be in touch with one person who will solve your problem."

When you can quickly connect the client with someone who can help and thereby avoid delays in ticket resolution, the client won't feel compelled to go back to their CSM. "The typical bad scenario is the client says, 'You told me to file a ticket. Now it's been sitting for ten days and nothing has happened.' Then the CSM is the one that has to drive the escalation and poke to get the ticket resolved. But now you've created this bad cycle of behavior where the client feels the only way to get help is to escalate to the CSM." Escalation is equivalent to dialing 0 on a phone tree, or yelling "Operator!" To avoid and break this cycle, the Support team must roll out their own escalation process so that clients know that raising their hand for more help will result in an action plan, driven by Support, not the CSM. The CSM can simply keep abreast of the escalation for context. (This also ensures that Support can work 24/7 on the escalation as needed, across multiple geographic shifts, which a CSM would not be able to do.)

The second thing you have to do to sustain this division of labor—with CSM being proactive and Support managing reactive cases—is to ensure the Support team has visibility into the client's context.

Get Visibility into Client Data

It used to be that Support teams would resolve tickets with blinders on. They'd be completely unaware of any other aspect of the client's context: Is the client's renewal due this month? Is the sales team working on a major expansion with them? Is this a generally happy client that ran into an issue, or is this support ticket the latest in a series of crises they've experienced? What Outcome was the client trying to achieve when they ran into this technical issue? Does this issue relate to a project that the Services team was working on with the client?

Without fully understanding the context, a Support rep might not prioritize the client's issue appropriately in their queue. They also might not resolve the root cause of the problem, proposing a Band-Aid solution instead, without realizing it. They may not talk to the other people at their company who could help them resolve the issue in a way that results in the best experience for the client and accelerates their path toward achieving their desired outcome.

Nowadays, the best-run Support teams ensure they have a 360-degree view of the client's context when resolving a ticket. Andrea Lagan, the former COO at professional services automation company FinancialForce and current chief customer officer at HR software company BetterWorks, made it a priority to ensure that her support team had the visibility they needed. "If I'm a support analyst working on a case, the first thing I see for that customer is whether they have a red health score. And, oh, by the way, their renewal is coming up in 45 days, and they've had five other high-priority tickets opened in the last ten days or so." In general, you'll want to make sure that your support team can see data on customer health, adoption, renewals, notes from recent conversations with the client, documented desired outcomes, and other information.

Give Visibility into Escalations

The most customer-centric organizations create processes so that CSM, Professional Services, and Sales can work closely with the Support team during a sensitive client situation. For example, if a ticket arises with a client that has had a high volume of support cases recently, or if the ticket has been open for a while, or if it's especially urgent to resolve it, Support tickets trigger a Risk Escalation that keeps the CSM, Project Manager, and Sales rep in the loop and recommends a certain playbook of actions. These risky situations are often reviewed in a weekly executive team meeting.

Summers explains what happens when this visibility isn't given to other client-facing teams.

A typical scenario would be that an account executive is going to go onsite to a customer. So they want to be able to know, what are the most recent Support cases? Are there any longstanding issues? But if the Support team isn't tracking client interactions in a system that's accessible to other client-facing team members, then that information is often buried in someone's personal email or spreadsheets. The account executive is thinking, "I may get asked about something in an onsite meeting. I need my talk track ready. I don't want to look like I was blindsided by something I didn't know about."

Many of us know that feeling of dread. Integrating the Support ticketing system with the Customer Success solution and CRM can help ensure that escalations are visible to everyone without much effort from the Support rep.

Support Teams Can Be Proactive, Too!

Summers has found that besides helping to mitigate the impact of negative situations, Support reps can proactively help a portfolio of clients, beyond the client that submitted the ticket. Perhaps the Support rep found a creative way to solve a problem and also realized that multiple clients may be experiencing the same problem. They can give the CSM team a heads-up about the set of clients that could benefit from the solution, and the CSMs can then reach out to the clients about it. Specialized Support SME teams are especially in a good position to suggest solutions for specific groupings of customers that have experienced a similar challenge.

Support teams are also helping to accelerate the flywheel of the Helix. They're finding opportunities to sell services when the client could benefit from education or additional help on a regular basis, as we discussed in the last chapter. Support reps are also figuring out when a client is trying to solve a problem that their current contract doesn't allow them to solve, but that they could tackle if they bought an additional product or upgraded to a new level of partnership.

Indeed, the world of Support is evolving just like the domain of CSM. Bill Patterson is the executive vice president and general manager CRM Applications at Salesforce. He's seeing a marked change:

> When you think about customer service in the broad sense, most interactions are very transactional. You're calling about a problem—I'm fixing said problem. You're calling about a question—I'm answering that question. Today's service world often begins and ends in that transaction.
>
> But businesses are starting to recognize that these moments allow us to understand the needs of our customers. These moments are a treasure trove of information for understanding our customers in a way that's more personal. That's how the opportunity in customer service is changing.

Patterson sees another opportunity to turn formerly transactional communications into more valuable interactions, in that the Support rep can help the CSM become more proactive. "The CSM can take the transactional case and say, 'How can I help you get the most from the service?'"

He further sees an opportunity to leverage support data to predict churn. "If I have a question about my cable bill, I'm not threatening to leave every time I call, I'm just trying to unblock my problem. But if you didn't take care of me, my propensity to leave is higher. If I've had this experience many times, I enter the interaction with a negative attitude. And a CSM with a CSM platform can identify patterns leading toward churn. The customer is thinking 'I've been trying forever to make this work but I just can't and now I'm giving up.' The CSM can correlate the flurry of cases with the drop in product usage and take the necessary steps to retain that customer."

The end result of this isn't just reduced churn, it's a change in the way we think about service. "Today, for many service interactions, the customer is thinking, 'Do you even know who I am?' Now, I can start making them feel like we are authentically caring about the customer and their problem. Overall, we can take service from a transactional model to a human-centric one."

Collaboration with R&D

Support teams often become frustrated when clients encounter bugs in the product, and even more frustrated when there's a high volume of bugs, and even *more* frustrated when they can't share with the client a timeline for fixing the bugs. That frustration is understandable; it also echoes the client's frustration, which of course must be addressed in order to achieve the kind of renewal, expansion, and advocacy rates that we discussed in Part I of this book. Customer-centric organizations define processes for Support to work with Engineering to identify bugs, prioritize the resolution of bugs, and communicate timelines back to the client.

Besides helping to include bug resolution in the product roadmap, Support teams can help Product Management teams identify more holistic ways to improve the product. For example, analysis of tickets—as well as qualitative feedback from Support reps—can show areas of the product where clients are investing the most effort; perhaps that effort could be reduced with changes to the user interface or even larger-scale architectural improvements. This sort of analysis can also reveal the areas of the product that clients find the most valuable; after all, they wouldn't be struggling to use the product if they didn't believe in its potential. To aid in this analysis, Summers recommends tracking a Customer Effort Score through a survey that asks the question, "On a scale of 'very easy' to 'very difficult,' how easy was it to interact with [company name]?" Support teams are even getting involved in the Product team's design reviews to offer their input early in the development cycle. In general, advising the Product team on improving the product—which is the most scalable asset at the company—is a terrific way to deflect tickets. This way, Support teams are helping to resolve problems at their root cause, preventing tickets from occurring in the first place.

Ticket Deflection

Support teams can deflect tickets in other ways, too. Ticket deflection—ensuring that issues don't come up in the first place—has been a priority for our own VP of Global Support at Gainsight, Emily McDaniel. She notes that Support teams can assist Documentation teams in identifying technical articles that require an update (due to a recent feature release) or another modification, which can help clients better resolve issues on their own rather than submitting a ticket to Support. Likewise, Support teams can recommend improvements to training materials (perhaps owned by the Education team) that will help ensure clients don't run into issues in the first place. Communicating with customers en masse through the online community by sharing tips or a heads-up about issues can also help clients become more self-sufficient. Finally, sometimes Premier Support offerings (that the client pays for) include regular "support reviews," in which vendor and client can align on how to improve the way they work together on technical challenges.

Career Paths for Support

Because of the rise of the customer-centricity, Support reps now have more career paths than they've ever had before, says Summers.

> We have a shift from a traditional kind of on-premises support organization, where someone would have a support career and stay there for 20 years, moving through the ranks. In recent years, I've had people move from our support organization into product management, sales engineering, professional services, IT, technical operations, engineering, and CSM. This kind of movement was inconceivable even a decade ago. Today's Support reps gain valuable work experience and insights into the customer experience. This allows them to transfer into other disciplines and add immediate value from having that hands-on product experience.

Even as reactive Support models are described in contrast with the more proactive CSM model, the new focus on customer-centricity has elevated Support teams as well.

Summary

In this chapter we discussed how Support teams gave rise to CSM teams and also supported them in their quest to become more proactive. At the same time, Support teams have become more proactive, too—updating other client-facing teams on escalations, identifying ways to help clients avoid the fates of ones with escalations, finding upsell opportunities, and educating the Engineering and Product teams on how to improve the quality and value of the product. These trends have helped the Support team become more valuable in the eyes of CEOs and helped Support members achieve new heights in their careers.

In the next chapter, we'll cover another team that has had to evolve along with the rise of the subscription model: Finance.

14 | Finance: The New Scoreboard

One of the hardest, most expensive things to do is to convince a prospect to become a customer. Once that's done, the adoption period right after that is very important, because that's when the economics of the transaction actually start to finally benefit the vendor.

That's multi-time chief financial officer John Bonney, who has held that role at FinancialForce and most recently Harness. His statement shows his belief that Customer Success is instrumental to the profitability of a recurring revenue company. CFOs like Bonney are becoming critical partners to chief customer officers as they set targets for Customer Success, plan headcount, and think through the translation of client outcomes to vendor revenue and profits.

CFOs are increasingly jumping on the Customer Success bandwagon, expressing genuine belief that upfront investment in the success of a client will help generate the flywheel effect of the Helix that we discussed earlier in the book. Here's how Bonney describes how Customer Success helps you sell to *new* clients:

> Typically at the beginning stages, there will be some sort of onboarding which is pretty hands-on, and that can mean higher cost in the beginning. That's okay—actually we plan for that—because once the customer acclimates well to your solution, they will grow their relationship you with in the future. Our company can benefit from greater profitability as the customer gets further in their journey. And those customers who are successful are also typically your best salespeople. Even your strongest sales reps typically can't acquire new customers without good word-of-mouth from happy customers.

Christophe Bodin knows a lot of CFOs like Bonney. He's chief customer officer at Anaplan, a "connected planning" software company that helps an organization's functional teams such as finance, sales, supply chain, and HR drive strategic and financial planning across the enterprise for better, faster decision-making. Christophe knows the value of Customer Success because he's in the thick of it every day; but because he works with so many finance teams as his clients, he also knows how much those finance teams value their Customer Success counterparts. In particular, Christophe knows that an effective financial planning process requires a strong focus on customers: "When I've seen CS and finance working together well, it's when Finance actually understands how customer behavior is driving the metrics. It's about Finance being deeply cognizant of the customer journey, what both customers and CSMs are doing at each point, and knowing how that impacts the P&L."

In this book we've shown again and again that investing in CS results in strong revenue growth. As Finance teams get wiser on the value of CS and begin to spend more time on it in the budgeting process, they're digging into the mechanics of the return on investment in CS: What kind of bang do I get for my buck? More specifically:

- What "bang" should I be aiming for?
- How many "bucks" should I spend, and where?

In this chapter we'll discuss how Finance and CS are partnering together to answer those two questions.

What "Bang" Should I Be Aiming For?

"If you need more revenue, invest in Sales." Why is that the default—some might say "kneejerk"—response to the basic question of how to make more money? One of the reasons Sales is such an obvious economic driver for companies is because its core key performance indicator (KPI) is meaningful and well-defined: bookings.

But for businesses implementing Customer Success, many struggle with defining the final financial KPI. While everyone agrees that leading health score indicators (e.g. adoption, maturity, satisfaction, etc.) are what you should action day-to-day, every Customer Success team needs to define the final "lagging" indicator to use with executives and the board. Finance teams in particular need to know that ultimate financial KPI for Customer Success in order to work with CS leaders to properly budget for their function.

It shouldn't surprise you that that metric is retention. But unlike in Sales, there's debate over which retention metric to anchor upon: Gross Retention Rate (GRR) or Net Retention Rate (NRR). Here's how John explains the difference between these two metrics. "Gross Retention means, if you had ten customers paying you $10 one year ago, how much of that $10 did you retain today? And Net Retention means, if you had ten customers paying you $10 a year ago, how much are those same ten customers paying you today?"

GRR takes into account churn, but doesn't benefit from expansion—hence the max is 100%. NRR includes both expansion and churn, and therefore can (and probably should for most companies) be over 100%.

Gross Retention versus Net Retention

So how do you choose between GRR and NRR as an anchor KPI for your post-sales/CS organization? We've thought about this a great deal as we've met thousands of companies over the years and realized that there isn't a one-size-fits-all solution. But we are convinced there's a framework to help you make the right decision for your company.

At first glance, it's tempting to automatically assume NRR is the better indicator because it synthesizes two revenue streams—the renewal and the upsell. In a nutshell, it includes more information. But that's not necessarily the case. On one hand, GRR has an advantage over NRR in that it truly measures the long-term health of the business because gross churn erodes expansion opportunity over time. In other words, you can't upsell clients that you lose! On the other hand, an over-focus on gross retention and churn can lead to a point of diminishing returns. And this focus has practical effects every day. Do I focus on the nth at-risk client and try to save them (sometimes in futility) or take that energy and spend it on a healthy client ripe for expansion?

Three Dimensions to the GRR-versus-NRR Problem

There are a few core dimensions to consider in this problem:

- **Financing:** Are you private and needing to raise additional capital? In that case, investors may scrutinize your GRR. Alternatively, are you public or do you plan to go public? In that case, you likely will be reporting NRR.
- **Growth rate:** If you are growing fast and valued on growth, NRR may have a larger economic impact near-term. On the other hand, slow-growth companies can receive great ROI from optimizing GRR (and therefore churn).
- **Current Gross Retention:** In general, there is a bright line for GRR and you don't want to go below it. Depending on your target customer segment and Customer Acquisition Cost (CAC), that rate could be below 60% (for SMB) or below 70% (for Enterprise). Below a certain point investors look at a business as being not viable and the churn rate indicates more fundamental, systemic challenges.

It all comes down to how optimized you are around Gross Retention—or to put it another way, how optimized your renewal mechanism is. If that mechanism is fully optimized or very efficient, the higher-ROI focus might be around Net Retention. Our recommended GRR ranges are shown in Figure 14.1.

GROSS RETENTION OPTIMIZATION RANGES

IF YOU SELL TO SMB CUSTOMERS

IF YOU SELL TO ENTERPRISE CUSTOMERS

Figure 14.1

Do I Optimize for GRR or NRR?

If you're a private company needing more capital, work hard to get your GRR to the fully optimized level, since investors will notice. If you're public and reporting NRR, you can probably live in the zone of "room for optimization" for GRR and focus on improving net retention. Similarly, the higher your growth, the more you should focus on Net Retention versus Gross Retention.

It's certainly a continuum, but if you're a high-growth public company with a 97% GRR, you might take those incremental hours spent chasing the pesky few red customers and instead double-down on your successful ones to help them grow and expand. As an example, Brent Grimes, senior vice president of Global Customer Success at MuleSoft, a Salesforce company, is an advocate for using Net Dollar Retention as a key metric. "It allows you to make decisions both at a macro-level across the company and also within individual territories around where I spend my time—what is the tradeoff between the ability to retain one customer and grow another?"

How Many "Bucks" Should I Spend, and Where?

Now that you've figured out what "bang" you're aiming for—Gross or Net Retention, depending on your situation—you'll need to get into the details of the "bucks." We'll discuss the actual amount that you should budget for CS in a later chapter on budgeting. In the meantime, let's focus on the *how*: In what way should you invest to generate stronger Gross or Net Retention?

How Should We Spend the Bucks?

Smart Finance leaders know that it's not enough to simply hire a bunch of people in CS and expect strong retention. As Christophe emphasized, the great CFOs get into the details of the actual interactions between the CS team and clients across the customer journey. They're asking questions of their CS leaders such as:

- What type of CSMs do we have? What skills do they have?
- Where do CSMs spend their time?
- How much time are they investing in small business clients? In enterprise clients?
- What's the repeatable methodology that allows us to generate a particular retention rate?
- How should we invest the CS team's time to generate a one-percentage-point increase in retention?
- What types of root causes of churn can be addressed in the next year with CS execution? What types should be addressed through a structural shift (e.g. improvements in the product, or a change in our target market)?

When a CFO understands the mechanics of CS investments at the same level of detail as they understand Sales investments, they can truly command holistic knowledge of the revenue growth model for their company.

Bonney, the multi-time CFO, emphasizes the importance of Finance and CS being aligned on retention forecasts in particular. "Finance and Customer Success really need to be on the same page as you think about which customers are up for renewal. What's the client's likelihood of renewal? Are there any customers at risk? Those can obviously have a very material impact on your financial results." Like other CFOs, Bonney is looking to give his executive team and board visibility into the company's future revenue stream and cash flow, and the retention rate is a significant driver of those. As a result, Bonney has weekly touchpoints between Finance and CS to talk about customer health, including adoption metrics, which both departments consider a leading indicator of renewal. That alignment on forecasts helps Bonney work with the CS team to figure out the right investment in CS that will result in the retention rates they're aiming for.

Finance and CS will also want to align on principles for when to give customers discounts or refunds. Bonney has seen this go wrong:

> If there isn't collaboration between the two departments, you can have situations where customers that aren't happy ask for credits or refunds, and the CS team wants to grant them, but that can get out of control. In that case, you need to identify the root causes of the client issues and also get line of sight into future requests from clients. Otherwise, you can jeopardize really important revenue recognition rules that we have to follow. You can run afoul of your auditors.

How Should We Account for CS?

"Does CSM count as Cost of Goods Sold (COGS) or Sales & Marketing?" We hear this question in the Customer Success community all the time. The key to answering it is diving into one of the questions above: What types of CSMs do you have? We notice three categories of CSMs with different accounting categorizations:

1. "CSM for Value Gaps"

Because it's early days, your product doesn't deliver enough value out of the box, so your CSM fills the gaps. They're highly technical and create (sometimes ingenious) hacks to solve problems. Theoretically, this type of CSM could be charged for as a service, but your clients aren't willing to pay (so you need to invest the work as free), or else you haven't had the time or expertise to develop a services program yet. Over time, you may figure out how to package up this role as a paid recurring Technical Account Management (TAM) service. You categorize your CSM expense as COGS because the CSM is essential to delivering the product that the client purchased.

2. "CSM for Value Delivery"

Your product has evolved. The gaps are no longer large, and you've figured out how to plug the remaining ones by selling services to offset the cost of extra work that your team needs to do (and you specialize that work into a Services team). You realize that delivering value isn't just about getting feature adoption; it's also about managing client teams through the changes in behavior that the software prescribes. To achieve this, the CSM must build trust, reconcile different points of view in meetings at the client, communicate persuasively, mobilize the group behind a plan, and gain the respect of executives, who are often the decision-makers for renewing the product. You hire CSMs for their interpersonal skills. You focus them on a certain "lifecycle" of activities: kickoffs, milestone meetings, executive business reviews, and renewal conversations.

Your retention rates improve and your Sales team is happy because they can focus less of their time on escalations and more on hunting and expanding existing accounts. The CSMs count toward Cost of Retention (part of Sales & Marketing) since they contribute to the renewal, even if they don't have formal quota responsibility.

3. "CSM for Value Capture"

You have a strong methodology for delivering value to clients through your product (which may be very simple or intuitive) and/or through services (which are essential if the product is complex). Your CSMs are focused on monetizing the value that you're delivering (by upgrading clients to a new tier), selling into whitespace, by pitching new use cases, finding new teams to sell to, or selling new products. The CSMs' skills lie in exploiting opportunities: overages, whitespace, and organizational dynamics or politics. You hire CSMs who enjoy building long-term relationships and getting deals

	CSM for Value Gaps	CSM for Value Delivery	CSM for Value Capture
Product	Early	Robust	Mature; possibly multiple
Services Sold	Few to none; or else CSM is paid TAM role	Well-developed	Core competency, or else none needed
CSM Profile	Technical	Strong exec presence	Sales/"Farmer"
Cost	Cost of Goods Sold (COGS)	Retention (part of Sales & Marketing)	Expansion (part of Sales & Marketing)

Figure 14.2

done. They have a quota and may have the title Account Manager. They count toward Cost of Expansion.

One of the three models shown in Figure 14.2 isn't necessarily better than the others; your choice depends on your situation. Choose wisely!

Summary

In this chapter we discussed the value of Finance as a crucial partner to CS in understanding the impact of CSM activities and customer behaviors on the P&L. We covered the financial metrics that CFOs should use in budgeting—Gross or Net Retention Rate, depending on your financing, your growth rate, and your current Gross Retention. We discussed how much companies are spending on CS, how they are thinking through the types of CS investments they make, and how they are accounting for those costs. The bottom line? CFOs are no longer saying, "Need revenue? Hire another salesperson." Instead, they're becoming knowledgeable about the connection between CS investments and retention and how to optimize the bang for their buck.

15

IT: The New Mission for the CIO

The main thing that I always tell people is—early and often.

That's Karl Mosgofian, our own CIO at Gainsight, responding to the question of how Customer Success teams should engage with IT teams. Given that he has been a CIO across several large and small companies, Mosgofian has seen CS–IT collaboration succeed and also fail. "I think one of the mistakes that a lot of business leaders make is, they want to move quickly, but sometimes they don't bring in IT early enough. At some point, IT gets involved and says, well gee, why did you choose this product? Now you've got to go backwards and defend yourself."

But Karl also sees positive value from engaging with IT.

They can be tremendously helpful. SaaS is easy in that it's relatively easy now to fire something up. But typically you can't just flip the switch and everything works right. Data integration takes work and there are people who do it for a living and they're really good at it. They live in IT.

In this chapter, we'll discuss how we arrived at the point where the most successful companies aren't even questioning the value of CS-IT collaboration—especially when it comes to rolling out an insightful 360-degree view of your customers.

IT: An Essential Partner to Customer Success

Business, as with much of life, moves like a pendulum from one extreme to the other.

In the 1990s and 2000s, large corporate IT organizations emerged. Nothing got done without IT being involved. CIOs were on the fast track to becoming some of the most important leaders in the company. Then in the last five years, things feel like they reversed all of a sudden. With the "consumerization" of IT, technologies can now be purchased by line-of-business leaders—or even individual employees. We read many a quote from CEOs questioning whether they needed an IT department whatsoever. In fact, books were even written about the "End of IT."

More recently, we're seeing a new emerging trend. Companies—big and small—are suffering from technology indigestion. With SaaS and cloud, applications are so easy to buy that companies now own a ridiculous number of products. One friend who was CIO of an at-the-time 400-person company said his business had purchased 100 separate SaaS apps. Another CIO more recently told us his 700-employee firm had hundreds of cloud-based products. Both were brought in to rationalize the mess because:

- Multiple products were purchased to do the same thing.
- The technologies didn't work with each other.
- Much of the vendor functionality wasn't being utilized.
- Some of the services were over-purchased and over-provisioned.
- No one was sure of the security standards for each.

This isn't a one-way street. Some IT departments have earned reputations as "progress-blockers." This leads cloud application providers to circumvent IT because they may understand technology but not the core business. Instead of taking it personally, IT professionals should examine why the business does not view them as trusted advisors.

We see this situation from two vantage points:

1. As a growing company suffering many of the above challenges. Needless to say, Nick went from thinking "we'll never need IT" to staffing up a couple of years ago.
2. As a vendor selling a platform into this new world.

On the second point: Early on, our application was sold like the ones above—to "line of business" (in this case the Customer Success team)—and was often purchased without heavy IT involvement. But our business has evolved a great deal:

- Clients now view Customer Success platforms as technology to be rolled out across the entire company—CSM, Sales, Services, Support, Product, Marketing, Finance, etc.
- Clients realize that CSM platforms depend on data—the more data, the more value.
- Clients woke up to the fact that CSM platforms often house some of the most sensitive data in the business—data about their customers.

As such, we're seeing more and more companies looking at their CSM platform decision as an "enterprise" decision. And being an enterprise decision, they're involving their IT counterparts to:

- **Plan the roadmap of data integrations into the platform and assess:**
    - How data will get out of the source systems
    - How data will be mapped across source (e.g., by a common client ID)
    - How data inconsistencies will be resolved
    - What type of "ETL" (data processing) is required to push the data into the CSM platform
    - How the plumbing of the above works in terms of scheduling, logging, validation, etc.
- **Assist with the change management across the company in terms of:**
    - Data updates
    - Functionality rollouts
    - User adoption

- **Assess and manage the security posture around the application, including:**
  - Validating vendor security compliance (e.g. SOC II Type 2)
  - Understanding application permissions and controls
  - Determining how those permissions and controls fit with other enterprise systems (e.g. Salesforce.com)

To some extent, the customers that are the most savvy about involving IT are the ones that didn't involve IT enough in previous SaaS platform rollouts. Most frequently, we've seen these companies cite poor planning around early software rollouts as their "learning experience." The business departments may have driven the rollout for expediency, but years later the aftermath is a configuration that is hard to maintain, not up-to-speed with the latest-and-greatest functionality, and poorly adopted. In fact, many of these same companies are in parallel going through a "reimplementation" of existing systems, and they don't want to make the same mistake in the CSM world.

So if you're a CS leader looking at a platform decision, our advice to you is to involve your IT partners early on. They'll be great assets in the decision-making process and more importantly, they'll make sure you're set up for getting maximum value over time.

Here's how Eric Johnson, SVP and CIO at SurveyMonkey, thinks about partnering with CS teams on their technology needs.

In the last three to five years, the role of CIO has gone from more of a back-office function managing the technology, to one where you oper-ate more on the business strategy. As CIO, how do you actually help the line-of-business leaders drive better decisions? CIOs are getting so deep with their CS leaders that some of them are actually stepping into Customer Success executive roles. But as partners to CS, CIOs can help you understand how to stitch together the people, the process, and all the technology to truly have a better perspective of what's going on with your customers. Let's start by sitting down to truly understand, what is the chal-lenge you're having, or what is the business opportunity that you want to take advantage of? Let's talk through that before we even start discussing technology.

There's a big push now, more than ever, around improving the cus-tomer experience. To do this, you often have to make sure that behind the scenes you're automating the tracking of interactions and even the interactions themselves. You get to a point where you can't just keep throwing bodies at the problem. You have to find ways to drive scale. That's where CIOs can help.

To start, they can help with your Customer 360. Historically, companies had siloed data sets for their customer interactions. You're interacting with clients through customer support calls, through your product, through sales and marketing activities. You need to ensure that you're looking across all the different channels of how you're interacting with your customer to figure out which interactions are effective and which aren't.

That's the dream!

As partners to you in thinking through your business goals even before your technology needs, CIOs can help you roll out that 360-degree-view of the customer that you've always dreamed of but that never made it to fruition.

Three Reasons Your Customer 360 Is Stuck in the 1990s

Let's all just agree: The 1990s were awesome. Tamagotchis, Birkenstocks, Vanilla Ice—what more could you ask for? And even though Birkenstocks and fanny-packs are (incredibly) back in fashion, some things are probably better left in our memories. Let's take 1990s tech, for example: Dial-up modem tones and brightly colored iMacs may give rise to warm feelings of nostalgia, but waiting 30 minutes to download an email? We're super-glad we've moved on from that.

But how much have we really moved on? In some aspects of B2B IT, things haven't changed a ton in the last 20 years. Plenty of companies are tracking essentially the same data using similar systems funneled to the same teams—and those teams make use of that data the same way they did in 1998. Like, does anyone outside of Marketing know what content customers are engaging with? Does anyone outside of Product have any clue what daily active use looks like? Could anyone besides Sales even find a customer's basic contact info? And even if those pain points have been solved, they probably haven't been solved evenly across the company.

Around the turn of the century, pioneers like Tom Siebel, founder of pioneering CRM software company Siebel Systems, were talking about the need to bring all customer data together in one view—a "360-degree view of the customer." In this utopia, every employee in a company would fully understand what's happening with a client. Obviously, if we graphed the amount of customer data we're collecting and analyzing since the 1990s, it would look like the letter J. But have we really achieved the mythic 360-degree view?

Let's travel back in time to the 1990s to understand the original need for a Customer 360. The macro business trend of the 1980s and 1990s was consolidation. Private equity and debt markets opened up a world of megamergers from telecom consolidation to AOL-Time Warner. In this sea of conglomerates, customer experience suffered as employees struggled to get a full picture of what was happening with a client.

So IT departments embarked on consolidation projects—just smash together every disparate system with an acronym for a name: ERP systems, HR products, and CRM implementations. And the Customer 360 stood like an oasis, just beyond reach across a desert of multiyear IT projects. After all, just because you can route different data sources into one window doesn't make the information meaningful or even necessarily more accessible!

Fast-forward two decades and where are we? In some sense we still strive for the elusive Customer 360, with employees hunting and pecking across many systems to understand what's happening with a client. At the same time, a senior exec at one of our large Fortune 500 clients recently said, "Our problem isn't that we don't have a Customer 360. It's that we have 48 of them!" Another client recently asked us, "What use is giving employees data if they don't know what to do with it?" A third told us, "Beautiful dashboards become beautiful parking lots."

What if our premise around a Customer 360 is wrong? Or perhaps just stuck in time? We think there are three key ways customer data infrastructure is still sporting parachute pants and bucket hats—in other words, stuck in the 1990s:

1. **Data:** Customer data is no longer about static, manually entered information (e.g. customer contact information). It's about real-time, dynamic data sources like product usage and telemetry from IoT sensors.
2. **Structure:** Business changes are no longer one-way. Sure, there are a number of megamergers (hello AT&T!), but divestitures, spinouts, and take-privates are just as much en vogue.

3. **Pace:** The pace of updates has increased radically. New products are launched and revised continuously, and client sponsors change seemingly all the time.

Instead, the new Customer 360 has dramatically different requirements:

- **Personalized:** A Customer 360 needs to show us the products and businesses relevant to me, as an individual employee. And it needs to show us the information relevant to the person at the client org with whom we're speaking—not just at the company level.
- **Insightful:** And please don't make us interpret all of this data. Give us a simple red/yellow/green view of how this client is doing.
- **Action-oriented:** Tell us what we should do next based upon proven best practices.
- **Automated:** And as much as possible, do those actions for us at scale.

The new Customer 360 is no longer a dashboard or a report. It's an orchestration system to drive the client experience end-to-end. In other words, it's far more strategic than a workflow hack or an incremental time-saver.

If you're a CEO or IT leader and your Customer 360 is stuck in the 1990s, it's time to get really strategic and proactive with your processes and systems. We're seeing agile companies with 21st-century levels of sophistication in this area turning CX into a massive competitive advantage. In short, you really don't want to be caught wearing your Generra Hypercolor T-shirt in 2019 and beyond. It's time to update your Customer 360 to something a bit more current. (Full disclosure: We still think Hypercolor is cool!)

Summary

In this chapter we discussed why CS leaders have been most successful in scaling their teams through technology when they work closely with their CIOs. CIOs have become indispensable partners to their CS peers in translating business goals into technology requirements and evaluating CS platform decisions. As a result, companies have become savvier about how to purchase and configure a best-in-class Customer 360 that's personalized, insightful, action-oriented, and automated.

CS leaders seem to have more departments interested in partnering with them than ever before. Human Resources departments, too, have become allies to CS, as they have realized that making clients successful produces happier employees—and also that the stress of the Customer Success job can create unusual burdens on teammates. In the next chapter we'll discuss how HR departments are evolving in the Customer Success economy.

16

HR: Happy Employees Take Better Care of Customers

Let's face it, most customers aren't making their way to your Customer Success manager because they've already gotten a ton of value from your product. They're reaching out because they have a problem.

That's Tracy Cote, chief people officer at Zenefits, a cloud-based human resources software company. She's pointing to how difficult the role of CSM can be, because you're often taking care of challenging client situations. Her point of view isn't unusual. Some would go so far as to say that working in CS is the hardest job in the company. In this chapter, we'll explore what causes the CSM job to be hard and then discuss what CS leaders and their HR partners can do about it.

Why the Customer Success Job Is Hard—And Why That Matters

The CSM job can be super-challenging for six common reasons:

- **The "Glass-Half-Empty" Phenomenon:** Whereas Sales reps start at zero bookings every quarter—with a fresh canvas—and need to build up to 100% of quota from there, CSMs start at an assumed 100% default gross retention rate, and the only possible direction is down. When Sales closes a deal, we ring the gong, but a renewal seems more like a save—with sighs of relief and brow-wiping—than a victory to celebrate.

- **The "Downstream" Phenomenon:** CSMs are downstream from other departments, inheriting the consequences of those departments' decisions. When Engineering's quality assurance processes lapse, CSMs hear about it from their clients. When Product Management releases a new feature that doesn't deliver sufficient value, CSMs hear about it. When a Marketing event goes wrong, CSMs hear about it. When Sales sets the wrong expectations in the sales cycle, or sells to a customer that isn't within the target market, CSMs hear about it.

- **The "Buck-Stops-Here" Phenomenon:** CSMs handle the worst of the escalations. Your Support rep may be in the details of troubleshooting the ticket, but your client will hold your CSM accountable for their overall success and, therefore, for whether the ticket gets resolved.

- **The "Helper" Phenomenon:** CSMs often feel your company's challenges in a very personal way, because they're often the kind of people who by nature love to help others. When they can't help their clients in the way they want to, it's really tough for them.

- **The "Cost Constraints" Phenomenon:** CSM teams have to stay within budget even as their environment is changing at a dramatic pace due to frequent product releases, the market changing, and your go-to-market team making new decisions about who is the target customer. Keeping up with those changes while managing ever more accounts per CSM is very hard.

- **The "Is Anyone Out There?" Phenomenon:** All of these issues are compounded by the fact that many CSMs, especially those who serve enterprise clients, work remotely from their homes or from small offices separate from "headquarters." When they finish that tough call, they may not have anyone nearby to confide in.

If you're not careful, you can end up with a CSM team that's pretty miserable. No one wants a team that's unhappy, but having an unhappy CSM team is arguably worse than having an unhappy team in any other department. That's because when your CSMs are unhappy, that misery spreads to your clients. When we don't attend to our own emotional needs, it's hard to attend to the emotional needs of others, including our clients. In other words, when we don't experience empathy from our work culture, our own supply of empathy for others runs low. Conversely, when our CSMs are happy, they're radiating joy to our clients, who in turn have a better Experience. If we're accountable for generating strong Experiences for our clients, we'll take infectious joy over contagious depression any day!

As Cote points out,

> You have to always remember that your Customer Success team is the front-line experience for both your company and your brand. If your employees are engaged, happy, and empowered, they are going to do a much better job of ensuring your customers want to stay with your brand. The interactions between your CSMs and the customer, and the relationships they build, will have a long-lasting impact on the success of your business in terms of reputation as well as revenue. Empowered employees radiate competence and customers embrace that. Put simply, the happiness of our CS team is something that leaders have to care about.

Another reason (if you need any more!) to invest in the happiness of CSMs is employee retention—which seems so obvious, but it needs to be said. When you lose a CSM, their departure may not only be disastrous for the client relationship, but it also increases your people costs, because you need to invest in backfilling that CSM and training their replacement. In other words, unhappy team members affect your P&L. Remember JD Peterson, the chief growth officer at HR software company Culture Amp, the company focused on employee success from Chapter 6? Here's what he says about the impact of unhappy team members on your financials:

> There is plenty of data to show that happy employees spend less time out of the office. And of course, they stay longer. We all know how expensive it is to recruit and replace and train up employees. And when you have happier employees, you improve your employee Net Promoter Score, which is like Net Promoter Score for clients. They're going to be proud to work here. They're going to be motivated to tell others how great your company is. They're going to give referrals to new team members. This increases your brand.

Just like happy clients, happy team members can create a "Helix," a virtuous cycle of improvement where happy team members result in more team members joining, who in turn become happy. Let's explore this analogy between team members and clients in the next section.

Your Teammates Are Clients, Too

In an earlier chapter, we discussed the importance of generating strong Outcomes and Experiences for our clients. The fact that our CSMs' well-being so strongly influences the success of our clients means that we have to generate strong Outcomes and Experiences for our CSMs, too. Put differently: CSMs are clients, too. This analogy equating CSMs with clients holds true in many other respects. Certain concepts in Customer Success have direct analogues in the realm of managing team members. Check out these examples from the Table of Customer Success Elements:

- **Lifecycle Management:** How are we onboarding new team members, checking in with them after 90 days, scheduling regular one-on-one meetings, holding regular career development discussions, and reevaluating compensation?
- **Risk Escalation:** How are we monitoring signs that a team member may be at risk, such as not meeting a target, expressing frustration, anxiety, or depression, demonstrating a difference between their interests or skills and the nature of the role, or other signs?
- **Renewal Management:** At the end of the year, do each of the employees and the employer want to renew their relationship, and can we outline vision for that relationship next year that's beneficial to both sides?

These examples illustrate how a CS leader, in partnership with an HR team, can help team members have a great experience and achieve outcomes in their career and life from their job.

Applying Servant Leadership in CS

From the time Allison was little, her dad shared stories with her brother and her about heroes. There was a story about how the Wright Brothers, two little-known bicycle mechanics who worked tirelessly on their flight experiments for years, were greeted in France by unfamiliar praise from crowds of admirers of their innovation. There was another story about how Roosevelt secretly sent aid to the British before the U.S. entered World War II, even when faced with political opposition to getting involved, because it was the right thing to do. There were other stories that her dad made up at bedtime, sitting in the hallway between her and her brother's respective bedrooms, about heroic kids who saved the day. The stories varied, but a central character recurred: a leader with a vision to humbly serve others—a servant leader.

Nowadays, we don't hear many stories about servant leadership in the media. We could go on about the very different narratives of leadership that are told nowadays—carrying themes like narcissism, greed, materialism, workaholism, sociopathy, and others—but those have been well-documented elsewhere.

We think we need more compelling stories of leadership in our lives. We need to know what to expect from our leaders, and as we grow in our careers, we need to know what to aspire to and how to get there. We need more inspiration in general.

Servant leadership is the idea that leaders serve their teams rather than teams serving their leaders. Leaders don't sit at the top of the pyramid; they invert the pyramid, empowering everyone else. (The concept was created by Robert Greenleaf, who also founded the Greenleaf Center for Servant Leadership.) Although we're not perfect at Gainsight, we've witnessed and heard many stories of servant leadership among our managers. Among them:

- Whenever Nadav, our former director of Enterprise CSM, wanted his team members to try out a new motion to help our clients, he performed the motion himself first. This showed his team what's possible and trained them on how to do it. Nadav traveled literally around the world (multiple times) to support his team in this way.
- Allison was in a meeting with Daniel, our manager of Solution Architects, where we were discussing work–life balance for the team, which at the time wasn't great. Daniel took a stand in saying that he believes managers should formally take responsibility for their team's work–life balance in the same way they are responsible for operational results.
- Elaine, a thought leader in our Education team, led a session to document how to thoughtfully manage our teams through change, a permanent aspect of our lives at a growth-stage company.

To some, these activities might seem small. But imagine the world we'd live in if every action stemmed from a philosophy of servant leadership.

That's not to say leaders on our team don't make mistakes. We personally have made plenty of them. Sometimes we make mistakes due to our emotional state: We're stressed, threatened, or otherwise in pain. Sometimes we make mistakes because we don't have the right knowledge: It takes experience, creative thinking, and solid judgment to arrive at a win-win-win in any given situation. In either case our intentions aren't bad, but our actions are.

We think most people want to help others. Even if they're not aware of their desire to serve right now, they'll likely discover it later in life. And perhaps some inspiration would help. But an important root of the problem is that even when people want to serve, they don't know how. Servant leadership isn't merely about wanting to help; it's about taking actions that are effective in helping.

We need a playbook for how to be a servant leader in the context of a growing company. You've committed to your investors to achieve high targets; you know that change is a necessary constant; you need to do more with less. All of these factors make it difficult to serve your team.

Although we haven't written the playbook, we'll share eight frameworks that we've found helpful in trying to be servant leaders ourselves:

1. **Transparency:** Share more rather than less.
2. **Growth mindset:** Be a role model to your team by showing them that even leaders need to grow.
3. **Calm:** Reduce stress and create joy.
4. **Purpose:** Grow with a purpose in mind.
5. **Energy:** Help your teammates thrive.
6. **Self-compassion:** Be there for yourself so you can be there for your team.
7. **Vulnerability:** Bring your full self to work, inspiring your team members to do the same.
8. **Geographic inclusion:** Have a "no-headquarters" culture.

1. Transparency

Peterson from Culture Amp believes in the value of transparency because he sees his most successful clients embracing it. "First and foremost, the best cultures that we see in our clients start with gathering feedback and giving employees a voice. It starts with simply listening. And reciprocally, these cultures are focused on transparency and openness." Employees are sharing with management and management is sharing with employees.

At Gainsight, Nick has espoused transparency from the beginning. This has showed up in the normal ways: all-hands communications, "Ask Me Anything" Q&A sessions, and the like. But it's also showed up in unconventional ways, like Nick embracing vulnerability and sharing stories about his childhood loneliness, for example. One of Nick's favorite weekly rituals is his Sunday-night email to the company, "Mehtaphysical Musings," about what's happening in the company that people need to know, tips for teammates, his calendar for the upcoming week, and updates on what's happening for him outside of work with his family and with his second family, the Pittsburgh Steelers!

2. *Growth Mindset*

Allison says,

> In my view, no one is ever done growing. When we stop growing, we die inside. That's true for leaders as well as team members. Leaders should role-model this growth mindset so that team members emulate them and so that team members can support them in their own progression. So last year, I created a professional growth plan for myself and shared it with my entire team in an All Hands. I shared feedback I had received from across my organization, and then shared behaviors that I was going to Keep Doing, Stop Doing, and Start Doing. I've found the team really appreciates this. They know I'm not perfect, and they are grateful that I recognize it, too. They appreciate that I'm working on responding to their feedback, and even want to help me in my own growth. They sometimes even see it as courageous for me to be vulnerable with them. If we can "grow in public," our teams will be more likely to grow, too.

3. *Calm*

Given the stresses that CSMs can absorb from their clients and the internal dynamics of your company, CS leaders and their HR partners need to work to reduce stress. "Work–life balance is incredibly important," Cote says.

We all talk about it and yet so many people don't feel like they will ever achieve this goal. This is so important, particularly for higher stress jobs. Find ways to build flexibility into how you schedule your people. Trust that if you let someone leave early to attend their kids' school event, they'll make it up to you tenfold later, because they'll be appreciative. Allow time off to be actual time off—people shouldn't have to work on weekends or on their vacations—and this requires a lot of discipline in many environments, where technology allows us all to be "on" 24/7. As the leader, it is completely up to you to set the tone. When you sense someone is starting to experience burnout, pay attention. Stop. Listen. Offer time off, a special project, or some sort of change that will break them out of the cycle. It's often said that "a change is better than a rest" and that is never truer than when employees are hitting their burnout point.

At the same time, reducing stress isn't the same as motivating the team. Cote takes inspiration from the book *Primed to Perform*, by authors Neel Doshi and Lindsay McGregor.

At the core, they say that individuals are most likely to be successful and motivated when they are in an environment that allows them to be curious, to be empowered to implement change, where they understand the purpose of what they are doing, and where they can see the potential for them personally, connecting their current responsibilities with their future success. Practically speaking, this means you have to build some "play" into the workday. And while a ping-pong table is nice, it's more about creating an environment where your team is given the ability to solve actual business problems. This will give them satisfaction and help you and your business.

4. Purpose

Much has been written about how people want purpose in their work. They're not always inspired by the numbers, by operational initiatives, or by short-term wins. They want to feel they are contributing to a broader purpose. It's the job of a servant leader to illuminate that purpose.

At Gainsight, we espouse a purpose around how Customer Success is part of a more human approach to business. We describe this with our goal "to be living proof that you can win in business while being human-first."

Allison finds further meaning in the role of CS in helping humanity navigate technology.

> There's a particularly strong purpose in Customer Success. How humans interact with technology is a fundamental question of our time. Software is eating the world, robots are more capable than ever, and AI can replicate at least some human capabilities. Interestingly, Customer Success Managers are at the forefront of human–machine interaction in the business world. When software has bad UI, when it's imposed top-down, or when it's not natural to adopt, the CSM is on the front lines, empathizing with the poor human being who's struggling to use the software. It's the CSM's job to break down the barrier between human and machine, in a way that's human-first. To me, serving that purpose is among the most valuable causes we can contribute to in our lifetimes.

5. Energy

Name a personality framework, Allison has read about it: Myers Briggs, the Enneagram, Five Dynamics. She has found these frameworks invaluable in revealing how to help her team members define their roles in a way that maximizes their energy, how to create teams of people that complement each other so that every activity is performed by someone who is energized by it, and how to quickly get to know candidates she is recruiting. Servant leaders know how to empower every team member—and that means putting them in situations where they are highly energized.

6. Self-Compassion

It's hard to serve others when you're not serving yourself. You can recognize a burned-out leader by their emotional volatility, reactive decision-making, reluctance to work through conflict, or inability to feel empathy for others. When leaders burn out, their pain cascades through the entire team.

So it's critical that leaders serve themselves, too. That means figuring out how to optimize your own energy level throughout the week. Over the years Allison has developed a weekly schedule that she is laser-focused on maintaining. For example, she follows a rule to be in bed at 9:30 p.m. and asleep at 10:00 p.m. every day. She's a morning person, and she is also one of those unfortunate people who need at least eight hours of sleep. She wakes up at 6:00 a.m. and refuses to check her email until she has gone through her morning routine of reading and meditating. Whenever she makes an exception and checks her email before she has completed the routine, it puts her mind in a scattered state for the rest of the day—whereas reading helps her focus, think bigger-picture, and tap into creativity.

Taking this further, we have a rule at Gainsight that we don't send email on Saturdays. We have made this a core principle of the company, as a part of our value of driving "Success for All," since the beginning of our company. We take pride in the "no-email Saturdays" concept. We educate new teammates, and especially leaders, on it. The intention is that if one person sends an email on Saturday, others feel accountable to have to respond. So barring a critical client issue, we are all in it together.

Nick models this himself by disabling email (and other work-related apps) on his phone each Friday night, only turning them on again Sunday night to catch up on the coming week.

We spend our days trying to empower others—through coaching, persuading, comforting, reconciling, aligning—which, when effective, requires a great deal of emotional energy. To take care of others, we need to take care of ourselves.

7. *Vulnerability*

A key part of self-compassion is recognizing that none of us is perfect. Many of us at Gainsight were inspired by Brene Brown's powerful TED talk on how leaders can show vulnerability and become even more powerful. As such, we have pushed the boundaries as executives on our comfort level in being open with our stakeholders.

For Nick, this started with opening up with our team about the loneliness he felt as a child, and sometimes still does today. He took it further when he started speaking with vulnerability in front of the thousands of customers attending our Pulse conference every year. The year he spoke about eating alone every day at lunch in school was transformative. Other speakers—Gainsight and customers alike—embraced the concept, and now Gainsight events feature vulnerability front and center. As such, everyone in attendance is in a frame of mind of openness, connection, and growth.

8. Geographic Inclusion

Peterson at Culture Amp observes a big trend in companies building geographically distributed teams and investing extra effort to help those "remote" team members feel included. "More and more people are not working from headquarters, and more people are not even coming into the office if they're near one—they're doing their work on mobile devices. When you're building a culture, you need to account for that." This is especially relevant for Customer Success because as we discussed earlier in this chapter, the difficulties of the role can compound when there's no one physically nearby to help the CSM bounce back from an emotionally challenging situation.

At Gainsight, we embrace the idea of geographic inclusion. We were founded in the unlikely combination of cities of St. Louis, Missouri, and Hyderabad, India. Over the years, we embraced the idea that our best people are everywhere, not just in tech hubs like Silicon Valley. As such, we tell our teammates that we have no headquarters, that our HQ is wherever each of our employees—our Gainsters—reside. We try to live this value in as many creative ways as possible, from always prompting people on the phone in meetings to speak first to streaming our all-hands meetings from a studio so that no employee feels less included because they aren't "in the room where it happens."

What Does This Mean for a Chief Customer Officer?

So what does it take for a chief customer officer to adopt these behaviors of servant leadership, and specifically to help CSMs cope with their challenging roles? Let's come back to Tracy Cote, who has studied the attributes of CCOs who create successful teams.

Cote observes that great CCOs don't just spike on one attribute; they're multitalented. "The best CCO is high IQ and high EQ. Strategic, tactical, empathetic, and relational, chief customer officers must navigate not only the emotions of customers but also those of the extended internal team. There is a natural tension between Sales, Professional Services, Product, and Customer Success as each team does their best to navigate a complex business landscape internally as well as externally." This kind of navigational ability helps the CCO shelter their team from the worst of stress.

"For example, Sales is generally incented to bring in new customers, and move on. But the CCO is responsible for retention, expansion, and advocacy. This can sometimes create issues especially if the handover between Sales and Success is not clearly defined. Additionally, CCOs are frequently drivers of change, and they need to be great at that. Other internal teams don't always understand what the CCO organization really does, so communication is essential." When a CCO creates alignment at the top and across the company, they give the space to their team to get into the flow of doing their jobs. "And because of the stress level of the role," Cote adds, "a sense of humor never hurts."

Summary

Peterson from Culture Amp said it well: "It's almost cliché now to talk about how happy employees lead to happy customers. Honestly, there's simply no doubt about it." In this chapter we discussed the typical reasons why Customer Success Managers can have a tough time. And we discussed how treating CSMs like a kind of client, through certain well-known servant leadership techniques, can result in a thriving Customer Success team.

Now that we've discussed how major functions within a company—ranging from Services to HR—are evolving along with the Customer Success movement, we'll explore how to launch a Customer Success initiative at your company. This is the topic we'll focus on in Part III.

17

Avoiding Customer Success Silos

Now everyone in your company is involved in Customer Success. That's perfection, right? Watch out or it could turn into chaos.

Coming out of the pre–Customer Success era, when B2B companies largely ignored their customers post-sale, we have a risk of swinging the pendulum too far the other way. Today, many companies have:

- CSMs reaching out to customers to drive adoption
- Product teams putting guides into applications
- Marketing teams blasting existing customers

And for the vast majority of companies, the proverbial "left hand" and "right hand" don't talk to each other.

A customer can tell a CSM that a given new feature isn't a fit. Nonetheless, the next time the customer logs into the product, they get a "pop up" guide for that new feature. And then an email for a marketing webinar about the new feature might show up in their inbox the next day.

In this way, you might be simultaneously over-engaging with your customers and still missing engagement opportunities. So what's the answer? We need to stop thinking about CSM, in-product, and Marketing emails as separate strategies. We need to destroy those silos. Instead, we need a target customer journey for a given goal (e.g. adopting a new feature, onboarding) and a coordinated usage of channels (CSM, in-app, email) to help the customer get to the next best action.

Avoiding Silos around Feature Adoption

As a former Product Manager, Nick can attest that a big part of the joy of the job is "shipping" new features. But that term itself is anachronistic, dating back to a time when we "shipped" physical things like floppy disks (Google it!) and CDs to customers. With SaaS, "shipping" is instant and in many cases continuous.

But the same isn't true for adoption. Customers have their own cycles of quarters, cadences, meetings, change management, and the like. And sometimes getting your release cycle to align with their adoption cycle can be a challenge.

Most companies will do the basics to drive adoption—release notes, documentation, screenshots. If they're really good, they'll create videos or even GIFs! But recently, with the excitement around Customer Success, things have snowballed. Marketing might take the mantle and "blast" the clients with information about a new feature. Product might get excited and put in an in-app notification. And CSMs might eagerly reach out to clients to get them to "adopt."

What does that look like for the client? We've seen clients with the following experience:

- Patiently explain to the CSM why the new feature doesn't work for their business model.
- Then get an email from Marketing about the same feature—maybe they unsubscribe at that point.
- They log into the product to do their work and, *voila!*, a popup for the same feature appears.

That's not a recipe for a good client experience. Coordinated Customer Success strategies take a different approach:

- Have an email go out to the customer about the new feature personalized based upon their usage.
- If they engage (e.g. watch the video) and start using the feature, stop there.
- If they don't engage (maybe they aren't email people), show an in-app notification the next time they log in.
- If they dismiss the notification, have the CSM reach out and say, "I noticed you didn't use this feature but saw the guide—what can we learn?"

Avoiding Silos in Customer Feedback

It's one thing to have a bad experience and then receive a survey. It's another when the survey itself is a bad experience. It can leave a bitter taste in the mouth. In fact, based on what we know about memory, the last moments of an experience are often the most indelible and can redefine a person's point of view on the entirety of the experience.

The psychologist Daniel Kahneman referred to this concept as the "Peak-End Rule," but it just underscores the need to execute surveys with the same level of care and coordination as you do with the entirety of your customer journey.

Let's play this out using a Net Promoter Score survey as an example:

- I pass the scheduled completion of onboarding.
- I get a time-bound Net Promoter Score survey in my inbox.
- I ignore the survey. I'm busy still onboarding!
- Yet another email. Delete.
- I give up.

I've just deleted a bunch of annoying, out-of-context emails. And the vendor doesn't learn anything about how to make my experience better.

A coordinated survey experience would look like this:

- A Net Promoter Score survey is triggered in-app after achieving something of value in the product.
- I don't respond—I'm busy! An email gets triggered.

- I'm still busy, so you wait until another outcome is achieved in the product to present the survey, and only after an appropriate amount of time has passed since the last attempt.

Summary

Customer Success isn't just a department, it's a company-wide mindset. But if every department in your company is trying to help in Customer Success without coordinating, you can make the situation worse. Your clients can get overwhelmed, confused, and frustrated. True enterprise-wide Customer Success requires an integrated approach aligned to your desired customer journey.

PART III

Implementation
Issues

18

The First Step: Launching CS in an Established Business

Many leaders at established companies look at Customer Success and think, "Yeah, that's great if you founded your company in the last few years. But how can I make this transition in an existing business when I don't have venture capital dollars to fund me?"

Chris Bates is a great example of a leader who has succeeded in threading the needle of transformation. Bates is the GVP of Customer Success at Tableau Software, a visual analytics software company. He was given the tall order of launching Customer Success in an established business. And he made it happen.

Our CEO joined in 2016. We moved to subscription in 2017. And that was a big change, since we've been a perpetual license company. Now just a few short years later, the bulk of our customers are purchasing via subscription licensing. As part of that progression, our CEO asked three questions: "What does it take to make customers *technically successful?*" Then he broadened the question and asked, "What does it take to make customers successful *in general?*" And then he asked, "How do we create

197

customers *for life*?" Those three questions provided a galvanizing call inside the company. Over a six-month period, we assembled a cross-functional team to provide answers to those questions, which ultimately formed the bones of our Customer Success strategy. In 2018 and 2019, we added over 100 Customer Success Managers around the world. We invested in Gainsight as our Customer Success platform. We aligned incentives internally to better facilitate collaboration across the account team. We launched full engagement marketing for our tech-touch organization. And we've invested in our partners in helping our joint customers be successful.

The transformation that Bates and his cross-functional team spearheaded is remarkable. Fortunately, it's achievable in other organizations, too. As B2B companies innovate in their business models, offering flexible and customer-aligned delivery models like subscription, cloud, pay-as-you-go, and outcomes-based pricing, they are realizing the increasing power that their clients have—and the increasing ROI from investing in retaining and growing their customer base. In parallel, these B2B companies have implemented myriad systems over the last decade—from CRM to Marketing Automation to Online Support to Billing—allowing them to have greater insights into their client bases than ever before. With this convergence of business need and data availability, B2B innovators are going beyond the normal organizations of Sales and Service/Support to create a new Customer Success Management (CSM) team focused on proactively driving client outcomes using data.

In this chapter, we'll guide you in launching a CSM team in your established business. We'll discuss the decisions you'll need to make, how to align departments around the launch through strong communications and journey mapping, and how to avoid common mistakes.

Empower a Leader for This Transformation

For most mature companies, this Customer Success concept requires a great deal of consideration. Where should the team live in the company? What are its responsibilities? How does it relate to other functions (e.g. Sales/Marketing/Support)? How should it be measured? Where does the budget come from? We've worked with hundreds of large companies on the journey to Customer Success and have seen what works and what doesn't in terms of launching pilot experiments in Customer Success.

Before we get into the details of the decisions you'll need to make, it's worth emphasizing that you'll need a single leader accountable for driving the transformation. That person may be you, or it may be someone you're appointing. As Catherine Blackmore, the GVP of Customer Success at Oracle, says, "The CEO needs one person to be in charge of this transformation. They have to have a direct line to the CEO. They can't be buried within a department and someplace else. They don't have an operating responsibility; they have a transformation responsibility, because there are so many pieces that are going to have to shift and change in order for this move to happen."

The Decisions You'll Need to Make

Now that you have your mandate (or you've appointed the right person), let's dive into the 11 decisions that will make this transformation successful.

1. Define the Core Business Driver for Customer Success

Because Customer Success is such a "hot" concept, it has also become an overloaded term. Customer Success can be applied to adoption, renewals, expansion, advocacy—anything that involves getting more from your client base by driving greater results. However, in your first rollout of Customer Success, you need to think deeply about the specific goals for your business. For some businesses, a lack of Customer Success causes churn. For other, more sticky businesses, the impact is slower expansion. The table in Figure 18.1 articulates example pilot goals for different types of businesses.

2. Define the Starting Point Organization

Like most new initiatives in large organizations, innovation comes from a combination of situation (what group you sit in) and motivation (your desire to change). However, we've found some patterns in logical starting points for CSM teams (see Figure 18.1) in terms of which group might launch the

Unique Aspect of Business	Current Situation	Customer Success Pilot	Customer Success Outcome
Complex onboarding	Fiction during onboarding causing downstream churn	CSM team focused on onboarding phase	Less onboarding churn leading to higher renewals
Seat-based pricing model	Overselling and low adoption leading to churn and downsell	CSM team focused on adoption phase (deployment and adoption of unused seats)	Increased percentage adoption leading to less churn and downsell
Sticky platform-style product with "land-and-expand" modules	Slow adoption hurting expansion efforts	CSM team focused on adoption phase	Faster time-to-value leading to faster next sales opportunity at customer
Long-term contract product or service	Poor customer satisfaction hurting advocacy and new sales	CSM team focused on satisfaction and business value	Improved client business value alignment leads to higher client satisfaction (e.g. Net Promoter Score or referenceability), yielding greater advocacy and new sales
Competitive product category with less client commitment	Company surprised by churns to competitors	CSM team focused on early warning to risk	Earlier action on risk leading to reduced competitive churn
Large enterprise targeted product	Customer satisfaction low due to low adoption and product issues	CSM team focused on product adoption and collaboration	Greater client engagement and adoption leading to higher satisfaction, yielding increased advocacy and new sales

Figure 18.1

CS effort. In general, the "ideal" CSM is almost like a unicorn—hard to find in real life because the job involves a blend of:

- Product knowledge
- Domain knowledge
- Strategic thinking
- Relationship skills

- Project orientation
- Task orientation

We most frequently see organizations with technical offerings starting with the Technical Account Management or Professional Services groups and organizations with transactional offerings starting with the Account Management group.

3. Define the Product to Start With

For many large organizations, the vision for Customer Success spans across the entire product line. But where do you start? Successful pilots involve one or a few product lines and create proof points to continue scaling. Again, there is no perfect answer, but consider what's described in Figure 18.2.

Starting Point	Pros	Cons
Mature product	- Likely large source of revenue for the company, so impact would be big - Likely high-profile clients	- Involves significant organizational alignment across the company - Sometimes unclear what differential impact of CSM team will be, given others involved
Mature product in transition (e.g. perpetual moving to subscription pricing)	- "Burning platform" for change - Likely attention from IT and other stakeholders	- Significant degree of change management
New product	- Can "do it right" from beginning - Likely newer pricing model (e.g. subscription) that demands CSM - Because fewer people involved, easier to tell impact	- Less dollar impact and lower-profile clients
Recently acquired product	- Likely standalone team, so easier to drive change - Take one step toward integration of the acquisition	- May have existing CSM approach to rationalize

Figure 18.2

Customer experience software company Genesys launched a fast-growing cloud business and started Customer Success there. They subsequently saw that the model applied to their traditional business as well. Chief Customer Success officer Lucy Norris observed, "Companies that deliver software on-premises and companies that deliver software in the cloud are starting to think about Customer Success in a unified way. What we're really learning is that customers no longer self-identify as on-premises. Modern customer customers expect a level of engagement and the level of service independent of whether they're running on-premises or SaaS."

In general, we find CSM pilots starting with newer or acquired product lines or with product lines in transition and then expanding to the overall business over time.

4. Define the Segment to Start With

Even within a product line, you likely have multiple tiers of customers, as shown in Figure 18.3.

At Gainsight, we define three canonical models for Customer Success for these tiers:

1. **High-Touch Customer Success Management:** Strong coordination around a client's Success Plan and client journey across CSM, Sales, Services, Support, and Product

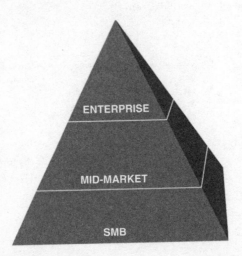

Figure 18.3

2. **Mid–Touch Customer Success Management:** Trigger-driven, "just in time" Customer Success based upon data (e.g. client is six months from renewal and only using one out of three modules)
3. **Tech–Touch Customer Success Management:** Fully automated, personalized Customer Success using email and other tools

Figures 18.4 and 18.5 illustrate these models.

We most frequently see CSM Pilots starting with the mid-touch segment, given the pros and cons in Figure 18.5.

Slicing the world further, you may need to take your segment of your product line and start with a limited set of clients. If you choose a high-touch or mid-touch model, you might be gated by the size of your initial team. As a rule of thumb, high-touch CSMs often manage 1 to 25 customers while Mid-Touch CSMs range from 25 to a few hundred. As such, companies pursuing high-touch Customer Success pilots often start with a subset of their top accounts.

How do you decide which clients to pick? Some progressive CSM pilots involve picking a cohort of clients for whom the company believes there is substantial "whitespace" or expansion potential. Other pilots are focused on A/B testing—taking a uniform group and dividing into a slice (e.g. 80%) that gets a CSM and a slice that does not. Regardless, be thoughtful in your initial client selection.

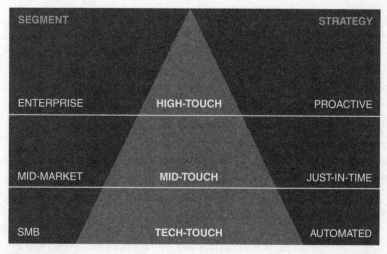

Figure 18.4

Segment	Pros	Cons
High-Touch	Impacts large clients	▪ Harder to tell different impact of CSM team ▪ Sometimes territorial issues with other groups
Mid-Touch	Significant dollars but usually gets limited attention	Requires process-oriented approach
Tech-Touch	Least amount of change management	Sometimes have to coordinate with Marketing (especially for automated one-to-many outreaches)

Figure 18.5

Whatever segments you choose, make sure your pilot is sized to your team's capacity. Jill Sawatzky at PROS has done this many times and shares her advice: "I would start a pilot with a small group of customers. What you don't want to do is have a brand-new small CS team trying to cover an entire large customer base. Then, after you've run the pilot for a few months, start to look at leading CS indicators. For example, did you get more references from the covered customer group? Did their Net Promoter Score go up? Don't focus on your renewal rate right away because it takes some time to make a significant impact on retention."

5. Define What Data Your Team Needs

Data is at once the greatest opportunity and greatest challenge for most large companies. Businesses are awash in data but often struggle to leverage it. For the CSM pilot, you need to define a practical and achievable list:

- **CRM**
  - **Customer name:** This is sometimes complex with customer "hierarchies" (e.g. parent and subsidiary businesses)
  - **CSM:** Where do you track the CSM assigned per customer? Is it a field in the CRM?
  - **Spend:** Where do you track the spend per client for the product in question? Is it accurate? Does it need to be 100% right or just directional?

- **Renewal date:** If you have contracted businesses, where is this information stored?
- **Tier:** If you want to focus on a specific client segment, how will you filter the data?
- **Entitlements:** Products/services under contract.
- **Support:** You may want access to support ticket history for the client.
- **Community:** If you have an online community, can you track how active a given client is?
- **Surveys:** Client satisfaction surveys are often essential for CSMs.
- **Professional services:** How can you see which client projects are on time versus running over?
- **Learning:** How can you track which clients have been trained versus not?
- **Marketing:** Can you see which clients are engaging in events, webinars, and emails?
- **Billing:** Can you view Accounts Receivable for a client to determine early satisfaction issues?
- **Telemetry:** If you have an online product or service, what can you see about client usage?

In our experience, CRM data is a must and organizations pick two or three other data sources (most commonly support and survey data).

6. Define What Systems Your Team Will Use

Depending on the scope of the pilot, you may want a formal system or you may start with a spreadsheet. Consider a formal system if you want:

- Sharing across the team and with other stakeholders
- Trackability and historical trending
- Process implementation and consistency
- Automation

7. Define IT Involvement

As we discussed in Chapter 16, depending on the data and systems needs, you might need IT help. In most companies, IT is a precious resource, so be sure to make your case early. Or you can consider third-party managed service providers that can run CSM platforms and data architectures on your behalf.

8. Define What's Out of Scope

By definition, a pilot is just a starting point. As such, make sure to clarify what you don't plan to accomplish in the pilot. We already covered focusing on product lines, tiers, and customers. But even within this, define what to "punt" for later. As an example, unless you have tremendous volume of client data, you probably want to punt "machine learning" and "predictive analytics" to a secondary phase once you understand your processes. Similarly, you might define the minimum viable product (MVP) for the pilot to be focused on the actions of the CSM team versus visibility to the rest of the organization. Finally, you may want to restrict the pilot to one region or geographical area.

9. Define How You Will Communicate

Brian Kaminski is the chief customer officer at Conversica, a leading provider of Intelligent Virtual Assistants for business. Brian has launched CS programs many times and points to the importance of communication.

> My tip is to raise awareness within the organization of the customer. That might sound ridiculous but a lot of times in software companies people forget that they're coming to work every day to build a piece of software that customers are using and getting value from. I share a customer story with a company every week. I think you need to spend time building the bridges with the other organizations in your company, particularly sales and product.

Speaking of the rest of the organization, successful CSM pilots require powerful and consistent communication. Define a communication program each of your stakeholders:

- **Team:** How often will you meet with your pilot CSM Team? Many pilots involve daily "scrum" meetings to ensure rapid progress. How will you coach each CSM in one-on-ones? How prescriptive will you be on processes? You may also want a weekly forum to recognize successes and share learnings.
- **Cross-functional:** How will you update the rest of the organization on your pilot progress? We'd suggest a weekly newsletter on highs, lows, and learnings from the pilot, along with a few formal review meetings.
- **Clients:** What expectation are you setting for clients? How do you introduce the CSM program? What's in it for them? Even in the MVP, it's important to have polished client-facing materials on the CSM program.

10. Define Success Criteria

Going back to the business goals, make sure to set expectations upfront of achievable metrics that can be used to measure the success of the pilot. At Gainsight, we try to distinguish *lagging indicators*—the financial outcomes of Customer Success like renewals, retention, and upsell—from *leading indicators* that can be moved more quickly. Leading indicators can include:

- A score measuring client adoption volume (e.g. Daily Active Users)
- A score measuring client sophistication (how well they use your product or service)
- A customer satisfaction metric like C-SAT or Net Promoter Score
- The percentage of clients that are referenceable
- The number of upsell leads sent to sales
- The number of at-risk accounts that were moved back to health
- A health score that aggregates several of the above into an overall indicator

Consider aggregating these into a scorecard for the overall health of the CSM pilot.

11. Define the Roadmap

While we emphasize focus, it's likely that Customer Success will become big in your company—if it hasn't already. As such, you may end up with multiple, overlapping, and confusing Customer Success initiatives across many product lines and departments. Consider a Customer Success Steering Committee or Center of Excellence to bring these initiatives together to ensure internal efficiency and a smooth external client experience.

Articulating the Benefits to Other Departments

Throughout the process of launching a pilot and translating it into a large organization from there, you'll need to be over-communicating internally. Catherine Blackmore, the GVP Customer Success at Oracle, emphasizes this:

> The first thing is you have to educate people on the problem you're solving. Your board has to understand it, because it's an investment to shift gears. Your C-suite has to understand it. And then the major lines of operational business and technology ownership have to understand it. Because as we found, it changes the way you do business. There's new infrastructure, new ways of operating, and a different way that you are even thinking about software. There has to be a talent shift. Can I train and upscale people to operate in a cloud environment? What are the key initiatives culturally we have to do?

Given the magnitude and breadth of the impact that this CS transformation will have on a company, senior folks have to understand the *why* behind it and be able to explain it to their organizations.

It's especially important to articulate the specific benefits of a CS transformation to the leaders of other functional areas. The following is a cheat-sheet on talking points by department.

Product Management

1. **Prioritize customers' requests for enhancements:** Product teams are often overwhelmed by client feedback. CSMs can help them figure out which enhancements would benefit clients most.
2. **Set up focus groups:** CSMs can advise on which clients would be most helpful in Product Advisory Councils and other groups that the Product team relies on for feedback.
3. **Announce product releases:** CSMs can promote the Product team's latest releases.

Marketing

1. **Proactively identify advocates:** You often spend a lot of time hunting down happy clients who can speak in favor of the product. With CSMs as your partners, you'll find it easier to identify clients willing to speak at an event, give a testimonial, or participate in a case study.
2. **Capture the narrative about how we drove an Outcome for a customer:** Even if you're able to get a client to agree to advocate, you often find it difficult to document in detail how the client got value. The CSM can be a partner in explaining the history of the client: how they got from point A to point B, and how we helped.

Sales

1. **Get visibility:** It's utterly painful when you call a customer and get blindsided by an issue that's troubling them. Having a CSM as your partner can help you have a 360-degree understanding of client health.
2. **Learn about new opportunities:** When an executive sponsor at your client leaves the company, it's a risk to the relationship. On the bright side, the new company that the sponsor joins is now a prospective customer. With a CS effort to identify these departures you can now track your "alumni network" and find advocates whom you can sell to at a new company.
3. **Learn where to focus prospecting efforts:** A CS initiative can make it clear what types of clients—by industry, location, or other attribute—are successful and which are not, which can help you with territory planning.
4. **Manage at-risk renewals:** Spend less time on escalations. That's the CSM team's job.
5. **Find more upsell opportunities:** Instead of hunting for upsell opportunities by crunching the data in a silo without customer context, collaborate with your CSM team to find them. The CSM team may even have a target for upsell leads that they pass over to you.

Professional Services

1. **Identify opportunities for selling new services:** CSM teams know what gaps in value the client is experiencing. So they can advise Services on which clients may be prime for purchasing education, managed services, advisory services, or other offerings.

2. **Scope projects more effectively:** The CSM is an ongoing point of contact with the customer, so they can help you identify the client's strategic goals and map the project plan to those.

Support

1. **Avoid being blindsided:** Get knowledge of the customer context from the CSM so you can resolve tickets more effectively, faster.
2. **Prioritize tickets:** Focus on the right tickets based on the CSM's advice on which tickets are more relevant to a client's success so as to maximize C-SAT.

Finance

1. **Drive collections:** When the Accounts Receivable team isn't getting a response from the customer, get help from the CSM, who likely knows someone who can push the payment along. The CSM can also inform you as to when it's better to hold off on the collection, or else risk a major escalation from a client who has refused to pay because they aren't getting value.
2. **Get visibility into cash flow:** CSM teams know more about the predictability of your revenue and cash than any other function in the business besides Finance, because they forecast retention rates based on an intimate understanding of the client base.

Bottom line: Think carefully about the WIIFM ("What's in It for Me?") for each department when you're pitching Customer Success at your company and you'll build a strong alliance that ultimately benefits your company and your clients.

The Value of Journey Mapping

Besides explaining the benefit to each department individually, consider how to help them see their role in the bigger picture of the transformation. ` great way to bring all functions together around Customer Success is `ugh a journey-mapping exercise.

Here's how Chris Bates from Tableau described his company's experience in creating a cohesive journey for the client with participation across departments:

> We assembled a cross-functional group of leaders and mapped out what should the customer go through across the entire life cycle, all the way from being a prospect to post-sale. It forced leaders across every part of the organization to look at the business and the relationship with the customer differently and see where the gaps are in the customer journey. It also prompts leaders to think beyond a particular silo and look at the journey through the customer lens.
>
> We defined a step-by-step guide called Tableau Blueprint to help customers become data-driven organizations, which is our goal at Tableau. It's really an opportunity to document the best practices that clients are hoping to receive from us. We do an interactive assessment of the client to help them see where they are strong and where they have gaps. Coming out of that assessment we set joint priorities and capture them in a Success Plan. Then, all client-facing team members can act in harmony within that roadmap.

When every function is aligned around a methodology—Blueprint in this case—for helping clients achieve their Outcome over a prescribed journey of steps, it ensures that the CS transformation is sticky.

We've discussed some best practices that can help you get CS off the ground at your large company. But there's a lot that can go wrong. We hope we can help you avoid those potholes in the next section.

Five Lessons from Failed Customer Success Programs

Customer Success Management is hot. But it's also new. So with the tremendous growth in the CSM world come some organizations that have failed in their quest toward success. While most companies are radically increasing investment in CSM, a few have pulled back. As the old saying goes, "last in, first out"; since many CSM programs are relatively new, they are sometimes cut when times get tough.

From our experience at Gainsight, here are five common ways that CSM programs can fail.

1. *Wrong Leader*

This might be the most common reason why anything fails in business. But to be specific, we're not talking about hiring a leader that's wrong for any company—we're talking about the wrong leader for a specific company. CSM is a broad job and the leadership need varies dramatically based upon the stage, scope, and the nature of your solution. Common patterns of failed hires include:

- A leader who's skilled at large-scale management in a job that needs someone to work as a "player-coach"
- A leader who's good with clients in a job (e.g. a low-priced offering) that demands time spent in the office with data
- A leader who's strong with data in a job (e.g. a high-priced offering) that demands time spent in the field with clients
- A leader who's great with experienced team members taking over a team of low-paid, entry-level CSMs

Gainsight Best Practice: Companies and candidate CSM leaders are mutually demanding practical exercises and projects in the interview process to get to know each other's styles better. For example, a company could have the CSM candidate analyze historical churn data or present a sample Executive Business Review.

2. *No Goals or Unrealistic Goals*

We've written about approaching "pilots" for CSM. Whether they are labeled that way or not, most CSM initiatives are experiments at this stage. ⸱ such, CSM leaders need to clearly specify how the results should be ʑured.

ʑou have a multiyear-contract business, it's unlikely that your renewal change dramatically 90 days after starting the CSM pilot, so you might need to measure a leading indicator like Net Promoter Score or adoption. Similarly, if your pilot is focused on a specific part of your customer base, zoom in on the success criteria in that segment (versus looking at overall metrics). If you don't talk about goals and achievement, it's easy for management to start imagining they can live without the CSM initiative.

Gainsight Best Practice: Create a scoreboard of CSM metrics and share it weekly with your company.

3. Unscalable Model

It's great to start small in CSM. You can run a pilot and learn a great deal. But make sure you are building a CSM model that can eventually impact your entire business. As an example, we've seen companies run an uneconomical pilot (e.g. one CSM managing $100K of revenue) and have no plan on how to scale beyond that.

Gainsight Best Practice: Choose the appropriate touch model (high-touch, mid-touch, or tech-touch) for your average selling price. Don't design a pilot that will forever be a pilot.

4. What Does the CSM Team Do Again?

Because CSM is new for most companies, it's also foreign. Many CSM teams fail because other key organizations (most notably Sales and Product) don't understand the value proposition of CSM. This means that when budgets get tight, those other orgs often fight for resources from the CSM group.

Make sure you are educating your peers in other leadership roles in your organization's charter, goals, and successes. We're big believers in following the data at Gainsight. You should be able to prove the value CSM is driving for the company as a whole and across the various departments (as we described earlier in this chapter). To do this, you can build out ROI dashboards for your CSM team based on criteria relevant to each role.

Bates at Tableau emphasizes the importance of clarifying what the CSM does in contrast with other roles, both for the sake of other departments and for the sake of your clients. "Sometimes clients can feel like they're watching a bunch of six-year-old kids playing soccer, where everybody's just chasing the ball rather than sticking to their own role on the team. Define clear roles and responsibilities among the account team. It will be powerful to talk with the client about how each person will support them."

Gainsight Best Practice: Create a "strategy deck" showing the charter and structure of Customer Success internally and dashboards per the above to show results. Create a client-facing deck to communicate roles externally.

5. No Sustainable Funding Model

Even if you manage to get a CSM team chartered and maintained, how do you grow it? It's critical that you have a clearly defined funding model so you can budget for the group. Think about how other groups are funded:

- Support: Case volume or a percentage of revenue
- Sales: Sales targets and sales quota/productivity
- Engineering: Percentage of revenue

The worst situation to be in is to have to argue with your CFO for every incremental headcount. A related question to ask your CFO is whether CSM is a cost of Sales and Marketing or a Cost of Goods Sold. We see an increasing trend toward CSM being a part of Sales and Marketing.

Gainsight Best Practice: We've seen three common funding models:

- Percentage of revenue
- Fixed ratio of accounts or dollars managed per CSM
- Self-funding P&L where you charge for Customer Success

Summary

The road to Customer Success is paved with good intentions. Hopefully, this chapter helps you avoid the potholes along the way. We discussed frameworks for making decisions, suggestions for gaining buy-in from other functions, and reasons why transformations fail. In the next chapter we'll discuss an important aspect of that transformation: What kind of CS leader do you need?

19

Leadership: What Kind of Leader Do I Need for Customer Success?

One of the best parts of our jobs at Gainsight is helping people in the field of Customer Success achieve their career aspirations. Because we meet so many CS people, we're often at the hub of conversations about hiring. CEOs come to us looking for "the best chief customer officer you know," and CCOs come to us wondering, "Have you heard of any job openings at companies that value Customer Success?" Sometimes we joke that if our business didn't work out, we would start a staffing firm.

It's been incredible to see the rise in the CCO role. Five years ago, we knew of only a few dozen CCOs in the world. Today, there are thousands of people whose title is CCO or else who have the same role but under a different title: for example, SVP of Customer Success, chief digital officer, and chief success officer, to name a few. Today, executive search firms are building major practice areas in recruiting for this role.

Given the new abundance of this executive role, many folks are wondering what aspects of that role are becoming standard. CEOs wonder, "Will my current CS leader scale with my company? What should I look for when interviewing CCO?" And CCOs wonder, "What skills should I develop and what experiences should I take on? How should I convey my experience when I'm interviewing for a role? And when I take that role, what will be expected of me?"

We'll answer those questions and others in this chapter.

The Next Generation of Customer Success Leadership

Calling all *Star Trek* fans: Which starship *Enterprise* captain is your favorite: Kirk or Picard?

We like them both, but it's so interesting how different they are. Captain Kirk would overcome any challenge through sheer will and indomitable optimism. He wasn't afraid to bend the rules for the greater good. In the "final frontier" there isn't a roadmap to follow. No one has gone there before, and you need a trailblazer and pioneer to make decisions—sometimes on pure instinct.

Captain Picard was different. To fans of the original series, he could come off as cold and calculating, but underneath he was just as committed to the mission and spirit of the Federation—and the humanism of Gene Roddenberry by extension. But in the world of *The Next Generation*, Picard knew the value of the Prime Directive—of adhering to a strategic framework in service of the overall mission.

We don't think one is better or worse in general, but we do think Kirk was right for the original series and Picard was the captain we needed for *The Next Generation*. In the Customer Success movement, we're in the middle of the same transition *Star Trek* made—from a Kirk-type leader to more of a Picard.

In a lot of ways, Customer Success is growing up. We've evolved from being mostly an individual department focused on churn avoidance to a growth engine predicated on a companywide strategic focus on the customer and their outcomes and experiences. That was the theme of Pulse (our big annual conference) this year: What does the future of business look like with the customer at the center? As CEOs and CS teams go through this transition, both sides are trying to determine the type of leadership needed for the 2020s versus what was needed in the 2010s.

So how do you sort out 2010 leaders from 2020 leaders? Check out Figure 19.1.

	Customer Success 2010	Customer Success 2020
Charter	Focused on defense (e.g. saves, prevention, etc.)	Focused on growth
Recruiting	Hires from support or account management exclusively; reliant on "rock stars"	May also hire from management consulting, customer domain, product, or other areas
Org Philosophy	Executes CS entirely from within their team	Proactively aligns with rest of company to make CS > CSM
Funding	Relies on headcount to scale or is inhibited by headcount restrictions	Understands larger financial model and helps with (1) self-funding paid CS or (2) delivering clear ROI from CS
Sales Alignment	Complains about the sales team	Deeply aligned with the sales team
Product Alignment	Preoccupied with filling gaps in product	Creates detailed process and analytics to collaborate with product team
Metrics	Measures NPS and retain solely	Looks at leading indicators (e.g. customer health) and growth metrics (e.g. net retention)
Compensation	A purist about what can/can't be included in comp (e.g. CSMs can't have incentive comp)	Evolves thinking on comp based upon stage/strategy of business
Customer Lifestyle	Interactions happen mostly on a scheduled, calendar basis (e.g. monthly check-in)	Augments scheduled interactions with data-driven triggers
Process	Thinks process is overrated and it's just about having people "use their gut"	Believes strong people can be augmented with repeatable processes

Figure 19.1

The 2010 leaders have played a huge role in shepherding the Customer Success movement into this new 2020 stage, but we definitely think it's time for a Picard-style 2020 leader in most companies. Consider: Which style leader does your company have?

The World's Top CS Leaders Are Doing These Four Things

We spend a lot of time trading notes with CS leaders, including at our Pulse Executive Retreat, an incredibly intimate event we hosted recently for less than a dozen of the top CCOs and Customer Success leaders in the world, from Genesys, Sitecore, Pearson, Kronos, Slack, PTC, ADP, Instructure, RealPage, and Zendesk. It was so inspiring and humbling to see how innovative each one has been in their organizations—but also to see how their innovations are also part of larger trends across the industry. Below we'll discuss the four strategies these leaders have implemented. If you're a CEO interviewing a CCO, ask them their perspective on these approaches—since they should have an opinion even if they don't agree with the point of view shared below. If you're a CCO looking to "up your game," reading the following four strategies will provide insight into what the industry luminaries are thinking.

1. **Successfully charging for Customer Success**

This has long been a point of contention within our industry: Can you (and if so, how do you) charge for Customer Success? Eduarda Camacho, executive vice president of Customer Operations at software company PTC presented a working framework at our retreat. It's called SuccessPoints and it's a program that gives a customer the flexibility to spend their points on a multitude of services—adoption workshops, training, technical services, etc.). They learned two things:

- The services could be deployed by many different teams—Solutions Consultants, Services, CSMs, Support, etc.
- Customers wouldn't ask for discounts. They had always tended to ask for them with specific Professional Services Scopes of Work (SoWs) or projects.

The takeaway: If you find yourself giving away a lot of hours of hands-on training or services engagements, you could create a flexible offering that drives better outcomes and doesn't leave money on the table.

2. **Standardizing more metrics**

Another company gave a great presentation on their standardized framework to quantify value. They've branded their CS team as "Proactive, Personal, **Proven**"—we bolded the last word, pointing to the move toward more standardization. CS is real, it's here to stay, and part of that evolution means moving away from ad hoc metrics. When you can benchmark yourself against a broader base of comparable organizations using the same metrics calculated the same way, you can build a much more solid base for incremental improvement.

Here's one example: Several companies present at the Retreat track the percentage of their customer base that is *referenceable*. It's a great proxy to know how healthy the customer base is.

3. **Moving from product-centric to customer-centric models**

There was a superb presentation by Dale Smith, SVP Customer Success at real estate technology leader RealPage, Inc., on how to break down silos between the CS org and the Product org. We believe the future of Customer Success (not the function—the larger philosophy) is a deeper relationship with the team most directly responsible for enabling the customer's success: the Product team. Customer Success and Product need to equally own it as a common mission and shared goal to strengthen cross-functional bonds and celebrate common wins together.

4. **Getting serious about personal development**

Personal development is pretty systematized at many companies. CS has in some cases lagged behind their peer departments, but that's clearly changing. Leaders at the Retreat shared how they were offering professional development days on a quarterly basis to just learn—read a book, take Udemy courses, sign up for live courses, go spend time with a customer to learn more, and so on. Or, they were using a profile test (like Myers Briggs or several others) to see where there were gaps in their leadership teams or to learn how to work better (or give feedback better) to teammates. And those leaders were increasingly sharing their 360-degree feedback with their entire team.

What Type of Leader Is Best for My Stage?

Even though we've noticed important shifts in the attributes of CCOs over the past decade, you'll need to hire the person who suits your situation. We find that the stage of your company is the defining factor for what type of CCO is best. David Skok, general partner at Matrix Partners, identified three stages for a business:

1. Finding the right product-market fit
2. Finding a repeatable, profitable and scalable go-to-market model
3. Scaling the business

These stages can apply to a startup, but it could also apply to a new business unit within a larger company.

We believe that in each stage, you'll need different types of people to help you achieve success in that phase. In this way of thinking, there's no concept of universal "A players"; rather, there is merely a concept of the degree to which a person matches the needs of their job. This is a notion of "person–job fit" (an analogy to product-market fit). The needs of the job are largely determined by the stage of the company.

Stage 1: Finding the Right Product–Market Fit

In Stage 1, you'll need people (regardless of function) who are passionate about the pain point you're trying to solve, curious enough to examine customers and your market deeply, willing to take risks in running experiments, and patient, given the many iterations it can take to achieve product-market fit. Now let's apply these criteria to determine what kind of people we need in CS. During this stage, your head of Customer Success may be the same person as your head of product, because the more this leader can speak with clients to understand the value they're achieving (and not achieving) from the product, the faster they can achieve product-market fit.

Stage 2: Finding a Repeatable, Profitable, and Scalable Go-to-Market Model

In Stage 2, the goal is to create a playbook for generating revenue that your company can execute consistently in Stage 3. To create this ultimate playbook, you'll need people who are effective in detecting patterns across many client situations (in pre- and post-sales), designing frameworks for explaining those patterns, exhibiting a loop of learning and iterating, and in general creating structure from ambiguity. Your head of Customer Success should exemplify these attributes.

Stage 3: Scaling the Business

In Stage 3, you'll need people who are results-oriented. They are hungry to meet targets, obsessive about forecasting, and expect their team to execute consistently against established processes. That said, they can't execute in a "heads-down" way; they'll also need to collaborate well with other teams to achieve a "symphony" of activity the company. Your head of Customer Success should model these behaviors.

What's Hot in the Job Market

In Chapter 3, we heard from Alexis Hennessy, the principal at Heidrick & Struggles, about how she has seen the market for heads of Customer Success take off. Here's what she looks for when she's evaluating candidates:

- **Tolerance for ambiguity:** "We want someone who has the ability to look around corners and do something that hasn't been done before, because the function is still very much being defined in how to do it well. Somebody who is unafraid to take risks, very forward thinking."
- **Cross-functional abilities:** "We look for people who are very proactive in their thought process versus reactive and really understand how Customer Success can influence the broader organization. They'll talk a lot about how they work collaboratively across functions in the organization even if those functions don't report to them. They have the ability to rally the entire organization around a solid customer journey, putting the customer at the center of everything that they do. That level of influence is highly important."
- **Revenue metrics:** "You need to look at the metrics. So I want to see growth. How did you move numbers up and to the right? They should be very fact-based."

- **Tenure:** "These days, three years at any company is a respectable period of time. Anything less than that and it's hard to really know if that person was able to make an impact. We want to see a certain amount of staying power so that we know that the story you're telling is actually yours. You had enough time to get in there and actually make a difference."
- **Cloud experience:** "Every company right now is going through some sort of transformation. If they don't have cloud-native technologies already, they are moving to the cloud."

Hennessy adds: "If there's ever going to be a tradeoff in experience, it would be on the technical chops. This person doesn't have to have managed a support organization before or moved up a technical or support track. But they have to know how to hire a really strong support leader underneath them. It's great if they have strong technical chops, but they should be overwhelmingly commercial and customer-oriented."

CS Leaders Won't Be Successful on Their Own

We've spoken a lot about the need to hire the right person. But simply hiring a great candidate and expecting them to make your company customer-centric won't work. Hennessy has seen this fail. "If a client is just recruiting a CCO because they feel like they're supposed to, because everybody else is doing it, then the Customer Success talent that's worth their salt will see right through it and won't be interested. It's up to the company to make it apparent how impactful the role will be to their organization, how valuable the executive team and the board views finding the right person. They really have to make sure that they're empowering these people. The entire executive leadership team has to be on board in order for this person to make a positive impact on the broader business." This reminds us of our discussion in Chapter 8 on why Customer Success can't be delegated—the CEO truly needs to own it.

Trends in the Customer Success Executive Search Market

Every week, several CEOs reach out to us at Gainsight asking for advice, intros, and background checks on hiring a leader. We've spent the last six or seven years growing the world's largest network of Customer Success leaders and we absolutely love using it to help professionals and companies connect.

Although we are not recruiters by profession, we've been able to learn a lot about Customer Success more broadly by facilitating some of these connections. And several of our colleagues have done the same.

We've learned five key things about hiring Customer Success leaders:

1. **Hirers need to clearly define what they want.**

"Customer Success" is such a buzzword that, not surprisingly, many LinkedIn titles have magically changed to it very recently. That means you need to cut through the noise and get specific about what you're looking for. Some key questions to consider:

- Do you want the role to own revenue (renewals and/or expansion) or not?
- Is the energy of the company "high-touch" (e.g. large enterprise) or "tech-touch" (e.g. SMB)?
- Do you need the leader to be technical by background (e.g. if you sell into the security space)?

2. **Companies want startup and scale experience.**

CS is a conundrum. On one hand, the teams get big quickly so leadership scale matters. On the other hand, the field is so new and evolving that leaders need to be able to innovate quickly. We've found that the candidates that resonate the most with hirers have a mix of large-company and young-startup experience.

3. **The increasing trend is to hire someone for all of post-sales—maybe a CCO.**

Customer Success Management often started as a siloed function. But CEOs across the world realized that for Customer Success to thrive, the entire customer journey needs to be oriented around it (from Product to Marketing to Sales to Post-Sales).

While CEOs can't usually put all of that under one person (because what's their job then?), we find that CEOs are increasingly putting all of "post-sales" (support, services, CSM, training, community, renewals, etc.) under one leader and sometimes calling them the "chief customer officer."

4. **Hirers are prioritizing D&I in job searches.**

We all know that tech as an industry has to get radically better on diversity, inclusion, and belonging. There are all kinds of great reasons why, but there's only one that really matters: It's the right thing to do.

The good news is that it seems like Customer Success as a function is ahead of the curve in this area. From a report we did with LinkedIn, the Customer Success profession shows promise in helping drive tech toward equality, given the near 50–50 gender balance in the job.

But gender balance is just one vector for diversity and it doesn't say anything necessarily about inclusion—which is just as important. Furthermore, leadership in CS is still skewed away from underrepresented groups.

We're encouraged that the thousands of CEOs with whom we've spoken lately have put diversity as a top factor in thinking about their slate of candidates. It's going to take deliberate action at all levels to do the right thing—and we're proud to say we see many leaders taking that action. We'll talk more about this topic toward the end of the book.

5. **Hirers want first-principles thinkers.**

Finally, CEOs are realizing that Customer Success is still a relatively new profession (no matter how much people have retroactively changed their LinkedIn profiles!). As such, there is much more to be figured out in the future than has been decided in the past. In addition, Customer Success is truly a little different in each company.

Because of this, we're seeing leaders emphasize learning agility in their hiring process. Can this person adapt and evolve? Do they have the strategic thinking skills to plot a course that's unknown?

At Gainsight, this is one of our company values—*Shoshin*, which is a Japanese word that means "A Beginner's Mind." In essence, it's about approaching each problem as if you're a complete beginner, no matter how much expertise you have. It helps you spot unconventional or unknown solutions that you might miss if you approach the problem with arrogance.

As the industry grows in unexpected ways, the hiring leaders we've talked to recognize they need people who will grow alongside it.

Summary

In this chapter we discussed how to spot CS leaders who are up to date on the latest best practices, how to choose a CS leader who is appropriate for your stage, and how to take a page from a top executive recruiter's playbook in screening candidates. We also noted the importance of setting up that leader for success. One important way to do this is to create an organizational structure that empowers CS, which is the topic of our next chapter.

20

Organizational Structure: Should Customer Success Be Part of Sales or Its Own Org?

If names be not correct, language is not in accordance with the truth of things. If language be not in accordance with the truth of things, affairs cannot be carried on to success.

—Lao-Tse, *The Analects of Confucius* (Chapter 13)

What does *Customer Success* mean, anyway? Is it the team of Customer Success Managers? The post-sales organization? A company-wide imperative? When we use *CS* as the name for so many different concepts, we can confuse ourselves. It's why CS people are often confused about what to call themselves. When we speak with leaders of "post-sales" in B2B businesses, one of the most candid, often-hushed questions we get (especially over a glass of wine) is, "What should my title be?" As the quote above illustrates, names matter.

The question of title goes hand-in-hand with the question of organizational structure: Where should Customer Success report? To dig into these two questions, we collected data from Bessemer Venture Partners' (BVP) Nasdaq Emerging Cloud Index (EMCLOUD),[7] a set of public cloud companies. The data includes the titles and responsibilities for the functional "Customer Success" leader and the overall head of the "post-sales" organization. There are three key takeaways.

1. Hire a VP of Customer Success

When we researched the org charts of the EMCLOUD, we found that 44 out of the 50 companies employed a functional CS leader. The other six may have an equivalent leader, but we weren't able to identify them with certainty, so we left them off. Figure 20.1 is a graph of those 44 companies' titles.

This chart is powerful because it's evidence of two things:

1. 88% of the largest (by market cap) publicly traded cloud companies employ a head of CS.

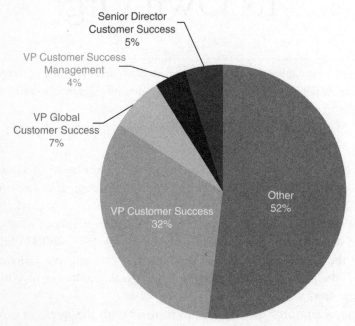

Figure 20.1

2. The most often-used title for that person by far is vice president, Customer Success.

Key takeaway: Every SaaS company of meaningful size should have a VP or VP-level person in charge of Customer Success. And many non-SaaS companies should strongly consider doing so as well.

2. Consolidate "Post-Sales" Under a Chief Customer Officer

Let's get one thing out of the way: What's up with the term *post-sales organization*? We're using "post-sales" as a catchall here even though we really don't like the term. Full disclosure: We've used the term *post-sales* in the past both in content and in marketing outreach as well as in internal and external conversations. If we don't really like it, why do we use it? Because post-sales is well-understood and all-encompassing. That said, it's also dated and doesn't truly reflect the mission of the function. It implicitly centers the sale as the most important moment in the customer lifecycle, which is a very inside-out way to look at the customer's journey. It's passive. It doesn't include a mission or mandate, which bolsters the misperception that once money has changed hands, the customer is just a cost center, not a precious resource. In addition, in modern businesses where the customer has power, the lines between pre- and post-sales are blurred. In a way, a customer is always in pre-sales—and post-sales, for that matter.

Going back to our research into organizational structures, 45 companies on the Index have an executive "umbrella" leader of the "post-sale" teams. (Again, the missing 5 out of 50 probably have a similar position, but we left them off in the absence of certainty.)

You can see in Figure 20.2 that SVP Customer Success and chief customer officer (CCO) are present in 15 out of 45 companies. If you group CCOs and anyone with an executive-level title and the words "Customer Success" in it, you end up with almost half the titles of these organizational leaders—48.9%. That means 90% of the world's most successful SaaS companies have consolidated "post-sales," and although none of them are using the words "post-sales," the "Customer Success" term isn't yet universal, even though it's the most-used name.

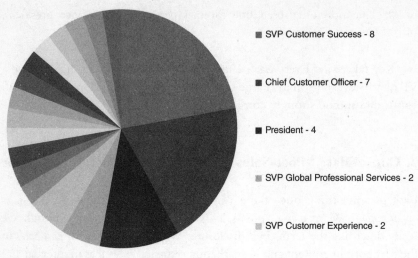

Figure 20.2

3. Customer Success > Customer Success Management

So why is *Customer Success* not already the de facto term? I think people sometimes find it confusing because it's a synecdoche. *Synecdoche* means when a part of a whole and the whole itself are referred to interchangeably. When you refer to "Customer Success" at your company, you may be talking about a VP Customer Success reporting up to a senior VP Customer Success.

That reporting structure—VP CS reporting to SVP CS—is actually the most common hierarchy on the BVP Cloud Index, but only with three total instances. We researched each hierarchical relationship between CS functional leader and the CS organizational leader and found that of 45 companies on the Index there were 41 unique combinations of titles. You can see how it gets confusing! We won't include a graph from our data to support this point because it would look like Figure 20.3, which is a ton of diversity.

Other departments are synecdoches as well. At the top of the Sales team there's the SVP Sales, and underneath you have VP Sales (North America), VP Sales (Operations), VP Sales (Engineering), and so on. People intuitively understand that the Sales org leader is responsible for a much broader

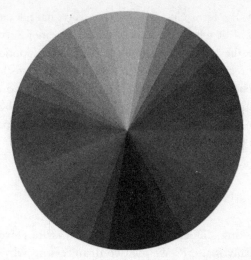

Figure 20.3

strategy. But in Customer Success, there's unfortunately still a lingering mentality that CS and CSM aren't synecdoche, they're synonymous. We think that's the reason why the most common hierarchy of VP CS reporting to SVP of CS (or CCO) is not yet ubiquitous.

To combat the confusion, we need to emphasize the broader scope of Customer Success beyond just Customer Success Management. To do this at Gainsight, we actually renamed our internal CSMs to *COMs*—Client Outcomes Managers. This preserves the term Customer Success as the name for the broader organization that reports into our chief customer officer. That organization encompasses Professional Services, Customer Support, and other functions that are generating success for clients. In other words, "It's not just the job of CSM to deliver success; we're all in this together, whether we're resolving tickets or driving onboarding projects." The COM naming convention also clarifies that the role of the CSM is to make sure our customers are achieving their desired outcomes with Gainsight, in part by quarterbacking across other functions (including Product, Marketing, and others) to ensure a coherent journey for the client.

Similarly, Lucy Norris, executive vice president, chief Customer Success officer at customer experience software company Genesys, rolled out the term *advisor* as a more precise title for the CSM role.

In the market, the term *Customer Success manager* has relevance when we recruit people. But when you look at what Customer Success managers do at the core, they "advise" customers to help drive adoption. They help customers appreciate the benefits of the product and the technology. They also advise their organization's product management function around what they hear from customers. So the role of a CSM is really about being that advisor to the customer and also advising their own company and what really matters to their customers.

4. What's in a Name?

You might be asking, "Does the naming of these various levels of CS within a company actually matter?" We see two main reasons why it does:

1. **Title conveys mission.**

When your title is, say, EVP Professional Services but you're actually responsible for the entire customer journey, why does your title only encompass part of that journey? More importantly, are your various post-sales teams united under the mission of making customers successful? Do other organizations (i.e. Sales) understand the full scope of your mandate?

Sometimes this misnaming happens when companies implement a siloed CSM team and then try to figure out who that team should report to at the executive level. Maybe this executive is a VP Sales whose mandate expands to include CSM. If this executive ends up hyper-focused on renewal and expansion without a strategy for first operationalizing overall Customer Success across all client-facing teams, they will certainly struggle to meet their numbers. Here's another example: Take a VP Pro Services who suddenly finds herself managing a CSM team. If she's still focused principally on achieving a Services Gross Margin target and considers the CSM team to be a tactical channel for driving new services bookings, she will neglect that team's ability to influence recurring revenue.

2. **Standardization > fragmentation.**

When we were building out our Elements framework (which we discussed in an earlier chapter), we did so with a deliberate eye toward becoming more prescriptive. We know there's a tendency for companies to view their client bases as fundamentally unique, but the danger is losing sight of the similarities. Customer Success as a discipline is mature enough that evidence-based best practices can be applied at any company no matter how "unique" it is.

Fragmentation is the enemy of sharing knowledge. The more we can speak a common language in business as in technology, the more modular our solutions can be. The solutions that are flexible enough to adapt to the widest variety of business models and yet rigid enough to be scalable and effective will naturally spread as the evidence proves them. The same goes for titles! Not only is it good to "rectify the names" as Confucius said, it's actually inevitable.

Should CS Report into Sales?

In line with the benchmarking data above, we see many benefits from CSM reporting into an SVP of CS or CCO. That SVP or CCO should then report to the CEO or general manager of the business unit. This ensures that:

1. Someone at the table in executive team meetings has knowledge of client experiences and outcomes, which allows them to share information that may not otherwise be top of mind for other executives, and advocate on behalf of the needs of customers.
2. The CEO can hold someone accountable for the Gross Retention Rate and Net Retention Rate, which are two critical drivers of company valuation, as discussed earlier in this book.

That said, there are certain circumstances in which it can make sense for CSM to report into a Sales-type leader, such as a SVP Sales. Those two scenarios are:

1. **Long-tail scenario:** The customer base is primarily a long tail of small clients. In this situation, the product is typically lightweight, professional services are not required to drive value, and the CSM role is transactional, focused on completing renewals and expansion. The CSM team may even be an Account Management team, for all intents and purposes

much like the "CSM of Value Capture" model that we discussed in an earlier chapter. Actually, CSMs may not be required for most of the customer base; it may be that the burden of driving outcomes and positive experiences falls on Customer Marketing, which manages one-to-many tactics.

2. **Startup scenario:** The company is small, with only a couple of CSMs and salespeople. In that case, it may make sense to have only one client-facing executive who manages both CS and Sales.

In both scenarios, it's critical for CEOs to hold their revenue leader accountable not merely for in-quarter new bookings targets, but also for leading indicators of renewal and expansion in future quarters. Many sales leaders are inclined to prioritize near-term bookings, since they probably grew their career in environments that rewarded this, and since, as boards of directors catch up to modern thinking on how to grow subscription revenue, those boards are often instinctively inclined to reward that short-term focus. The question is: What will that sales leader do on the last day of the quarters—try to help a rep close a new deal, or get on the phone to handle an escalation from an enterprise client? Sales leaders will typically focus on the former, but if they neglect their customers too much this quarter, they'll find themselves trying to plug a leaky bucket next quarter. That difference in time horizon between Sales and CS is notable; a great leader who manages both functions will need to have their eye to both horizons.

Where Does the CRO Role Fit In?

Like the title *chief customer officer*, the title *chief revenue officer* is a relatively new one. Often this executive reports into the CEO and manages Marketing, Sales, and a Customer Success organization (which may include Professional Services and Support). Therefore, the CRO manages essentially the set of functions that are most directly responsible for driving revenue throughout the Helix.

We wanted to gather data on the typical scope of responsibility for a CRO, so we launched a survey to revenue leaders in the Gainsight community, with 44 responding that they had the specific title *CRO*. As would be expected, all of them owned New Logo Sales, and almost all of them (43) owned Upsell, demonstrating the role of the CRO in managing new business across the client journey. Thirty-six (82%) of them owned Renewals, and 30 (68%) owned CSM. The trail-off in ownership for Renewals and CSM probably indicates the presence of a Customer Success leader who is a peer to the CRO or the fact that CSM is not yet present at every company. At the same time, CROs are paying more attention to CSM than they used to. We asked the CROs, "How has your organization's focus on Customer Success changed in the past three years?" Ninety-three percent had increased their focus, with only two respondents answering that their focus had stayed the same, and only one answering that their focus had decreased.

Is it a good thing that CROs are meddling more in Customer Success? Christina Kosmowski thinks so. She is the VP, global head of Customer Success at Slack, the collaboration company that is one of the fastest growing SaaS companies of all time. Kosmowski oversees CSM, education, professional services, and renewals—a broad scope typical for a "post-sales leader." But she sees the value of having sales and CS report into a single leader who then reports to the CEO, which is how it works at Slack. "I think that that's extremely beneficial, because the way Slack started out was very consumer-oriented. So the enterprise motions were built later. Having sales and Customer Success work together to tackle the movement into the enterprise has been extremely valuable."

She emphasizes,

> I don't see myself as reporting to sales. I think there's a leader who has both sales and CS in one organization in which we're equally represented. He said, "I can't do this role without Customer Success." He was the one who really spearheaded and sponsored bringing it into the organization. So he's got that mindset. If I look across various companies I know, I think that mindset is becoming more popular among CROs. But CROs were traditionally hired from sales. It doesn't have to be that way. Why can't the CRO be a CS leader, or a marketing leader, or another profile?

They can also have the broader mindset to be effective in the cross-functional CRO role. Dennis Dresser, chief revenue officer of product analytics company Heap, agrees.

> I think it's pretty well researched that customer-centric companies typically win the market that they compete in. If you invest properly in customer

success and being customer-centric, it's likely that you're going to have a higher win rate in opportunities, much higher retention, and much higher net dollar retention and expansion with your customers. No longer can you sell a piece of software and then leave the customer to its own devices to make sure that they have great adoption and business value. It's critical that the vendors also stay involved in that part of the journey. That's why it's so critical that the chief revenue officer owns the CSM function and makes sure it's integrated with the other go-to-market functions.

We see the benefit of a leader looking across multiple customer-facing functions along the customer journey—particularly when the CEO cannot spend their time creating coherence across those functions, perhaps because they need to focus their time elsewhere or because they're a product-oriented CEO. That said, we wonder about the staying power of the CRO title, because it's inward-focused. How will a client feel when they're meeting with a *chief revenue officer*? Will they believe that the CRO is meeting with them with the primary goal to generate revenue, as opposed to support the client's objectives? There's an element of navel-gazing in the term *revenue*. And as you know from the quote at the start of this chapter, we believe names matter.

Yamini Rangan actually took the title *chief customer officer* at Dropbox even though she also oversaw sales, marketing, and other traditional revenue-oriented functions, precisely because she wanted to convey her focus on customers through her title. That might seem extreme, but we expect to see this kind of thinking spread more broadly. In fact, when she moved over to HubSpot as CCO, she kept the same title and org structure. Alison Elworthy on her team believes this integration of roles is critical. "We have a new org structure at HubSpot where we have what we call a *chief customer officer*. Marketing, sales, and customer success all are under this umbrella."

Will the CRO and CCO roles blend in the future to manage the entire customer journey? The jury is out!

Summary

In this chapter we discussed the rise of the chief customer officer role, spanning a multifunction organization that includes CSM, Professional Services,

Support, and potentially other teams. We considered specific alternative scenarios in which it could make sense for CSM to report into Sales—in the case of a long-tail customer base, or at a startup. We explored the role of the CRO in managing all revenue-related functions and wondered about the staying power of that inward-focused title. In the next chapter we'll cover another question about how these revenue-related functions should work together: Who should own post-sales revenue?

21 | Roles and Responsibilities: Who Owns Renewals and Revenue?

Sometimes when people hear the question, "Who should own renewals and expansion?," they roll their eyes. It's probably the most hotly debated—and long-debated—CS topics of the decade. Some people are tired of talking about it. But others are in the thick of making this decision on ownership at their company. (Will this chapter resolve the question once and for all? Time will tell.)

Let the games begin! To represent the side in support of CSMs owning renewals, we'll bring in time-honored champions Christina Kosmowski of Slack and Samuel Lee of KeepTruckin. To represent the side against CSMs owning renewals, we'll bring in Jane Graham at Kronos, Inc. and Anthony Reynolds of Altify. Then we'll have an overtime match to determine who should own expansion.

CSMs Owning Renewals: The Arguments in Favor

We've gathered three major arguments: (1) ensuring accountability for the CSM, (2) giving renewals a focus that Sales wouldn't give them, and (3) keeping a single point of contact.

1. Accountability for the CSM.

Kosmowski, the global head of Customer Success at Slack from the previous chapter, believes that the CSM should do renewals.

> Ultimately, the renewal is the byproduct of that value realization from all the work that the Customer Success team has been doing. As a matter of fact, being a trusted adviser is about talking about the business value that your customers are achieving, which is what renewal conversations are all about. The "trusted advisor" claim [which we will explore in the next section] could be an excuse to not have accountability with your customer. I think the renewal should be this event where you're saying, hold me accountable. We need to be able to show that we in Customer Success actually deliver enough value that you want to continue to use our product and have this partnership with us.

2. Sales is focused elsewhere.

Kosmowski says,

> I'm a big believer in CS owning renewals, because it helps create the focus on retaining customers and not just landing them, which is what Sales is typically focused on. Also, those are two different skill sets. I spent 15 years at Salesforce and CSM owned renewals there. When I joined the company, Salesforce was around $20 million in revenue. When I left, we were close to $10 billion. Having that focused team on renewals was fundamental to driving that growth. The renewal dollars in my last two years superseded the new sales. It was so important that there was that infrastructure and cultural focus on retaining revenue so that when we hit that massive scale we were in a really good spot to handle our enormous installed base.

She believes Salesforce wouldn't have been as successful if Sales had owned the renewal, because they're more interested in closing new business (due to the typical sales culture, skill sets, and executive focus) and would have inevitably deprioritized renewals.

3. **Single point of contact.**

Some thought leaders in Customer Success say that introducing too many different people from the vendor to the customer can confuse them, and that a single point of contact can also execute more effectively given their knowledge of the relationship. This is Samuel Lee's view. He's head of Customer Success & Support at KeepTruckin, a fleet management SaaS company that's on a mission to modernize the transportation industry. Lee explains, "CSMs are with the customer through the lifecycle. There's nobody else in the company who has the understanding of the client's pains and challenges, their business goals, and what it's going to take for them to renew next term. So the CSM should own the renewal. That said, if there is a heavy negotiation piece to the renewal, or there's a large upsell opportunity that coincides with it, then it can make sense to bring in the salesperson." (We'll add: Finance teams may also get excited about the idea of reducing specialization. Combining workflows into a hybrid role may result in lower headcount costs.)

★★★

These are compelling arguments from Kosmowski and Lee, but there's always another side to a debate. Let's explore the counterarguments next.

CSMs Owning Renewals: The Arguments Against

We've gathered three major counterarguments: (1) preserving the coveted "trusted advisor" status, (2) reaping the benefits of specialization, and (3) allowing CSMs to focus on upfront efforts that pay dividends later.

1. **The "trusted advisor."**

Some CS professionals believe that giving the CSM commercial responsibilities could risk compromising their position as trusted advisor to the client. Jane Graham is VP of Customer Success and Renewals at Kronos, Inc., overseeing both the Customer Success and renewals teams, for about $1 billion in recurring revenue and over 15,000 customers. CSMs at Kronos don't manage renewals, but the team that does reports into Graham as the head of Customer Success. "The renewal is a transaction that can muddy the waters between what the CSM is there to accomplish, which is helping the customer achieve business outcomes, versus what your company wants to accomplish, which is getting them to renew." So Graham sees the benefits from separating the renewals team from the CSM team at her company.

Anthony Reynolds, CEO at Altify who appeared in Chapter 8, endorses that argument. "I'm a big believer that CSMs should not be selling to the customer. Salespeople should sell to the customer and Customer Success should focus on the customer's success. The CSM should be driving the adoption, the enabling, the engagement, the training, and all the things to enable value realization. I don't believe Customer Success people should have a motivation to drive cross-sell or upsell opportunities. Those will be the result if they do their job effectively and win the hearts and minds of customers." In his view, contributing to renewals and expansion doesn't require owning them.

Reynolds knows the downside of giving CSMs selling responsibilities, as a client of some vendors himself.

> There's nothing more frustrating when we have a meeting with our CSM, and we think we're going to spend time being educated or informed on best practices around adoption or value realization, but that person is just masquerading as a seller and trying to sell us some other service or some other piece of technology. Don't disguise just another seller as a Customer Success manager.

2. **It's too much for one person.**

Jane Graham believes that specialization between the CSM and Renewals owner helps to optimize workflows, especially when a company reaches around $200 to $300 million in recurring revenue. That's the point when she believes the two functions should diverge.

> The bigger you get, the more customers you have and the greater the need for specialization to optimize both the renewal outcome and the Customer

Success outcome. We're asking the CSMs to do the complex job of helping clients leverage our tool in the most beneficial way possible, auditing their current product footprint and connecting with their executive leadership to figure out where our products fit within a broader landscape of their IT infrastructure. This requires a lot of product knowledge and muscle that you have to build, a lot of executive presence, and even vertical-specific knowledge of how our products address that vertical's specific needs.

It's a tall order to also ask those CSMs to know how to negotiate our commercial terms, understand our standard sales agreements, and understand how a deal construct might impact revenue recognition. The renewal team can get really good at understanding how to work with procurement, negotiate the right terms, identify when our commercial terms need to be updated, and recognize trends and patterns and competitive pressures we're seeing at point of renewal.

3. Different time horizon.

There's a third reason why it can make sense to give renewals to Sales or a Renewals team instead of the CSM. In order to set up the renewal for success, the CSM needs to be "at cause"—doing the things early on in the customer's contract that bring them to an Outcome and a terrific Experience. If the CSM is asked to also manage the renewal, too much of their focus could be diverted to the transaction itself—given the typical focus on dollars from their managers and executives—and away from the early-stage activities that will actually ensure successful transactions months or years later. Therefore, the time horizons that both a CSM and a renewals person need to focus on are different and it's hard for a single person to operate on both time horizons.

Executive Ownership versus CSM Ownership

Sometimes the CSM team won't own renewals, but an Account Management team reporting into the head of CS will. (This is the structure of Jane Graham's organization, for example.) In addition, sometimes the CCO will be held accountable for the Gross Retention Rate, even though renewal execution is handled by the Sales team. Alexis Hennessey, the executive recruiter from Heidrick & Struggles, observes, "The majority of the time the sales leader still owns the revenue. I'd say maybe 20 or 25% of the time, we see chief customer officers owning renewals even if they don't own the execution of the actual transactions." We've seen that percentage increase over time.

Kevin Meeks from Splunk is an example of an executive owning both. As VP of Global CSM and Renewals, Kevin sees the value in both specialties. First, he sees the CSM's role as being all about business outcomes. "If the CSM does their job the way they should, really managing that customer post sales experience and managing toward outcomes and success that they're looking for, the renewal should be a non-event."

For Kevin, the renewals team then becomes a natural complement.

A great renewals team can take the renewal readiness inputs from the CSM and continue that message with the customer. So being intimate enough with the accounts to know what they've done over the last couple of years, to understand the value, understand what they've done with the product, the success that they've achieved, and really position a strong renewal based on all those inputs. In the old days, renewals were very much operational. As we move into subscription models, where you're actually renewing the license itself, you have to be focused on outcomes and value and what the customer is doing with the product. So the renewal motion itself is very different.

And Kevin sees a strong argument for having these teams under one leader. "So the reason that we brought these two teams together recently was we needed to have a really fluid motion between the two organizations. They need to be talking, they need to be collaborating. The RSRs should hold the CSM accountable to that renewal readiness. And the CSM should hold the RSR to accountability of closing the renewal. There needs to be a really tight partnership between the two organizations."

CSMs Owning Expansion: When Does This Make Sense?

We see two scenarios in which it makes sense for CSMs to own upsell: (1) when the product and pricing model result in normal CSM activities leading to upsell and (2) when CSM ownership is limited to upsell lead generation.

1. **Adoption = Upsell Revenue.**

Let's bring back Kosmowski (from Slack and Salesforce):

> I think it depends on the nature of the product and pricing model. At Slack right now, expansion is truly driven by the Customer Success team, because increasing product usage results in upsell in our pricing model. It's very easy for our renewals team to capture that upsell. That's a very frictionless experience for the client. If instead the CSM says to the client, "Oh, I can't help you with that, I've got to go bring the salesperson back in," even though the CSM can do it, that's not a great experience for your customer.

Kosmowski does see the value of bringing a salesperson back in for a different kind of upsell: "In situations where there's a new sales cycle with a net executive who has a whole new value proposition, it's more like acquiring new business. So it makes sense to bring sales back in."

Similarly, for Brent Grimes at MuleSoft, adoption and proliferation of MuleSoft's technology are key to both retention and expansion. Brent's team is uniquely impacting expansion revenue: "This is something that we focused on figuring out for a while, but I think we cracked the code a few years ago and it's allowed us to accelerate our net retention rate."

> For us, it was all about being data driven and understanding why customers expand. And if we understand that, then we can determine which customers are currently most likely to expand and spend the most time with them. Then we can further understand what actions lead to expansion. So let's say that you find out that having a success plan for an account and hosting an onsite visit are really important to your expansion, then being able to systematize that is critical.

2. **Lead (not dollar) target.**

Some companies hold CSMs responsible not for an upsell quota, but for developing a pipeline of upsell opportunities for the Sales team to close. That's how Sam Lee divided up ownership at KeepTruckin. Lee explains, "CS is responsible for identifying the upsell opportunity within customers and then passing that lead over to sales so that sales can then close that down. Sales has a new logo revenue target as well as an expansion target, and the CSMs have a target for leads (CSQLs)." *CSQL* stands for "Customer Success Qualified Lead," analogous to the Sales Qualified Leads that a Sales Development team (pitching to new logos) is often responsible for.

Where We Net Out

What's the bottom line? In Figure 21.1 we bring back the three types of CSMs that we explored in an earlier chapter.

CSMs for Value Capture are responsible for revenue generation (renewals and expansion) in existing clients. Whether you can have this type of CSM depends on your answer to this question: *How much CSM effort is required to get clients to achieve value from your product?*

If the answer is "low," then CSMs should be able to handle renewals and likely also expansion. Typically the effort required to get clients to value is low when both (A) and (B) are true:

(A) The product is easy to set up due to a strong user interface, in-app walkthroughs, zero or easy data integrations, and limited product complexity.

(B) There is zero or limited human involvement in the process for getting value (e.g. in terms of change management, strategic decision-making), or else Professional Services can very effectively cover these needs so that CSMs don't have to get involved.

	CSM for Value Gaps	CSM for Value Delivery	CSM for Value Capture
Product	Early	Robust	Mature; possible multiple
Services Sold	Few to none; or else CSM is a paid TAM role	Well-developed	Core competency, or else none needed
CSM Profile	Technical	Strong exec presence	Sales/"Farmer"
Cost	Cost of Goods Sold (COGS)	Retention (part of Sales & Marketing)	Expansion (part of Sales & Marketing)

Figure 21.1

When (A) and (B) are true, the CSM has the time and mental bandwidth to fulfill some of the criteria that our champions mentioned above. They're able to:

- Handle the workload of both value delivery and renewals.
- Learn multiple skills—both helping clients get value (which is relatively straightforward) and sales techniques that are helpful for renewal transactions.
- Manage clients simultaneously on two different time horizons (early stage and renewal stage).

And they achieve some of the benefits mentioned above:

- Single point of contact—great for the client
- Reduced headcount costs—great for your Finance team
- Accountability for financial results—great for everyone (usually)

But, it's important not to force this. If (A) and (B) aren't true—which is likely in a huge percentage of companies—keep the specialization.

One other point: Many companies change this ownership over time as their business matures. In the early days, it may make sense to launch a CSM organization with a singular focus on adoption and value. Over time you may be able to layer on renewal responsibility. As an example, many private equity firms now have a playbook where they move renewal responsibility to the CSM team post-deal.

What about Upsell Specifically?

Let's parse it out: What *is* upsell, exactly? If you ask CEOs what upsell means to them, you'll hear a wide range of definitions:

- A customer paying more for the same service
- A customer adding one user or license
- A customer adding a bunch of licenses
- A customer adding a new product module
- A new stakeholder buying a product
- A new division buying a product

From supersizing your fries to getting premium floor mats in your new car to buying a bigger island, upsell covers a lot. But if everything is upsell, how do you determine how to handle it? Who does the upsell? Who gets comped on it? How do you comp? These questions are impossible to answer if upsell is such a big bucket.

So we're proposing an expansion taxonomy:

1. **Price increase:** Same business unit, same economic buyer, same products, same licenses—just more money
2. **Small upsell:** Same business unit, same economic buyer, same products, small number of additional licenses
3. **Big upsell:** Same business unit, same economic buyer, same products, big number of additional licenses
4. **Cross-sell:** Same business unit, same economic buyer, new products
5. **Cross-stakeholder sale:** Same business unit, new economic buyer
6. **Cross-division sale:** New business unit

Note that the levers for each type of upsell are totally different:

1. **Price increase:** Contractual terms or limits on price increases; investment in R&D to justify price increase; market competitiveness
2. **Small upsell:** Ease of adding licenses; whitespace in stakeholder
3. **Big upsell:** Whitespace in stakeholder
4. **Cross-sell:** New product development
5. **Cross-stakeholder sale:** Number of stakeholders you appeal to
6. **Cross-division sale:** Number of business units within the customer

Broken down like this, questions about "who owns what?" become easier to answer because the answer changes for the situation. Let's take a look at who might handle upsell in each of the following circumstances:

1. **Price increase:** Specialized renewal rep, Account Manager or Customer Success Manager (if the CSM meets the criteria of "CSM for Value Capture," above)
2. **Small upsell:** Ditto, and define a line for easy upsell
3. **Big upsell:** Define a line above which it goes back to Sales
4. **Cross-sell:** Sales

5. **Cross-stakeholder sale:** Could be an Account Manager, "CSM for Value Capture," or Sales
6. **Cross-division:** Sales

In any of these cases, the CSM could be responsible for CSQLs.

A Final Word on the "Trusted Advisor"

We do think it's absolutely critical for clients to consider CSMs to be trusted advisors. In vendors where there's a strong emphasis on execution in transactions that doesn't take into account the success of the client, having a hybrid CSM/Renewals/Expansion role can compromise the relationship. That said, many of the best salespeople in the world have always functioned as trusted advisors, keeping their clients' long-term interests in mind. As such, there is no reason to think that owning revenue and being a trusted advisor are at odds as long as companies and individuals have a long-term orientation.

Summary

In this chapter, we discussed one of the age-old debates in Customer Success: Who should own renewals and expansion? We explored divergent points of view on this topic in order to showcase the full breadth of opinions in the industry, then offered frameworks for how to consider which points of view are most relevant for your situation. We don't believe there's a universal right answer—but we do believe certain patterns of thinking can help you make the right decision for you. In addition, over time the clear trend is for Customer Success to own more overall revenue.

In the next chapter we'll explore how much money to spend on Customer Success—and when you can't get your desired budget, how to do more with less.

22 | Budget: How Much Should I Spend on Customer Success?

The job of the CEO is to maximize the upside while protecting the downside. Depending on the phase of our business, the mix between greed for the upside and fear of the downside can ebb and flow.

The good news is that Customer Success is becoming an important part of the strategy in all seasons of business, good or bad. That said, because Customer Success is one of the newest disciplines in business, we've seen companies consistently make mistakes in planning that come back to bite them. As Albert Einstein famously (but apocryphally) said, "Insanity is doing the same thing over and over again and expecting different results." This chapter is all about avoiding the same old errors next year. In the following, we list 13 budgeting mistakes to avoid.

Fail #1: Underfund Customer Success

Have you ever shown up for a family dinner late, only to see your relatives smiling and full, their plates clean, and only scraps left for you? Sometimes that's what it can feel like when trying to secure your budget as a Customer Success leader. While prominent thought leaders like McKinsey, Bain, BCG, Accenture, Deloitte, PwC, Gartner, Forrester, and Geoffrey Moore have all talked about the ROI of Customer Success, and while we at Gainsight have shared massive improvements in revenue growth from investing in Customer Success (as discussed earlier in this book), many companies are still underinvesting in the area.

The former investment bank Pacific Crest (which is now KBCM Technology Group) showed that the typical growth-stage company invested 13 points of recurring revenue in Customer Success/Renewals in 2017, which was the last year they published this data. (Note that this metric refers to the "cost of renewal," which could include the cost of a Renewals or Account Management team as well as CSM.) Anecdotally, we've seen this metric scale down to 4 to 8% as companies grow, but many businesses are at less than 1%, so there is still a big gap. Phil Nanus, who leads the research on Customer Success at the Technology Services Industry Association (TSIA), found that the full range is between 0 and 15%, with the average about 3%. He tends to find that the percentage is lower for larger, scaled companies, with a higher percentage for smaller startups.

In general, Nanus sees CFOs pushing back less and less on requests for CS budget. "I saw 2018 as a tipping point. In the data it was obvious to see that the walls were coming down. We had many conversations with CFOs, and it wasn't necessarily the conversation about 'Do I need Customer Success?' I think we've gotten past that. However, the very next question or statement out of the CFO's mouth would be something along the lines of, 'Well, Phil, don't you dare tell my chief customer officer that we need 2,000 CSMs, because we have 2,000 salespeople.' They don't want another very large field-based people organization." Many CSM teams are still trying to carve out their space, and it may not be as large as the space afforded to Sales.

As a positive success story, let's look at customer experience software company Genesys. Lucy Norris, executive vice president and chief Customer Success officer, developed a strong business case for Customer Success. "At Genesys we treat Customer Success as a cost of sales. Our investment there is primarily to raise retention rates and to minimize time to get our customers referenceable. That's the tone at the top, right?"

> **Tip #1:** Agree early with your CFO on a target ratio for Customer Success as a fraction of revenue.

Fail #2: Stretch Customer Success Thin in Budget

With a limited budget, companies often sign up for more than is feasible in terms of Customer Success. They want a Customer Success Manager for every account. They want to radically improve onboarding. They want to overhaul the entire Customer Experience. Using another powerful—but anonymous—quote from the past: "You and what army?"

You need to be able to give something up if your budget is limited. Rather than skimping on the items that make your team more efficient and effective, we recommend curtailing what you can cover:

- Maybe CSMs only get involved post-onboarding.
- Maybe CSMs can't do renewals anymore.
- Maybe CSMs don't cover some accounts, with a pure "tech-touch" model instead for those.
- Maybe CSMs need to push more work to Support and Services.

> **Tip #2:** Constrain your plans for next year based upon your budget available—and clearly communicate those plans to the rest of the company.

Fail #3: Mixing Entering and Exiting Costs in Budget

Because Customer Success is relatively new, there is a great deal of building to be done. As such, during a year, a lot may change in terms of your cost structure:

- Team members will be hired and ramped.
- New clients will be signed and come onboard.
- New products will be launched.

While you may target 12% CSM cost as a fraction of recurring revenue by the end of next year, it may take starting at 16% to get there.

Tip #3: If you agree with your CFO on a cost model, be clear whether it's an entering or exiting cost target.

Fail #4: No Business Case to Support Your Budget

Enough about costs already. Customer Success is *not* a cost center—it's a growth driver. That's easy to say, but what's your business case?

How much evidence do you have to prove to your (possibly skeptical) CFO that this has an impact? In 2017, did you:

- Break down a cohort of clients into a "test" (A) and "control" (B) group to compare results when you intervene versus when you don't?
- Track the key growth drivers from your team—namely:
  - Renewals: At-risk accounts saved
  - Expansion: Upsell/cross-sell leads sent to Sales
  - Advocacy: Case studies and references sent to Marketing
- Identify early indicators of churn or expansion with statistical validity that your team can act on?

Customer Success pros like Kim Peretti, global vice president of Customer Success: Adoption and Enablement at DocuSign, take this scientific approach to the next level: "We defined cohorts of customers where we had a CSM engaged versus those without one. We found a double-digit improvement in attrition rate with CSM involvement."

Tip #4: Build a financial model (your CFO likely speaks Microsoft Excel) showing the impact of your team.

Fail #5: Bad PowerPoint to Support Your Budget

Even if your CFO lives in Excel, your exec counterparts will eventually pitch their plans to the CEO in slides. While it may be trivial, great slides make people feel like the strategy is sound and well thought out. Do you have a Customer Success pitch deck? We'd recommend including:

- Your charter from your team
- Looking backward
  - Results from last year
  - Learnings from last year
- Looking forward
  - Targets for next year
  - Strategy for next year
  - Budget for next year

Tip #5: Even if it involves getting a design contractor, make a nice deck for your plan for next year.

Fail #6: Customer Success Not Being in the Right Part of the Financials

Is Customer Success cost a Cost of Sales and Marketing (S&M) or a Cost of Goods Sold (COGS)? Is it a revenue driver or a cost center? We did some research and the answer is there are companies out there that put it in either bucket.

No matter what the accounting says, however, there is a fundamental superposition in Customer Success between impacting these two buckets:

- **COGS:** Some of Customer Success is inherently part of your core offering. People buy your product or service assuming they will get help. Some of that help might come from your Customer Support, Services, and Training teams. But some may also come from CSMs. The more you have other scalable resources (support, training, professional services, community, etc.), the less CSMs probably do "delivery" work. One way to think about this: If your CSMs were all on vacation for a year, would your clients still be able to get value?
- **Sales and Marketing:** On the flipside, much of what your team does is also about revenue. Are they doing work to make sure the client gets enough value to renew/retain? Are they identifying leads for the Sales team? Are they creating advocates for Marketing?

Per Chapter 14: If your type of CSM is "CSM for Value Gaps," they likely count as COGS. If they're of the type "CSM for Value Delivery" or "CSM for Value Capture," they likely count as Sales & Marketing.

Tip #6: Do a quick time study of how much time your CSM team spends on COGS-related activities versus S&M-related. Share this with your CFO.

Fail #7: Hire CSMs with No Ops Support

We remember the days when you used to have to convince leaders to hire Sales Operations. "Why do we need Sales Operations? Here's the phonebook—start calling!"

As they learned the benefits of consistent process, automation, enablement, and data, companies started realizing that Sales Operations is a critical part of Sales. In fact, we recently talked to the president of a rapidly growing public company who budgets 0.2 FTEs in Sales Operations for every account executive.

In Customer Success, we're still in the old "phonebook" world. CSMs work in spreadsheets, live with bad data, have no consistent processes, and get very little training. Meanwhile, their aggregate headcount cost dwarfs a relatively small amount of spend on operations.

Some companies might say, "Oh, we let the CSM team share resources from Sales Operations." How is that working out? If your job title says "Sales Operations," it's pretty clear what you prioritize first.

In the last few years, one of the top trends we've seen is Customer Success teams investing in operations.

Tip #7: If you don't have a Customer Success Operations person, budget for one. If you have one already, grow the team.

Fail #8: Not Talking to IT in Your Planning

Per the above, you are likely to have IT needs next year, whether it's:

- Process implementation
- Tool setup
- Systems cleanup

In general, as discussed earlier in this book, we've observed that Customer Success teams don't partner enough with IT—to their own peril. If you have projects next year (surveys, playbooks, onboarding, etc.), is IT aware of them? Are you giving them advance notice on what they need? Oftentimes the limit won't be your budget—it will be IT's.

> **Tip #8:** Meet with your IT lead now about your needs for next year.

Fail #9: Not Aligning with Sales and Marketing in Budgeting

What are your Sales team's plans for next year? Going International? Expanding to SMB? Where sales goes, CSM needs to follow. Every new customer needs support from CSM in some way. If you haven't met with your head of Sales by now about next year's plan, you are behind the curve. Where do you need to staff up? Where can you defocus? Is sales reorging? Do you need to? And don't overlook how Marketing will impact your budget next year. Are they hiring someone to support customer engagement or customer marketing?

> **Tip #9:** Get an early view of your sales and marketing plan for next year now.

Fail #10: Not Investing in Developing the Team

So now you have a great budget with new hires, IT help, and maybe an ops person or two. If you're like many CS teams, you'll end up spending all of your precious budget on the business and very little on developing the individuals. Your CS team will be watching the Sales team having:

- An expensive "kickoff" and maybe even another at midyear
- Professional sales training coming in
- Attendance to major sales thought-leadership events
- Maybe even a full-time enablement resource or team

What about the Customer Success team that's talking to your clients every day? It's not a lot of money, so plan for it upfront. Budget for:

- Customer Success to be at your Sales kickoff
- Professional Customer Success training
- Customer Success conference attendance
- Building a Customer Success enablement function

Along those same lines, we send AEs all around the world to build face-to-face relationships with prospects and clients, and those costs are baked into the Sales budget. Your CSMs' relationships are equally valuable, and you'll need to plan ahead for the expense.

Tip #10: Plug training, travel, and bonding into your budget from the start.

Fail #11: Not Leaving Room for Experimentation

Let's be honest—very few of you reading this even had "Customer Success" teams a few years ago. The CS space has grown rapidly and no "ways of working" are fully baked yet. Should you tier your customers by ARR? Should you have both CSMs and AMs? In this book, we've presented a number of practices that we've seen work, or that the data shows are commonly adopted, but that doesn't mean you shouldn't run an experiment to test an idea you have. But most CS leaders get to midyear and wish they had the resources to try something new. Maybe you hear an idea from a colleague at another company? Maybe you want to experiment with a new technology? If you commit your annual budget upfront, you will only evolve on an annual basis.

Tip #11: Leave room for experiments in your budget.

Fail #12: Not Investing in Systems

[*Shameless commercial warning*] While Customer Success is certainly about People and Process—like all areas of business—it can still greatly benefit from technology. Almost every new business process (like CS) is piloted on spreadsheets and Google Docs. The question is, can you scale faster at some point through systems?

While the classic benefits of systems are the same in any field (consistency, automation, tracking), one of the unique benefits of systems in CS is in enabling the experimentation that's needed in a relatively new field. Do you A/B test approaches to onboarding? Can you compare time to value for different products? Can you look back consistently at patterns in churn or growth? Figure 22.1 depicts the old adage.

Tip #12: Plan for systems investments next year.

Fail #13: Starting Budgeting Too Late

As we have seen, CS leaders are often brought into the process at the end, leaving them with the proverbial scraps at the dinner table. If your budget year starts on 1/1 or 2/1 and we are sitting here in August, you're on the verge of running out of time. Even if you're reading this in the thick of summer, the New Year is upon us. Get ready.

Figure 22.1

How to Spend Less Money

Let's say you do all the things above, and you're still left with less budget than you want—which is often the case. Phil Nanus from TSIA says that as a result, "One of the hottest topics and trends in Customer Success is scaling Customer Success." You'll learn a lot more about our advice on scaling in Chapter 25.

How to Prepare for a Recession

Nanus from TSIA says,

Specifically when it comes to budget, I think the biggest challenge is going to be the macro conditions. The reason I say that is, if you look at the typical Customer Success organization, they really haven't done a good job of establishing their ROI. Only 45% have a direct funding model today in terms of charging for Customer Success as a service. If the macro conditions deteriorate, the rest of them may not have a good ROI or funding model to fall back on. The whole CS movement has been riding a wave of growth. I certainly would expect some culling of those organizations over the next 12 to 24 months if there is an economic downturn. Now, hopefully the good times continue to roll and we won't see that, but every day we are working with CS organizations to make sure that they have a solid backing and economic models so that when times get tough they are ready for that.

If you haven't already accumulated metrics that prove the ROI of your team, now is a great time to do that.

Summary

In this chapter we discussed how much companies are spending on CS and how CSM teams can scale their impact with fewer people when they don't get the budget they wanted. We also discussed the importance of developing strong ROI models to defend CS budget in a potential future downturn. One of those ways to justify CSM spend is to charge clients for it as a service, which we'll discuss in the next chapter.

23 | Monetization: Should I Charge for Customer Success to Boost Profitability?

You've heard from us in this book—over and over again—how much CS drives growth. But let's come back to Phil Nanus from TSIA, who was featured in the previous chapter. If you asked Nanus about how large companies measure the ROI of CS, he won't point to growth as his first answer.

> The first way that I see companies proving ROI is by monetizing Customer Success. They're charging a fee for their adoption capability. We see about half of our member companies, which are typically large organizations, doing this today. The impact is significant. It's the clearest way to demonstrate an ROI, because if you get a dollar in the door, you can walk up to your CFO and tell her, can I spend 40, 50, 60 cents on that dollar? You may have a margin target just like other service capabilities.

For Nanus, charging for CS is the fastest and easiest way to demonstrate ROI and protect the budget for your team.

Other CS leaders choose to charge for CS because it allows them to spend more to get their clients to value. Eduarda Camacho is executive vice president of Customer Operations at PTC, a global software company that enables industrial digital transformation. "We're charging for CS not because we want to run it as a P&L," she explains, "but rather because it helps us to secure the budget and grow the CSM team. The primary measure of the success of our paid program is whether we're protecting PTC's recurring revenue, facilitating expansion, and helping our sales team grow new logos by delivering customer outcomes." So she's measuring the ROI of her paid CS team by pointing to its impact on subscription revenue as opposed to a gross margin metric.

Regardless of your motivation for monetizing CS—whether you want to prove its ROI or to drive recurring revenue growth—there are a few questions you'll need to answer:

- *When* are you ready?
- *What* are you selling?
- *How* should you roll it out, price it, and measure success?

These are the questions we'll explore in this chapter.

When Are You Ready?

We spoke with two experts on monetizing CS to learn what questions you should ask yourself when considering whether to launch a CS offering: Catherine Blackmore, GVP Customer Success at Oracle, and Omid Razavi, VP of Customer Success & Services at SupportLogic, Inc. (which uses machine learning to help support organizations) and former global head of Product Success at publicly traded cloud company ServiceNow. Those conversations illuminated three questions:

1. **How mature is your software?** If it's a new product, you probably don't know enough yet about how to drive value for your clients, so you won't know enough about how to package up a CS offering.
2. **How mature is your CS?** You'll need a well-defined baseline (i.e. free) CS plan before adding a paid version. The customers who consider the paid version will want to know what specific *additional* benefits they will receive beyond what they've already been getting.

3. **How mature is your buyer?** If your clients haven't bought the type of product that you offer before, they may not be accustomed to asking for this type of budget. It was probably challenging enough for them to buy your product, and it will be even more challenging to request budget for a CS offering on top of the subscription they're already paying. You may need to prove the value of your product before you can pitch the value of your CS service. On the other hand, more mature buyers may want to progress beyond the basic use cases for your software by getting more help from you. They'd be happy to pay for a high-touch CSM as a partner.

Naturally, you'll want to make sure that your clients are willing to pay for the extra benefits that come with a paid CS program. Typically, the companies that are charging for CS have a significant enterprise segment. We'll come back to pricing later in this chapter.

What Are You Selling?

First of all, you're likely not charging for *all* CSMs. Most companies that have monetized CS offer a free CS tier side by side with a paid one. Razavi from SupportLogic, Inc. emphasizes, "It is the customer that should opt for the right plan for them, and they should never be forced to pay. If they are forced, the customer may simply ask the salesperson to work within their budget, which essentially requires you to bake the CS fees into the license costs." That means you risk cannibalizing your subscription revenue by making the client pay for CS. Instead, Omid recommends that you give the client the choice by offering a free tier.

You may offer CSMs who are more senior in the paid version. Charging for CS may help you afford to hire people with the advanced skill sets that could deliver the true transformation that your clients are looking for. Catherine Blackmore from Oracle often finds clients saying,

I want my CSM to not just be a generalist, but really understand this industry that I'm in. If I'm in the financial sector, I want that CSM to know how to get me to success. I want them to talk just like me, and I want them to deeply advise me on roadmaps and basically be a business analyst to my company. That looks like a whole different person from the generalists we hired out of an undergrad program. That's the moment where you're looking at the finances and saying, gosh, there's no way we're going to be able to afford these people unless we increase price. Or, unless we do what I call a very un-customer-centric approach, which is you say every year, the customers that spend more on our software will get the more expensive resource. But what if a client doesn't spend a lot of money and they want that resource?

That client should be allowed to work with that high-caliber person if they pay for it separately, says Blackmore.

Camacho from PTC recommends not charging for a CSM specifically, but rather charging for a holistic program, or Success Plan, that includes the CSM (who could be dedicated to the account or shared across many accounts, depending on the package) as well as other resources that will help the client get to an outcome. PTC offers a "digital currency that allows the customer to get access to training, specialized experts, and all types of other services that the customer would require. The high-end bundle also includes access to a Technical Account Manager." In summary, she explains, "It's not about monetizing your CSMs. It's about monetizing that whole support infrastructure for your customers so that you can help them get to that business outcome faster." Razavi from ServiceNow agrees. A paid CS program "can encompass, for example, customer support with higher SLAs, premium education (training and certification), and some aspect of expert services (e.g. health check and optimization). It should be designed and delivered as a collaborative effort by all involved in the post-sales customer journey. As such, the revenue should be shared among those teams to create better processes, content, and engagement models that will ultimately benefit your customers." You can drive bigger outcomes for your clients with this kind of cross-functional effort, particularly when you can invest further in it as a result of monetization.

A word of caution: Make sure that the introduction of the paid program doesn't distract from the ultimate purpose of CS—to help grow revenue faster. You don't want your CSMs to merely check the boxes on the items you sold to the client. Concurring with this point, Camacho emphasizes that PTC's CSM program is different from a traditional professional service. "We leverage our CSM team to do many other things that are not about delivering against the monetized program. For example, we monitor our clients for risk, we intervene when we see issues, we replace our client's products with newer, better versions." This allows them to deliver against their ultimate internal goal of protecting and expanding PTC's recurring revenue.

How Should I Roll It Out?

In speaking with Razavi and Blackmore, you'll download a host of tips on how to roll out the monetized CS plan effectively. We captured 14 takeaways here from the design stage through to ensuring accountability:

1. **Involve your clients:** Blackmore notes, "We brought our customers into the design of the new program. We did a lot of discovery, so that when we did get to the point of educating our customers about the new offering, it was what they were looking for."

2. **Define the target:** With any new offering, know which audience you're optimizing for. Says Razavi, "You may arrive at enterprise accounts that spend > X dollars on licenses."

3. **Clarify the products:** "If your company offers more than one product, make sure either all or none of the products are covered by the premium CS plan," Razavi explains. "It will be confusing to both the customer and your CSMs if you offer paid CS only for a subset of your products."

4. **Get smart on pricing:** We've dedicated an entire section to this topic later in the chapter.

5. **Create a beta program:** Razavi recommends, "Offer the monetized CS to beta customers, then get their feedback to improve the plan. Double-down on services that add value and trim others that don't."

6. **Decide who's selling:** If you have a professional services sales team that's selling side by side with product sellers, you'll likely want them to pitch this new CS plan, too. That said, Razavi sees the benefit of product sellers taking the lead: "Make the monetized success plan simple enough that your product sellers can sell it, and that you do not need an overlay of services sellers, which will add to your cost. The product sellers should be fully compensated on CS plan sales, as they do with product sales. It should help them make their number and qualify for President's Club." Given that a monetized CS plan will have a lower margin than your product revenue, you may get pushback from your Finance team on the idea of compensating equally for the two types

of revenue. Explain that the CS plan is similarly recurring revenue and that it's critical for product subscription growth.

7. **Educate your team:** "You have to educate all the people that touch the customer," says Blackmore, "and ensure they know why the change is happening and what the change involves."

8. **Focus on new clients:** Start by selling the offering only to new clients until you're ready to sell to existing clients. "The plan has to be the right fit for your customers and for the company," says Blackmore.

9. **Offer a grace period:** Blackmore recommends a grace period in which nonpaying clients can stick with their CSM.

10. **Make it an upgrade:** Make the new CSM that clients are paying for a true upgrade from the previous CSM, by assigning someone with greater seniority or with experience that's more relevant to the client's industry. "We explain to our customers, this isn't the same resource you've had before," says Blackmore. "It's not about charging more for what you got before."

11. **Align contracts:** "Make sure the monetized plan is co-terminus with your license agreement," Razavi suggests, "so the two will start and renew at the same time."

12. **Introduce it early:** Razavi emphasizes that training your sales team to sell the monetized CS plan early in the sales cycle, together with the product, will help communicate its value. You'll also have more luck defending your price, since introducing a product later in the cycle might have the effect of cannibalizing the subscription contract that the client was already securing budget for.

13. **Make it agile:** "Update your plan every year to delight your customers and stay ahead of the competition," says Razavi. "Your CS program should be a differentiator for your company."

14. **Track outcomes and deliverables:** Charging for Customer Success can actually make the client value your help more. Blackmore says, "Customer Success becomes way more valuable if it's paid." So they may respond more rapidly to emails from your CSMs and do the things you've wanted them to do all along. It's a double-edged sword, though: Now that the client is paying for CSM, the CSM is really on the hook. "When it's free, the client probably doesn't pay as much attention to what that CSM does every day. But, when you start to pay for it, how that person delivers becomes so important. The CSM program is effectively a consultancy that has deliverables and the client wants signals to understand the value of what they're buying."

How Should I Price My CS Offering?

When pricing your offering, Razavi suggests looking at four types of benchmarks that will determine the boundaries of your pricing decision.

1. **Cost:** What you need to price to make your margin target
2. **Competitor:** What the competitors are charging
3. **The market:** What price your clients are willing to pay
4. **Value:** What value you are delivering for your client with this offering

For Benchmark #1, work with your finance department to ensure you understand how revenue will be recognized. Benchmarks #3 and 4 are particularly advantageous in the case of a CS service relative to other recurring services. Clients typically aren't willing to pay much for Support services (e.g. a designated Premier Support Representative). They're also not willing to pay much for Adoption Services, even though we as the vendor might believe that especially the latter delivers significant value to the client, since in this new Age of the Customer, the client believes that the vendor should take responsibility for ensuring that its product is adopted by the client team. On the other hand, clients have shown a high willingness to pay for mission-critical support services, since they want to make sure they don't get stuck in the case of a massive issue. That said, the strategic value of that type of service is low. What's great about a CS service focused on outcome realization is that the client often perceives it as mission-critical—"We need to get value out of this product if we're going to buy it"—and also the strategic value is high. As a result, CS offerings tend to command a pricing premium to other recurring services offerings. Razavi created Figure 23.1 to illustrate this point.

When you're evaluating your clients' propensity to pay, make sure to assess whether their purchase of your CS offering would reduce their willingness to pay for your subscription offering. Your SaaS revenue is far more valuable than any revenue from your CS offering, because it's higher margin and also likely will grow over time at a faster rate (via higher Net Retention). The first people to tell you this will be your Sales team. You'll want to prove to them, perhaps through a few initial pilot sales, that the CS offering won't cannibalize their subscription sales.

Here's an example of where you may end up on price. You may require a minimum, below which it's just not economical to serve a client. From

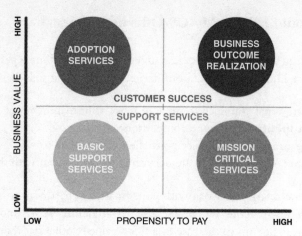

Figure 23.1

there, we often see companies pricing their offering as a percentage of the subscription contract (Annual Contract Value, or ACV). You could choose to discount the percentage for larger contracts if the market demands it. Alternatively, for your larger clients, you may want to offer an even higher-touch model of CS—an even more premium tier of the offering— and you may be able to charge a larger percentage for it. Figure 23.2 shows how Razavi envisions the pricing curve.

Blackmore also knows of companies that offer CS as a fixed fee completely independent of the product purchase. Camacho from PTC adds

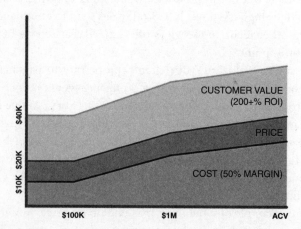

Figure 23.2

further that the price of CS may have nothing to do with the size of the client (which is often correlated with the size of the product subscription). She notes,

> The price has nothing to do with the client's size. It has nothing to do with whether the company is spending more than a million, or less than a million, or $100,000 a year, or $10,000. The price has to do with the client's strategic intent. What are they trying to do? What is the degree of digital transformation that they want? It's about what's required for the customer to get to the outcome. That's how we think about it.

You should also ask yourself, do you want your offering to be recurring revenue? On one hand, recurring revenue is valued more highly by investors, and it's nice that the contract can line up with the subscription contract for your product. On the other hand, you'd have to believe strongly that clients intend to renew at high rates; otherwise it can't really count as recurring revenue from investors' perspectives. That said, you probably have bigger problems if clients aren't renewing this offering at a high rate. In that case, you wouldn't be living up to the concept of CSM as an ongoing resource for the client, delivering value for the client in perpetuity, to ensure and expand that recurring revenue stream. It's a problem when clients (at least of a certain size) don't have a CSM. As Blackmore says, if I'm a CSM,

> I'm not a project team burning down hours in a statement of work and then leaving. Customer Success emphasizes business continuity. This team of resources stays with you for life. The value is in not having to spin up new project teams and educate them on everything you just went through with the last team. A CSM says, I understand what you've been through. I have the long term path for you. And if anything, I'm the quarterback of these short-term consultants who will sometimes come in to help out.

How Should I Measure Success?

Razavi recommends tracking several metrics to determine the success of your CS offering besides the sheer bookings and revenue:

- **Attach rate:** % of new target accounts that purchase the offering
- **Upsell rate:** % of existing target accounts that upgrade to the offering

- **Renewal rate:** % of dollars of sold CS offering that actually renew when eligible for renewal
- **ROI to the client:** a measure of Outcomes (as discussed earlier in this book) that shows the impact to the client from purchasing the offering

You should also consider how to measure the benefit of your monetized CS program to your company. We do recommend tracking the gross margin of this program, as Nanus from TSIA mentioned, to show that you're covering the cost of your CS team. In addition, you're likely charging for CS because you want to cover the cost of a program that you know is valuable to your clients and therefore to your company's recurring revenue. As a result, we recommend tracking the difference between the Gross Retention Rate, Net Retention Rate, and an Advocacy metric for target accounts that purchased the CS offering and those accounts that declined to purchase.

Summary

In this chapter we discussed how to decide whether to launch a paid CS program, how to roll it out and price it, and how to measure its effectiveness—to your clients and to yourself as the vendor. At the end of the day, investors will evaluate your business based on subscription growth, not services. But if charging for CS is a means to an end—allowing you to deliver more value and consequently faster growth—it could be a great move.

24 | Metrics: How Do I Measure Customer Success?

If you can't measure it, you can't manage it.

—Peter Drucker

It's all about the Benjamins, baby.

—Puff Daddy

Whether you take your leadership lessons from Drucker or Diddy, you know that a huge part of the CCO's job is to help your colleagues understand the "scoreboard" for measuring Customer Success.

Over the years, we, as leaders, have developed various methods to quantify most aspects of business such as:

- Finance: GAAP (or IFRS) accounting rules
- Sales: Bookings methodologies
- Marketing: "Marketing qualified leads"
- Personal ego: Twitter followers

273

And yet, with all of these statistics, we still can't measure what is usually the greatest "hidden" asset in our business—our customer base. How are we doing with clients? Are we delivering value for them? Are they likely to stay with us? Are they fans of ours?

If you've studied the field, the Net Promoter Score was created to partially address these questions. But with the trend toward *digital transformation,* companies are awash in data about their clients that they could be using to measure client health.

Customer Health Scoring is the concept that you can integrate various signals about your clients in order to quantify your customer base. Our goals for this chapter are to show you how to build a Customer Health Scoring framework and point out what mistakes to avoid.

But just to motivate you first, let's go back to Kevin Meeks from Splunk. We asked Kevin how he sleeps at night running such a huge Customer Success and Renewals Organization.

> How do I sleep at night? How I've slept well is continuing to improve and evolve our adoption and health scores. The data is king: if I have good telemetry; if I have good adoption and health scores; if I understand what my renewal pipeline looks like; if I know the status of it from a health and adoption perspective. I then know where we have our biggest risks and our biggest bets. I can assign my resources appropriately to mitigate those risks and then I can share that with our sales team. That level of visibility and data is important to the renewal business.

There's the fast way to do Customer Health Scoring, and the super-thorough way. We'll start with the fast way—which is more than a stellar starting point. But if you're an advanced CS leader and you want to be challenged to think more deeply, you can skip ahead to the thorough version.

The Fast Way to Measure Customer Health

The most important Customer Health Score you can create is one that signals the degree to which the customer is getting value from your product. In other words, are they getting that Outcome that we began to discuss in Chapter 6? You'll want the best measure of ROI that you can find.

You might have a measure of ROI that your product tracks automatically. For example, we spoke with an invoice management company whose clients wanted to reduce the amount of time it took to collect on invoices from their own customers. The company's ROI metric is "reduction in number of days to collect on the invoice." The greater the reduction, the greater the Outcome for the client.

Not every business has a clear ROI metric, though. In that case, you'll want to pick a measure of product adoption that is a strong proxy for whether clients are getting value. This metric isn't likely to be the sheer number of logins or page views; rather, it should capture the kinds of behaviors that you expect successful clients to perform in your product. If the ultimate milestone of client activity in your product is to create a dashboard, then that dashboard creation can become your ROI proxy. If you don't actually have product telemetry (adoption data), then you can use a measure of client engagement that you believe is a strong signal of ROI. It could be the client's usage of the online community or portal, or their engagement with marketing emails. The point is to take a stand on a single metric that's a proxy for ROI.

Using that ROI metric or proxy, you can create a Customer Health Score that uses a traffic-light analogy: green when the metric is strong, yellow when mediocre, and red when problematic. If you want to get even more granular in your assessment of client health, include additional colors—light-green in between green and yellow, and orange between yellow and red. Then define the metric's range for each color.

The nice thing about creating a Health Score that's based on ROI is that it tends to correlate with other metrics that matter, even if not always (and if you prefer to achieve perfection, move on to the next section in this chapter). Clients with a green ROI metric are likely to renew at faster rates (because they can justify the renewal to their CFO or Procurement department), expand at faster rates (because they have proof of success with you), and advocate more frequently (because they have real success stories to share).

The Advanced Way to Measure Customer Health

Let's say you've got the fast way under your belt and a little complexity doesn't scare you. Read on, friend, or skip to the next chapter.

Why Measure Customers

As with other areas of measurement, we'd break the value of quantifying your customers into three conceptual buckets. We've drawn an analogy between CS and Sales in Figure 24.1, to give you the gist.

Did you pay close attention to the table? Did something weird jump out? Did you notice that we said "Customer Health *Scores*," not "Customer Health Score?" One of the biggest mistakes companies make when implementing Customer Health Scoring is thinking everything can be distilled down to one number.

One way to think about it is to consider the old parable of the Blind Men and the Elephant, as shown in Figure 24.2.

Customer Health is the "elephant." But there are many views into health and each is like one of the people grasping at the elephant. In our clients, we see seven common types of views into Customer Health:

1. **Vendor Outcomes:** Track the overall ROI of Customer Success to your business.
2. **Vendor Risk:** Get an early warning on risk in accounts.
3. **Vendor Expansion:** View how the Sales team is expanding accounts.
4. **Client Outcomes:** Track your impact on customers.
5. **Client Experience:** Voice of the Customer team wants visibility.
6. **Client Engagement:** Marketing team driving Customer Success.
7. **Client Maturity:** Company effort to get clients at higher levels of sophistication.

Value	Sales	Customers
Report	Report on trend of overall bookings and pipeline to the company, board, and investors.	Report on trend of overall Customer Health Scores to the company, board, and investors.
Incent	Incent sales rep with commission based upon bookings.	Incent team members managing clients (e.g. Customer Success Managers, Account Managers) toward growth in Customer Health Scores.
Act	Take action on individual "deals" in the pipeline to convert them to bookings.	Take action on customers where you can improve Customer Health Scores in some way.

Figure 24.1

Figure 24.2

Vendor Outcomes Scorecards

Clients provide multiple areas of value to vendors and you should measure these separately. As we discussed in Chapter 5 on growth, for a typical vendor the desired outcomes for the vendor include:

- Value if the client stays with them
- Incremental value if the client expands with them
- Incremental value if the client helps the vendor acquire new clients (e.g. as a reference)

So a Vendor Outcomes Scorecard could have the following top-level dimensions:

- **Retention:** Are they likely to stay with us?
- **Expansion:** Are they likely to expand in spend or consumption with us?
- **Advocacy:** Are they likely to be an advocate for us?

And here's the confounding thing that you know if you've managed clients for a long time: Clients can be guaranteed to stay with you near term (because they are stuck) *and* be a negative advocate (a detractor).

Clients can be engineering you out long term (not "sticky") *and* short term be planning to expand. Clients can be about to churn (Retention Risk) *and* be an advocate! It's important to separate out the various "outputs" of a client relationship into separate metrics.

As an example, see the sample Vendor Outcomes scorecard in Figure 24.3. We've created "groups" for Retention, Expansion, and Advocacy, with sample indicators for each:

Retention Indicators

- Adoption Sophistication score: Number of advanced capabilities used
- Sponsor score: Relationship with exec sponsor
- Support Health score: Presence or lack of recent poor support experiences

Expansion Indicators

- Marketing Engagement score: Attendance to recent marketing events
- Open Opportunities score: Presence of open sales opportunities in CRM
- Utilization score: Percentage of contracted products or services used

Advocacy Indicators

- Sentiment score: Recent survey feedback (e.g. Net Promoter Score)
- Reference score: Recent reference activity
- Community score: Activity in online community

Figure 24.3

In general, vendor-centric scorecards are the types you'd want to share internally or with your board (or your CFO).

Vendor Risk Scorecards

Pivoting a different way, some companies may want to measure client risk by functional owner—so you can define clear accountability by department (see Figure 24.4). Examples could include:

- **Support health:** Does the client have too many cases open? Repeated cases? Cases aging too long? This could be owned by the head of support.
- **Product health:** Does the client have open bugs or critical enhancement requests? Similarly, the head of product would be responsible for this score.
- **Marketing engagement health:** Is the client engaged in vendor marketing activities? The marketing leader would be accountable here.
- **Product/service adoption health:** Is the client using the vendor's product/service actively and well? Often, the Customer Success team would directly drive this.
- **Services health:** Have the client's services projects with the vendor gone well (on time, on budget, on quality, etc.)? A head of Professional Services might take this on.

Figure 24.4

Vendor Expansion Scorecard

On the positive side, some companies want to easily expose opportunity—or whitespace—for their sales team. You can imagine taking each product/ service area and using logic to define the unsold opportunity to sell that offering into the given customer. For example, imagine you have two product lines:

- Lightsabers
- Tricorders

You could define rules for what you expect a client to purchase:

- If industry = *Star Wars*
  - For Lightsabers
    - GREEN = 10+
    - YELLOW = 1–9
    - RED = 0
  - For Tricorders
    - GREEN = 2
    - YELLOW = 1
    - RED = 0
- If industry = *Star Trek*
  - For Lightsabers
    - GREEN = 2
    - YELLOW = 1
    - RED = 0
  - For Tricorders
    - GREEN = 10+
    - YELLOW = 1–9
    - RED = 0

You could have further overrides based upon health. If a client has risk issues in a given product, the expansion score for that product could be set to "NA" until the issues are resolved.

You can then put a very sales-friendly view in front of your reps of the "selling opportunity" in their accounts, as shown in Figure 24.5.

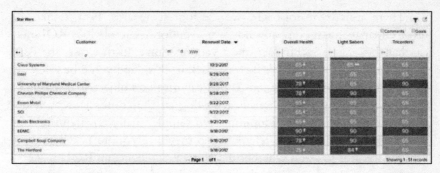

Figure 24.5

Client Outcomes Scorecards

Conversely, you could imagine putting yourself in the shoes of your clients and asking how *they* measure the success of the relationship. As we discussed in the earlier section in this chapter on the Fast Way to start measuring customer health, we're looking to measure to what degree the client is achieving an ROI. To solve this problem more deeply, we're going to use four scorecards, using what we call the DEAR framework:

- **D = Deployment:** Is the client activated? This scorecard could represent licenses activated as a percent of all licenses entitled, or a binary Yes or No on whether the onboarding has been completed.
- **E = Engagement:** Is the client engaged? This could be a binary Yes or No on whether there has been a check-in, whether live or by email, with a decision-maker in the last three months. (By the way, vendors that are very product-oriented often underestimate the value of checking in with their executive sponsor at the client. It's usually extremely valuable.)
- **A = Adoption:** Is the client using the product? This could be a measure of the quality of usage (e.g. the percentage of users who complete a high-value action), depth of usage (e.g. the percentage of users that are daily actives), or breadth of usage (e.g. the percentage of features that are regularly used).
- **R = ROI:** Is the client seeing value? To illustrate this, remember the example of the invoice management company that we discussed earlier, with the ROI metric "reduction in time to collect on an invoice."

There are two reasons why we use four scorecards. First, unlike the invoice management company, not every vendor has an obvious ROI metric that they can track. In fact, most vendors don't. In that case, the ROI metric may be subjective (we'll come back to this), and you'll be referring to other hard metrics (D, E, and A) that can give you objective insight into the degree to which the client is achieving an Outcome. Moreover, not every company can track Adoption; for example, many on-premises software companies don't have telemetry, so they'll rely more heavily on the other scorecards to assess whether the client is achieving an ROI.

The second reason we use four scorecards is that these measures tend to come in order: A client can't achieve ROI without first adopting the product; they can't adopt the product without first engaging with your company in some way, at least during onboarding; and giving the client access to the product is obviously a foundational step that needs to happen. Tracking progress in these scorecards over the course of the client's journey can help you understand whether the partnership is heading in the right direction.

Let's come back to the ROI scorecard. If you don't have an ROI metric that you can track, consider tracking what we like to call "Verified Outcomes." These are testimonials from the executive sponsor at the client that attest to the client's belief that they have achieved an ROI. For example: If that invoice management company weren't able to track the reduction in collection time for some reason, they could send a survey their client and ask about their ROI attainment. The client could respond, "Vendor X was extremely helpful to us. Because of our use of their platform, we were able to reduce the time to collect on invoices from Y to Z." That would count as a Verified Outcome, and the scorecard could reflect the existence of that Outcome within the past year.

Client Experience Scorecards

But it's not *just* about the Outcomes. It's also about how you make a client *feel*—the Experience—as we discussed earlier in Chapter 6. To envision a Client Experience Scorecard, think about all of the bumps in a typical client experience:

- Poor expectation setting in sales
- Long onboarding
- Rocky onboarding experience

- Bad support experience
- Repeated support experiences
- Outages
- Weak relationship with account team
- Product/service quality issues

A sample Client Experience Scorecard might look like Figure 24.6 and include the following:

- **Sales experience:** Survey client after sale to see how rep did in expectation setting.
- **Onboarding time:** Measure actual onboarding time versus promised.
- **Onboarding experience:** Survey client after onboarding.
- **Support experience:** Survey client after cases.
- **Support frequency:** Measure frequency of tickets.
- **Uptime**: Measure service uptime for client.
- **Relationship:** Regular Net Promoter Score survey.
- **Quality:** Count of bugs affecting client.

Client Engagement Scorecards

For many organizations, the focus on Customer Health is managing leading indicators. Often, the leading indicators for customer retention and

Figure 24.6

Figure 24.7

expansion tend to be around the level of engagement between the client and the vendor. A Client Engagement Scorecard, shown in Figure 24.7, might include:

- **Product/service engagement:** How sophisticated is the client's usage of the product/service in question?
- **Marketing engagement:** How often does the customer attend webinars, events, etc.?
- **Community engagement:** Is the client active in the vendor's online community?
- **Advocacy engagement:** Is the client an active advocate for the vendor?

Client Maturity Scorecards

Some businesses, particularly high-touch ones, want to drive clients toward increasing levels of "maturity" with their product or service. At the same time, they want to assess and staff clients differently based upon that maturity level. A Client Maturity Scorecard like the one in Figure 24.8 could include:

- **Business processes:** Does the client have business processes implemented around the vendor's product or service?
- **Sophistication:** How sophisticated is the client's usage of the vendor's product or service?

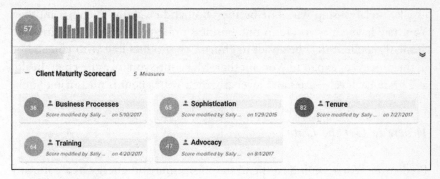

Figure 24.8

- **Tenure:** How long has the client been using the vendor's product or service?
- **Training:** How many people at the client have been trained on the vendor's product or service?
- **Advocacy:** Is the client an active advocate for the vendor?

What (Parts of) Clients to Measure

Continuing the theme, if you have large customers and/or multiple products, it gets even more complicated (see Figure 24.9). You may have a

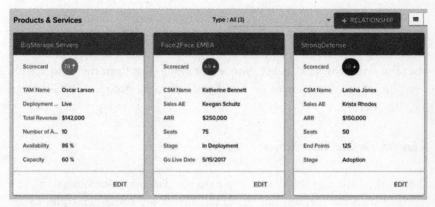

Figure 24.9

"sticky" relationship with one business unit and be about to churn another. You may have an advocate in one business unit and a detractor in another. Similarly, a client may be about to churn one product line with you and be in the process of expanding on another. Make sure you measure client health at a granular level—the same level at which your client is measuring you!

Where to Get the Data

Prediction: You're going to spend the most time and energy as a company on the easiest problem. You'll spend months and quarters of precious time talking about how your "data isn't clean" and waiting until you "figure out your data." In fact, you're reading this right now thinking, "We're not like the typical company—our data is a mess." Without knowing anything about your business, we can tell you that you have enough data to start. You likely have some combination of:

- Sales data in a salesforce automation (sometimes called CRM) system
- Financial data in an enterprise resource planning (ERP) system
- Customer feedback data in a survey system
- Services project data in a professional services automation system
- Marketing engagement data in marketing automation system
- User engagement data in a community system
- General customer data in data warehouse
- Website activity data in a marketing analytics system
- Support data in a support ticketing system

If you're lucky, you may also have *product telemetry* of some kind.

Now, if you have none of those, stop reading this and go get yourself some data! But if you're like most companies with a bunch of the above data but with issues in quality, you're not alone. Just from the most readily available of the data sources we listed you can make progress on Customer Health Scoring.

How to Define Your Scores

This is the hard part. Now that you have the data and your objectives, you need to turn the former into the latter. Below are some principles to get started:

1. **Define Customer Health *scorecards*, not scorecard:** Per the previous section, define multiple ways of measuring client health. The beauty is you don't have to choose! You can mix and match the same atomic data points (e.g. usage, Net Promoter Scores) into these separate views on client health.
2. **Define scorecards at the level your clients experience:** Per the previous section, whether your clients buy at the business unit level or at the product line level (or both), make your scores equally granular.
3. **Distinguish leading indicators from lagging indicators:** It's okay to have scorecards that track both leading indicators (e.g. how engaged is the client in marketing) and lagging indicators (e.g. renewal forecast), but don't average them together and expect meaning.
4. **For each scorecard, mix and match data:** For example, your Marketing Engagement scorecard might include a measurement of their attendance to webinars (from your Webinar system), their open rate on emails (from your Marketing Automation system), and their registration for in-person events (from your Event Management system).
5. **Automate wherever possible:** Manual inputs on Customer Health (e.g. a CSM's subjective perspective/scoring on customer sentiment) are sometimes necessary, but such inputs create more process for CSMs and are seldom objective. Pull in hard data from sources (see above) wherever possible to minimize subjectivity and the need for CSMs to make time-consuming inputs.
6. **Define an understandable grading scheme:** While eventually a numeric system (0–100) may be appropriate for visualizing a trend, you may want "bands." We recommend color bands for intuitive understanding (e.g. red/yellow/green), as we discussed earlier in this chapter.
7. **Leverage trends, but be careful:** You may want to look at "changes" to measure health (e.g. a client dropping in usage could be a bad sign), but you need to watch out for "false positives" (e.g. a usage drop due to vacations).
8. **Look for "absence of data":** One of the most powerful signals you can look for is the negative. Which clients haven't attended an event or webinar recently? Which clients didn't open the roadmap release email or attend the roadmap webcast? Which decision maker didn't respond to your recent survey?
9. **Vary rules by customer segment or maturity:** You can't treat all customers the same in terms of measurement. Make sure you are defining rules based upon the unique segments of your business.

10. **Leverage benchmarking where appropriate:** If you have a common value (e.g., transactions/day) across clients, you can use benchmarking rules to compare a given client against the average or median of its peers—and then score based upon this benchmark.

11. **Use overrides (but sparingly):** While you may normally take a combination of measures to determine a score (e.g. a combination of webinar attendance, event attendance, and open rate to define Marketing Engagement), you may need an override in cases where, no matter what the other measures say, a selected variable trumps all others. For example, if you get a Detractor Net Promoter Score response from an executive decision maker, that may trump all other objective data. That being said, don't have too many overrides or your scoring system will be for naught.

12. **Focus on actionability:** A big part of driving Customer Success as a company is identifying early signs. But equally important is finding *actionable* early signs. A client that stopped using your service is interesting, but what do you do about it? Perhaps more interesting is a client who is actively using your service but not reading your release notes. Near term, they are healthy. Long term, they may not perceive your innovation and may leave you. And you can do something about it.

13. **Don't have too many measures:** While I gave you many examples here, don't overwhelm your team with too many scoring measures overnight. Start with a few (I've seen 6–12 work).

14. **Keep old scores:** While you may decide to change the rules in terms of how you measure an area, I encourage you to retain the old data. Hide it, for sure, to not confuse your team. But keep the old data, as it may come in handy down the road.

How Not to Do It

These are pretty much the inverse of the above, but just for completeness:

- **Don't average averages:** Don't take all of your data about all aspects of customers, average them together, and expect meaning out of it. It's the same with averaging data across products and business units within a client. You wouldn't average your Balance Sheet and Income Statement together and expect useful information, would you?

- **Don't practice false precision:** I like color coding because numbers sometimes lead you to a false sense of confidence about how much you know (87/100 health going to 86 is likely noise).
- **Don't overdo trending:** If you want to see "red" every time a client drops 10% in some metric, you will see a lot of (*false*) red.
- **Don't wait for perfection:** The beauty of having multiple scorecards is that you can start now and keep adding incrementally.

Next Steps

Your mind might be swimming right now with ideas (and maybe anxiety) about how to build and roll out scorecards at your company. You might be wondering, does it have to be this complex? Fortunately, it doesn't. We went *way* down the rabbit hole in discussing the multifaceted question of how to measure customer health. But we don't know a single company that has implemented every suggestion this chapter. And making your clients successful doesn't require that. What it does require is thoughtfulness about what aspects of customer health matter most to your business.

So what do we do next? We'd recommend parallel processing:

- Run an offsite with your team to define a roadmap for how to measure different parts of your client base.
- In parallel, pick just *one* of the concepts in this chapter (such as the simple health score based on an ROI metric, discussed in the first section) and get going so you have a starting point.

One final thought: Let's circle back to the "elephant in the room." The elephant in this chapter is technology—specifically software. We've intentionally tried to keep this chapter completely agnostic vis-à-vis software, but if you've read this far, you probably understand that measuring your customer base according to the framework we've laid out is completely impossible without some sort of software solution.

Some companies choose to do this through a patchwork of tools (and lots of spreadsheets). Others look to all-in-one platforms or home-built solutions. As the CEO and COO of a Customer Success software company, you might be surprised to find out that we don't actually recommend Gainsight to every company—even though we are wholly convinced we're the most sophisticated and full-featured offering in this category. No matter what size or stage your company is in, the last step (and a crucial part of each prong of the parallel process we talked about above) is a software evaluation. We'll come back to choice of technology in the next chapter.

Correlation versus Causation in Customer Success

We think this question of causation or correlation is relevant as the industry analyzes the impact of Customer Success. As we write that statement, we realize we've been asked that question as much as almost any other.

- "How do we quantify the impact of Customer Success?"
- "How do we justify the need for Customer Success?"
- "What's the ROI of Customer Success?"

What the questioner (sometimes your CFO, sometimes your CEO) is asking is, "Why should I invest in Customer Success?" And more subtly, "How do you know there is a causal relationship?"

This dialog often comes up when CS teams present correlations:

- **Time-based correlation:** "We invested in Customer Success this year—look how much our retention rose!"
- **Account-based correlation:** "We focused Customer Success on these accounts—look at the saves we made!"
- **Leading indicator correlation:** "Check out how much adoption has gone up!"

Now, if your CFO is like many with whom we've worked, they might lean to the skeptical side:

- "Sure, retention went up, but how do we know your team is the *cause*?"
- "Sure, those accounts did well, but were they going to do well anyway?"
- "Sure, adoption went up, but wouldn't that happen naturally?"

In *The Book of Why*, the author, Judeah Pearl, talks about the near-impossibility of the *counterfactual*—namely, analyzing what would have happened in the alternate decision path. What would have happened if you hadn't invested in CS, if you hadn't focused on those accounts, or if you hadn't driven adoption?

Pearl would argue that sophisticated CS teams (with a lot of volume) might design a controlled experiment to truly figure out the causality. As in the drug industry, CS teams could run an A/B test. They could perfectly separate out a set of accounts upon which to test an intervention (e.g. having a CSM) versus a control group where no CSM is assigned. They would need to be careful to make sure there is no "bias" in the group design. For example, you couldn't have the test group be the customers who wanted to engage with a CSM (since those might be more likely to stay anyway). And the good news is several companies have done this. In fact, athenahealth presented at our Pulse conference event on experimental testing in their client base.

But the reality is that most companies don't have the volume, consistency, or processes to perform a real-life A/B experiment. And don't forget about the "harm" issue. Just like it's sometimes unethical to put a patient into a control group if the drug is lifesaving, it's often challenging to imagine ignoring a certain set of clients.

So what do we do—throw up our arms and say, "CS has no provable ROI"? No! We look to our colleagues in other functions to realize how they analyze their own impact. From our vantage point, there are five models:

1. CSM Is Like Support: CSM as a Cost of Doing Business

For some companies, CSM has become part of the product and part of the value proposition. The customer needs the CSM to get value and to work with the vendor. Over time, this cost looks a lot like a Customer Support cost. It's often categorized as a part of "Cost of Goods Sold."

Given this, CSM as Support lowers Gross Margins. Hence, the pressure will be about automating and reducing costs to the barest minimum that still works.

2. CSM Is Like Services: CSM as a Product

Many companies are trying to break the logjam of budgeting by self-funding CS out of their own pockets. Specifically, they are creating premium "Customer Success Plans," which often include premium support, training, professional services "points," and advanced Customer Success. So in a way, Customer Success becomes another product (though a service product). The great thing is that this approach is easier to justify at the CFO level. Indeed, Salesforce pioneered this model. At Pulse events, Splunk and PTC have presented about similar concepts.

One challenge to wrestle with is, "What about customers who don't sign up for the plans?" The answer from some of these companies is that they use profits from the plans to fund a "for-free" Customer Success service at scale.

3. CSM Is Like Pre-Sales: CSM as a Sales Enabler

Some companies have evolved their thinking to look at CSM as a cost of the sale (renewal). As such, they may have a renewal rep and a CSM working on a given client and they look at the combined cost as a cost of the overall transaction. These models look a great deal like the justification of a *sales engineer* (SE) or "pre-sales" resource to partner with an *account executive* (AE) for a new sale. Indeed, just as companies establish target ratios of "SE:AE," they may have a ratio of "CSM:Renewal Rep." In this approach, the CSM makes the overall renewal and/or expansion more effective just like a great SE helps an AE close.

4. CSM Is Like Marketing: CSM as a Sales Input

The concept of a "lead" was brilliant. Marketers created a well-defined (though often debated) output metric that could be quantified. Sophisticated companies measure a "cost per lead" and a lead-to-sale conversion rate.

We've seen some more sophisticated teams look at their CSM team this way. Allison articulated the concept of three leading indicators for CS: Customer Success Qualified Save (CSQS) for clients that the CSM team helped bring back to health, Customer Success Qualified Lead (CSQL) for upsell generated by the CSMs, and Customer Success Qualified Advocate (CSQA) for references and case studies generated by the CS team. If you have the appropriate formulas of conversion from each of these to lagging indicators (e.g. new business, renewal an expansion), you could come up with a funding model for CS.

5. CSM Is Like Sales: CSM as Obvious

We can get to the point where CSM is so fundamental that we don't even question it. Isn't that how sales works? Most companies have a "capacity model" spreadsheet. You input the number of account executives to hire along with assumptions around attainment, ramp time, quota, and other factors, and the model spits out a bookings number. Sales reps create sales—it's like magic!

We think many of us have been in situations where it wasn't so easy. Sales reps can't succeed without leads—or happy clients—or products/services. Sales reps often drive deals and make them happen—but rarely on their own. Sometimes they get lucky and get a "bluebird."

So maybe one day, far into the future, your CFO will ask, "How do we know those Sales reps caused the expansion versus just being there to facilitate? How do you know it wasn't the CSM that made it happen?"

Maybe we're dreaming? Or maybe we've seen the future!

Summary

In this chapter, we discussed a fast way to get started with a Customer Health Score that's based on an ROI metric. Then we dove deep into the different aspects of customer health that you may want to explore as you evolve your CS program over time. Finally, we discussed conceptual ways to think about the impact of Customer Success. Most businesses say "our customers are our greatest asset." And yet, those same companies have no way to measure this asset. It's time to fix that.

25

Scaling: How Do I Grow Customer Success without Throwing People at It?

The end of the calendar year for many businesspeople means three things:

1. Holiday fun
2. Closing Q4

and . . .

3. Microsoft Excel!

What we mean is budgeting season! Who's fired up? Anyone?

Thousands of Customer Success leaders around the world enter "fun" discussions with their CFOs. They debate ratios, cost structures, and scaling models. They are asked for the thousandth time, "How can you prove your team is having an impact?" (We've heard a rumor about some CFOs having "amnesia"—forgot where we heard it, though!)

But most notably, CS leaders and CFOs are annually faced with an almost impossible challenge. How do they scale their businesses and continue to get the benefits of CSM without breaking the bank?

Customer Success and the Rule of 40

This problem is particularly acute for companies trying to hit the "Rule of 40." As context, the Rule of 40 is a financial concept in SaaS that's all about balancing growth and profitability. Simplistically, the Rule of 40 is a calculation of your revenue growth minus your loss as a percentage of revenue, the idea being that number should be greater than 40.

So if you grow 100%, you can lose 60% of revenue $(100 - 60 = 40)$. If you grow 40%, you should be breakeven. If you grow 20%, you should make 20% margin on your business. As companies mature and their growth goes from 100% or more to 20–40%, the math starts getting intense.

How Do You Get Your Company to Break Even or More?

If you assume a normal SaaS gross margin of 70–80%, that leaves 70 to 80 cents on the dollar for all Operating Expenses—just to break even! But let's assume 70% margins for this simple exercise.

Most companies spend 10–15% (or more) on G&A (general and administrative) and 15–25% on R&D (research and development). Let's assume 35% combined. That means you have $70\% - 35\% = 35\%$ left over for Sales, Marketing, and Customer Success. That's not a lot.

If you're like most scaling SaaS businesses and you spend 5–15% of your revenue on Customer Success, you end up with very little money left over for Sales and Marketing. So how can you get the benefits of CS in terms of retention, growth, and advocacy without making it a linear scaling problem?

We are seeing more and more CFO and CS leaders digging into this very problem, which at its core is an efficiency problem.

Ten Ways Innovative Leaders Are Scaling Customer Success

Across the thousands of leaders we've met, we are seeing many methods for scaling, including:

1. **Improve the product and leverage it for virtual customer success:** Work with the Product team to ensure that the roadmap (especially in the short-term and at the beginning of next year) includes certain enhancements that will reduce the amount of effort that it takes for clients to get value from the product. In addition, make sure the Product team is giving you the data around product usage and adoption that your team needs to understand client health. Finally, consider using the product as an extension of your Customer Success team through in-application guides and walkthroughs. We spoke in Chapter 9 about ways to work more closely with your Product team. Those are important to do on an ongoing basis, but especially during the budgeting process, so that the degree of product complexity is aligned with the CS investment next year.

2. **Build a community:** Could your successful clients answer at least some of the questions that others are asking your CSMs? That's usually true. Build an online community where clients can help each other out.

3. **Centralize content:** The CSMs at most companies, particularly ones in growth stage, find themselves reinventing the wheel that their peers already built. Two CSMs may have each separately created a deck to address the same use case, and they don't even know it. Want a more efficient solution? Have someone on your CS Operations team own content, soliciting input from the CSMs and formalizing your team's methodology in its materials. You may find when doing this that you don't really have a methodology for how to help clients get value—in which case, you should build one!

4. **Re-segment your customers:** Focus your CSMs upmarket while ensuring that you're covering your bases for small clients (see the next tip). In addition, many companies are taking this further by incorporating potential spend and client need into the segmentation model.

5. **Expand your tech-touch strategy:** Are you already orchestrating thoughtful journeys for your clients that include a deliberate sequence of in-app walkthroughs, human interactions, emails, and surveys—all catered uniquely to each user? If not, now's the time. This approach

can drive success for your long-tail clients as well as automate some of the work that your overburdened CSMs are currently doing.

6. **Expand your support team:** If your CSMs are overworked in part because they're spending time resolving technical issues, hire in Support instead. The compensation for Support reps is typically less than that for CSM, and Support teams can also be located in lower-cost locations, because they don't need to be in the same place as clients.

7. **Hire in a low-cost location:** Let's say you haven't been able to automate away a lot of work involved in serving your clients. It's still there, waiting for you. As you promote CSMs to management positions and others move on to other roles at the company (or outside your company), backfill their positions in lower-cost locations. Those new locations could be in the same geographical market as your clients or they could be somewhere else. When we built our CSM team in India several years ago, we found maybe one or two examples of other companies that had done this. Today, it's commonplace. To set up this new location for success, consider ways to minimize the time zone difference, find team members who don't feel strongly about working during typical working hours, and create training sessions to ensure that knowledge is transferred from the old location to the new one. You'll also want to make sure you first hire a strong local leader.

8. **Sell services—and CSM in some cases:** You may not be able to do all the work you need to do from another location. In that case, consider selling your clients services to cover the cost and expanding your Professional Services team to deliver those. The work that can't be moved to a low-cost location may involve onsite advisory, high-touch education, and deep or technical guidance. Enterprise clients are typically accustomed to paying for services in these areas. You could also consider charging for the CSM role itself, which we'll cover in the next chapter.

9. **Hire earlier-career CSMs and use technology to help them:** CSM is still a relatively new field. Some of the most efficient and scalable CS organizations "grow their own" by investing in hiring, enablement, and systems.

10. **Reduce waste:** Not every activity a CSM performs is valuable. Some don't impact the client at all. Some don't correlate with retention, expansion, or advocacy. Find and eliminate situations where you are "pushing on a string" and you will scale more effectively.

Summary

Eventually, Customer Success switches from PowerPoint to Excel. By that we mean it switches from a theory to a model. And the question is, how do you scale the model? In this chapter, we reviewed ten strategies for scaling your Customer Success approach without throwing people at it.

26 | Technology: What System Do I Use?

Just as companies have invested in sales automation and enablement to drive sales productivity and in marketing automation to increase lead generation and brand awareness, hundreds of organizations have invested in Customer Success Management solutions to maximize client lifetime value and advocacy. In our benchmarking study of over a hundred Customer Success leaders (which we mentioned earlier in this book), we found a 33-percentage-point increase in Net Retention by optimizing Customer Success operations. If implementing a CSM solution can help you achieve this increase, anyone would be crazy not to do it.

In fact, we recently met one CEO of a large private equity–backed software company who connected CSM software with his company's strategy in the following way. This CEO had undertaken a massive transformation of his company from a traditional on-premises perpetual license model to launching a brand-new cloud offering. He had made significant changes in culture and leadership to embrace this new mindset. He felt that the last mile was "industrializing Customer Success." In this CEO's mind, it wasn't enough to have the right people with the right culture. "Our customers are telling us that our people are great but they still aren't working off of a consistent and coordinated set of playbooks."

And many companies are acting on this insight. Consulting firm Deloitte published a report, *2019 Enterprise Customer Success (CS) Study and Outlook*, in which they found under the heading of "What CS capabilities are seeing the greatest increase in investment?" that the "top-two areas where nearly one-third of CS leaders indicated that they plan to increase investment by greater than 10% are talent acquisition and technology enablement."

But just as Customer Success needs to transcend your organizational silos, so does your Customer Success technology. That means Customer Success teams need to think carefully about when, where, and how to deploy a CSM solution for maximum business impact. That said, most mature Customer Success organizations have found that there is no point of "perfection"—that you need to move fast and iterate as you go. Ed Daly, senior vice president of Customer Success and Growth at Okta, notes, "Perfection is the enemy of progress and waiting to implement Customer Success until it's perfect is a guaranteed approach to losing revenue. Much like an agile software development process, an effective Customer Success effort requires fast iterations, failures, learnings, and improvements."

In this chapter we share the steps companies should take before buying a CSM platform based on our learnings from more than 700 Gainsight deployments. These steps will help you put in place the strategy, data, and processes to drive success.

Is Customer Success Art or Science?

It seems like something from a different lifetime, but we still remember the old days when Sales was all chalkboards, steak knives, and "gut feeling." Okay, maybe chalkboards were before our time. Also, Nick is vegetarian and doesn't really need steak knives. But gut feelings—those were definitely the name of the game back in the day.

There was a time when the prevailing attitude was that selling was an art—unquantifiable, nonsystematic. Sales has gone through a "Moneyball" transition just like baseball—the art is still there, but the science has developed so much more.

Fast-forward to today. If you're starting a new company, you often define your sales process, identify your key metrics, and set up your Customer Relationship Management (CRM) system before you hire your first rep. That's an important development because companies are now able to start testing and learning in their sales process at a much more rapid rate.

The problem with the rock-star seller who somehow just closes is that it's not repeatable. It doesn't scale. And it will stop working eventually and leave you with no answers and no way forward. But that's a well-known and broadly accepted premise—at least in Sales.

So why is this functional initiative called Customer Success Management—a peer org but an evolutionary successor—reliving the 1990s (and not in the feel-good-music way) in its approach to hiring and processes?

We've met with thousands of new CSM leaders from teams all along the spectrum from startup to enterprise and from every industry, and we (surprisingly) frequently hear things like:

- "My team isn't comfortable with process."
- "It's not really about metrics—it's much more about gut feeling."
- "We're hiring a team and then are going to figure it out."

Let's address each premise individually:

- **"My team isn't comfortable with process."**
  Much like their colleagues in Sales, we think these new CS leaders will realize over time that, unlike what Alec Baldwin says in *Glengarry Glen Ross*, coffee isn't for closers. Instead, coffee is for consistency. By that we mean that the most effective businesspeople in Customer Success will develop consistent and data-driven ways to execute, and more importantly, to learn.
- **"It's not really about metrics—it's much more about gut feeling."**
  Consistency is important because Customer Success has another thing in common with Sales: It's a results-oriented business. It might not be as brutally quota-driven, but retention is a critical number to make for any company to grow. No CSM should be fired for "losing" a customer. But every CSM should be able to understand and explain why it happened and how to improve the process going forward. You can't do that without data.

- **"We're hiring a team and then are going to figure it out."**
  Many practitioners of the "gut feeling" school of CSM feel like "you need to get people right and then you can figure out process and tools." To the same coffee closers, we say this: If you hire a team with a mandate of "figure it out," then good luck getting that team to then embrace data, process, and systems down the road. You may get lucky, but more often than not, you'll get an army of people who believe nothing can beat their magical intuition.

Intuitive CSM vs. Predictive CSM: We see this mentality in the real world all the time, and we want to consciously push back against it: while it's true that nobody knows a customer as well as their CSM, you cannot make accurate predictions without objective measurements. This is true in science as it is in CSM. In this book's language, we're talking about health scores, but you can call it what you will.

Because of this fact, we've noticed that many of the newer and earlier-stage CSM teams are far more sophisticated than the ones that have been running for a while. Earlier CSM teams were often built like earlier sales teams—where swagger and heroics were rewarded and careful analysis was laughed off as "we're not ready for that yet."

Newer CSM teams are realizing that the foundation you build at the beginning is the one you will live with years from now. Our advice is, if you are starting a new CSM team, start it with a scientific approach from day one.

Project Plan: What Does a Best-in-Class Evaluation Process Look Like?

Buying a Customer Success solution isn't (and shouldn't be) done with the same level of spontaneity you might buy a one-click point solution for something that solves a very specific, limited business problem. Entering your evaluation process with a well-thought-out plan will get you to driving outcomes much faster and with better results. Here's our recommended 11-step process for purchasing a CSM solution:

- ☐ **Evaluation Team:** Identify the cross-functional evaluation team.
- ☐ **Business Case:** Create a business case to quantify the value of a potential investment.

☐ **Project Plan:** Create your plan for evaluating solutions.
- This outline is a good starting point.
- In addition, if you haven't been through a procurement process in your company, research what's been involved for comparable decisions.
- Do you have a standard vendor audit process? A security review? A compliance review?

☐ **Vendor Research:** Determine your short list of vendors to evaluate by reading online reviews, talking to peers, and reading analyst reports.

☐ **Request for Proposal (RFP):**
- Create evaluation requirements for the RFP.
- Send the RFP to potential vendors.
- Review responses.
- Score responses.
- Select finalists.

☐ **Solution Presentations:** We recommend breaking it up into three meetings—ideally on the same day for logistical convenience.
- Management/End User Demo + Roadmap Review
- Technical Architecture + Demo
- Executive Demo + Business Case Presentation

☐ **References:** Conduct reference checks and read online reviews of the finalists.

☐ **Proof of Concept:** If needed, we recommend conducting a Proof of Concept (POC) to make sure the solution works for you. We highly recommend this if you have a nontraditional business model.

☐ **Solution Design and Scoping:** Define a detailed scoping of the project to understand costs and timing.

☐ **Selection:** Select the final vendor.

☐ **Commercials:** Finalize the commercial agreement.

In the rest of this chapter we'll offer tips for ensuring that each phase is successful.

Evaluation Team: Whom Should I Involve Internally in the Evaluation Process?

One of the biggest mistakes you can make in a CSM platform rollout is to operate in a silo. As we've discussed at length in this book, transforming your company to be more customer-centric requires cross-functional

RACI	ROLE	QUESTIONS
Responsible		
	Customer Success or Business Operations Lead	a. Will this meet our business requirements?
		b. Are we ready for this?
	IT Project Manager or Business Analytics	a. What's involved in launching this and running it?
		b. How will this work with our existing stack of systems?
Accountable		
	Head of Customer Success/ Account Management	a. Is this the right partner now and long-term?
		b. How long will this take to get up and running?
	Head of Sales	Will this help drive revenue?
	Head of IT	Will this scale?
Consulted		
	Pilot Customer Success Managers or Account Managers	Will this improve our efficiency?
	Pilot Sales Reps	How will this fit with my existing sales workflow?
	Data Team	Can this handle our data?
Informed		
	CEO/GM	a. How does this help us strategically?
		b. Will we be successful with this?
	CFO/Finance Lead	a. How much does this cost—directly and indirectly?
		b. Is this worth the investment?
	Head of Product Management	Can this help me make better product decisions?
	Head of Marketing	How can this help us scale our customer engagement and customer references?
	Head of Services	Can this help me drive services revenue?
	Head of Support	Can this help me prioritize and better handle cases?
	Head of Training	Can this help me drive training revenue?

Figure 26.1

buy-in. We'd recommend using the RACI decision-making framework (see Figure 26.1) by defining who is:

- **Responsible:** The team conducting the evaluation
- **Accountable:** The team that will own the business process related to Customer Success
- **Consulted:** The team that will be using the CSM platform daily
- **Informed:** The team that needs to approve the investment and will be affected by the results

Business Case: How Do I Define the TCO and ROI for This Project?

Frequently, business leaders go too far down the path of an IT project without understanding the cost of ownership or the value they should expect to derive. We recommend doing the heavy lifting of projecting the ROI and Total Cost of Ownership (TCO) upfront, before you dive into the details of the technology itself. A business case could involve several components:

- Assessment of the current state of Customer Success processes across the company
- Benchmarking of current state versus "best–in–class"
- Proposal for improvements
- Calculation of TCO of improvements, including:
  - CSM platform licensing costs
  - CSM platform vendor or partner onboarding services costs
  - CSM platform vendor or partner ongoing services costs
  - Internal IT and operational onboarding time and implied costs
  - Internal IT and operational ongoing time and implied costs
  - Change management time and implied costs
  - Data preparation and integration time and implied costs
- Projection of ROI of improvements by customer segment, including:
  - Reduced churn
  - Increased upsell/cross–sell
  - Enhanced operational efficiency
  - Strengthened customer advocacy

At Gainsight we offer Strategic Advisory Services to help our clients define a business case, including by benchmarking the client against a set of best-practice processes. In addition, many third-party consultants can help with this process. We find this external advice helps Customer Success leaders gain the buy-in of the CEO, the CFO, and other stakeholders, and also helps the champion crystallize in their own mind the outcomes they want to achieve by using the software—a sense of clarity, which will contribute to the success of the deployment later.

Vendor Research: What Are the Available Options?

When was the last time you made a major purchase without doing some online research? When our Sales & Marketing teams interact with potential

Gainsight buyers, it's extremely—and increasingly—rare that they haven't read at least a few third-party assessments of our software and technology. It's not purely peer-generated content, either. Most of the leading analyst firms, such as Gartner and Forrester, have published research on CSM platforms. In addition, verified online review sites such as TrustRadius, G2, and AppExchange can be very helpful. Finally, we recommend checking out the market comparison charts that show the differences between vendors, available on G2 and similar sites.

RFP: What Functional and Platform Requirements Should We Look for in a CSM Platform?

CSM platforms, if implemented well, integrate deeply into your data stack and business processes. At best, they're capable of transforming your operations on a fundamental level with cascading improvements throughout your company. As such, we recommend a careful evaluation of your requirements and of vendor capabilities. Some companies make decisions based on merely one demo and "gut feel." While that can sometimes be effective, in the end the client often doesn't achieve the outcome they're looking for. In fact, they may not even really realize what outcome they wanted to achieve until their platform has failed to achieve it.

The most sophisticated buyers of CS platforms are focusing their assessments on the following three capabilities:

1. **Functionality (Driving ROI):** Our customers consider six types of functionality to be the core "pillars" of a CSM platform:
   - **Health:** A capability to view a "scorecard" of the health of a customer across many dimensions (e.g. Support health versus Adoption health versus Relationship health) and across the various entities within a customer (e.g. by product, business unit, geography, etc.). Furthermore, you should be able to drill into the details of customer health, such as account notes, support history, survey responses, key sponsors, or usage statistics.
   - **Workflow:** Tools to translate insights about customer health into action. These typically include a system for identifying actions that need to be taken, defining best-practice steps for those situations, parsing out work between CSMs and other team members, and integrating with other task management systems like Salesforce. Furthermore, Workflow often involves providing visibility into these

actions in internal communication systems like Slack. Finally, CSM platforms increasingly include proactive ways to define desired client outcomes and plans to achieve them.

- **Communication:** Tools to automate and personalize communications throughout the Customer Success lifecycle. These should enable all "touch models," from high-touch capabilities like automated Executive Business Review (EBR) PowerPoint creation to mid-touch tools like prewritten trackable emails, data-driven email nurturing, and in-application messages.

- **Analytics:** Most customers buy CSM platforms not only to optimize day-to-day operations but also to make strategic decisions across their business. As such, best-in-class CSM platforms include deep analytics capabilities, such as fully customizable reporting with graphs and tables, integrated data processing/aggregation/pivoting/trending, simplified cross-data-set joins and views, and personalized per-user dashboards.

- **Surveys:** Customer Success is about looking at data, but only in the service of understanding and gaining insight into customer relationships. Your data is only useful as far as it can uncover meaning that you can take action on. Most CSM efforts involve bringing together an objective (data-driven) and subjective (sentiment-based) view of client health. Therefore, most buyers want functionality to capture customer feedback via surveys. Surveys may be sent after individual transactions (e.g. after the sale, a support case, a project closure, etc.) or on a regular basis to assess the overall client relationship. This category of functionality also includes capabilities to close the loop in following up on survey responses in a consistent way. Because customers are typically all over the world, surveys need to be sent in multiple languages and aligned to multiple time zones. Finally, many companies look for analytics tools to process and assess survey results—including survey text analytics.

- **Apps:** Finally, customers want to make sure CSM doesn't become an "island" in a company and that it's exposed to all of the parts of the company that can drive Customer Success. CSM platform evaluations often include evaluating the app and experience for each stakeholder:
  - CSM
  - Sales rep (in systems like Salesforce Sales Cloud, HubSpot or Microsoft Dynamics)

- Support rep (in systems like Salesforce Service Cloud and Zendesk)
- Services manager (in Professional Services Automation systems like FinancialForce)
- Marketing manager (in terms of reference management capabilities, for example)
- Product manager (in terms of product usage analytics)
- Finance team (in terms of revenue and renewal forecasting)
- Partners

2. **Platform (Managing TCO):** While the end-user functionality seen above is what the business users care about, IT and Operations will only be able to deliver based upon the depth of the platform itself. We've seen companies look at these aspects of platforms to understand them better:

- **Data Integration:** CSM platforms depend on data. How does data enter the system? What data sources are supported? Sources to consider include:
  - Data via Amazon S3
  - Data via API
  - CRM (Salesforce Standard Objects, Salesforce Custom Objects, Salesforce Third-party Apps)
  - SFA (e.g. Salesforce Sales Cloud, Microsoft Dynamics, HubSpot)
  - Support (Salesforce Service Cloud, Zendesk)
  - Marketing (Marketo, Salesforce Marketing Cloud, Salesforce Pardot, Oracle Eloqua)
  - Professional Services Automation (FinancialForce)
  - Web Analytics (MixPanel, Segment, Google Analytics)
  - Finance (Netsuite, Zuora)
  - Surveys (SurveyMonkey, Medallia, Qualtrics)
  - Human Intelligence/Scoring
  - Social Media Data (LinkedIn, etc.)
  - Company News Updates

- **Open Data Model:** Because CSM systems are truly platforms, customers often need to constantly expand and evolve the data model. Make sure you verify that the platform allows you to add custom tables, fields, calculations, and other factors in administrative UI. Also determine if the platform can handle data processing (e.g. aggregation, pivoting, trending, etc.) or if you need data to be preprocessed. Finally, determine how flexible the customer model is. How many levels can the hierarchy handle? Can you add multiple dimensions (e.g. products) at various levels of the hierarchy? Does the scoring model allow you to granularly track multiple elements of a health score (e.g. support health, services health)?

- **Salesforce Integration:** Every CSM platform should integrate with CRM systems like Salesforce. As with most technology, the key is to get really specific about the depth of the integration. Is the data in the CSM platform integrated with the data in Salesforce? Are all custom objects available at all times to users? Is the CSM platform available 100% through the Salesforce UI? Is it available through Salesforce apps like Service Cloud and Community Cloud? Can your users update Salesforce fields directly from the CSM platform?

- **Self-service:** Customer Success is evolving rapidly and CSM teams want to stay on the cutting edge. As such, they need to be agile in changing the platform configuration. Leading customers demand a CSM platform that allows for easy configuration of reports, dashboards, rules, custom attributes, formulas, tables, and other factors without having to call the vendor. Furthermore, they look for online resources like a knowledge base, support chat system, and online community to get fast assistance.

- **Best Practices:** No CSM team wants to reinvent the wheel. Customers are looking for platforms with built-in best practices— preconfigured playbooks, email templates, surveys, reports, and the like that represent the best of what's possible in Customer Success.

- **Role-based Access:** A CSM platform should be able to reconcile the dichotomy between having role/team/function-based tailored view and access and the free exchange of relevant information across teams. Your CSM platform should have:
    - **Page layouts tailored to the needs of each function:** The ability for different teams to have a tailored view of the customer is essential to bubble up the right issues and opportunities to the relevant person. Custom page layouts also eliminate clutter while promoting cross-functional collaboration.
    - **Federated access:** Any reasonably sized business that has multiple business lines faces a tough choice: deploying each of its business lines on its own customer management system or forcing them to operate within one restrictive, shared environment. It does not have to be a choice if each team can configure and use the platform to meet their specific needs while remaining within one overall environment.

- **Security:** You are entrusting the CSM platform with a lot of sensitive information, such as customer data and business critical information. Any CSM platform should have:
  - Sophisticated user access permissions based on roles/profiles
  - Independent security certificates such as SOC 2 Type 2

3. **Company (Partnership with the Vendor):** Because the CSM platform is a long-term decision, customers often evaluate the company as much as the product. CSM platforms are evolving rapidly, so they want to assess not only where the technology is today, but also where it will be over time. Key questions include:

- **Customers:** Who are the vendor's customers? How big are they? In what industries are they? How relevant are the customers to your business?
- **CSM profile:** What is the background and profile of the CSMs with whom you'll be working from the vendor? How many people work in their CSM organization?
- **Services:** What initial technical services are available from the vendor to set up the platform? What advisory services are available to help with CSM strategy? What ongoing Technical Account Management and other services are offered? How many people work in Services?
- **Partners:** What partners are enabled to deliver services around the platform?
- **Community:** What kind of community exists around the vendor? Does the vendor have local chapters in my area to interact with like-minded peers? What customers are in the community? How robust are the company's events? How active is the vendor's online community?
- **Vision:** What is the vendor's three-year roadmap? What is its investment in R&D to enable innovation? What's the pace of release and recent release pattern?
- **Viability:** How big is the vendor today?

Since most of the above aren't yes/no questions, we recommend scoring each response—for example:

5 = Vendor has strong capability with strong demonstrated evidence.
4 = Vendor has strong capability with demonstrated evidence.
3 = Vendor has strong capability.

2 = Vendor can customize/stretch to meet need.

1 = Vendor doesn't have capability.

Solution Presentations: What Should We Cover During Our Reviews with the Vendors?

Since the CSM platform decision is a cross-functional choice, and therefore many people may be involved, it's important to break up the reviews into manageable chunks. When Gainsight demos software for prospective customers, we're extremely intentional to understand and document the outcomes they want to achieve. Often, they might not be sure, which is why it helps to have a prescriptive approach based on many hundreds of success implementations. To get a sense of what that prescriptive process might be, you can always start up a demo process with Gainsight today at gainsight.com/demo.

The most successful clients have already internally discussed their desired outcomes coming into each of the following three recommended meetings:

1. Management/End User Demo + Roadmap Review

This is a meeting (typically two hours) for the head of Customer Success/Account Management, head of Sales, and Pilot Sales reps/CSMs/AMs to understand the business value of the platform and user experience. This includes covering:

- Customer experience impact from platform
- Quick view of CSM/Sales Rep experience
- Management experience and dashboards
- "Day in the life" of a user
  - Looking up information on a customer to prepare for a call
  - Managing your workload and action items
  - Collaborating with others
  - Sharing information with clients
- Having the vendors demonstrate how best practices are built into the product and experience
- Roadmap and vision

2. **Technical Architecture and Demo**

Given the technical platform considerations above, clients typically review the platform in detail with IT, Business Operations, and the Data Team. This includes:

- Architectural overview
- Integration overview
- Security overview
- Administration demo

3. **Executive Demo + Business Case Presentation**

Finally, the savviest clients tee up a quick (30-minute to one-hour) presentation for senior executives (CEO/GM, CFO/head of Finance) to see the output of the system:

- Executive dashboard demo
- Business case overview
- High-level project plan

References and Proof of Concept: What Steps Should We Take to Vet Our Preferred Choice?

Even once you've developed a preference for a vendor, you're not quite done. We recommend pursuing the following four steps to build your conviction:

1. **References:** As in hiring, vendor reference checking is an art. We recommend extensive diligence in references to make sure you understand the true customer experience. In particular:
   - Ask the vendor for references that are similar in size and business model to you.
   - Look for "backdoor" references via LinkedIn.
   - Find customers that have left the vendor.
   - Find customers that moved to the vendor from other solutions.

2. **Proof of Concept (POC):** While not always necessary, a POC can be helpful in assessing technical fit. In particular, if you have:
   - Complex source data
   - Sophisticated customer hierarchies
   - Diverse user populations
   - Variable workflows

   POCs can be helpful to get beyond the demos to the details. If you conduct a POC, we highly encourage you to load "real" data (perhaps anonymized) into the platforms.
3. **Selection:** We recommend taking all of the data above and bringing the Evaluation Team back together to make a careful decision.
4. **Solution Design and Scoping:** Finally, make sure you understand the services scope of work and project plan in detail. Meet the onboarding team, understand their backgrounds, and assess the validity of the methodology.

The Importance of Getting This Decision Right

When we put together this evaluation process, we were very careful to stick closely to an "outside-in" perspective. What would be most valuable to a buyer agnostic of their ultimate selection? As important as it is for us to sell people on the value of Gainsight specifically, it's even more existential for us to help Customer Success teams and leaders succeed in delivering on their customers' desired outcomes as part of a broader movement. What's good for customers is good for Customer Success at large, which is good for us in the long run.

And make no mistake: Of all the technology or services purchases your company will make, the stakes have the potential to be uniquely elevated when it comes to a Customer Success solution. In some cases, companies can afford to (relatively) casually or indiscriminately invest in software because either the cost or impact or both are low compared to more costly or transformative implementations. It's not so—nor should it be so—with Customer Success. Your technology vendor could be an essential strategic partner to you in transforming your company.

Summary

In this chapter we recommended pursuing a thoughtful plan when aligning your company around a choice of CS technology. We emphasized the importance of certain functionality in that technology, but we emphasized equally the importance of choosing a vendor who can be a long-term, strategic partner to your business. Your CS platform, when supported by the right partner, can be one of your greatest assets in bringing all functions together around the success of your clients.

Another great asset in your CS transformation is your people, the topic that we'll address in the next chapter.

27 | Professional Development: How Can I Develop My Leaders and My Team?

Writer Tim Urban's blog, *Wait But Why,* is a popular one among people who love questioning everything in life. Urban posted a puzzle[8] that continues to fascinate us to this day:

"It's the year 2045 and you and your partner are ready to have a child. So you head to the clinic so they can extract your gametes and prepare to conceive just the right child (then they grow the fetus in a machine with optimal conditions—only the biggest hippies still engage in old-school-style pregnancy)." In this hypothetical world, you can design your child to have different levels of three traits: IQ (classic intelligence), EQ (emotional intelligence), and grit (perseverance). Urban explains, "Each of these traits can be assigned to your future child on a human population percentile scale of 1–100. So an IQ of 100 would put your child in the top percent of all humans in IQ. An EQ score of 50 would give the child average emotional intelligence." Then you're given 250 points in total. How will you distribute them across the three traits?

This question has sparked hours of conversation among our friends and family. Give it a try at dinner tonight or at your next cocktail party! In the meantime, let's redirect your mind from thinking about your future or current children, back to contemplating the world of Customer Success. You could just as aptly ask the question: "If you had 250 points to dole out for your ideal Customer Success Manager, how would you distribute them across IQ, EQ, and grit?"

Even though it's quite possible that folks are born with some initial level of IQ, EQ, and grit, we also are fervent believers that these qualities can be cultivated, including among CS folks, and that professional development programs should target them specifically. Although we could debate the split of points across the three capabilities, at minimum we believe that all three of these capabilities are critical ones for Customer Success folks to develop. Here's how we think about the types of skills pertaining to each of the three.

For the CSM

IQ → Product Knowledge

It can't be overstated: CSMs need to know the product well. "Product expertise is the backbone of the CSM role," says John Gleeson, the head of several CS teams at KeepTruckin, the fleet management platform company. "No amount of training on communication or escalations will compensate for a CSM not truly understanding the ins and outs of the product. It's the foundation for building trust with your customer. So first and foremost, you want to start with building true product experts on your team." Todd Massey, who has helped enable CSM teams at tech companies Mindbody and Delphix, emphasizes that product knowledge is not merely knowledge of features, but also of use cases. "You need to see how your customers use your product. Especially, find the customers who love your product and ask, what are they doing with it?"

The type of required product knowledge will vary depending on the particular nature of the CSM role. For example, the "CSM for Value Gaps" type will be hacking workarounds to compensate for gaps in the product, so they'll need to be quite technical. On the other end of the spectrum of CSM types, a "CSM for Value Capture," focused on monetizing clients' success by booking renewals and driving expansion, will need to be primarily familiar with how the product can help the client get more value; they'll be selling by (1) playing back for the client how their feature usage resulted in ROI for them and (2) translating new product use cases into theoretical value that the client could achieve.

EQ → *Prescriptive Persuasion*

As a CSM, you're responsible for ensuring that the client achieves their desired Outcome. This requires a certain level of assertiveness. Gleeson at KeepTruckin says, "As a CSM, you need to ask the hard questions in a thought-provoking way, because you need to understand the deeper value that the client truly wants but maybe hasn't fully recognized on their own." Once you're aligned with the client on the value that they truly want to achieve, you will need to be prescriptive—in other words, to proactively recommend certain courses of action for the client. That will sometimes entail pushing back (thoughtfully) when the client tries to go down a path that's not actually beneficial to them. As Gleeson says, "Great CSMs succeed in having those challenging conversations."

A common example of prescriptive language is: "Client, I know you're planning to do action A, and I'm hearing from you that you believe that's the right decision because of X and Y. But, I've worked with many clients who decided to do something similar, resulting in meaningful harm to them, in the form of these specifics. On the other hand, clients that are similar to you and who have performed action B were able to generate the following outcomes. As a result, I'd strongly recommend action B, and look forward to your questions and feedback." You'll see in that example that prescriptive persuasion requires strong abilities in asking questions and listening, as Gleeson pointed out. To effectively convince the client of a different course, a CSM will need to deeply understand the client's assumptions, beliefs, and goals.

Nils Vinje, founder and CEO of Glide Consulting, advises many growing companies on their CS strategy. He believes that strong planning is essential to the art of prescriptive persuasion. "A reactive CSM will bounce from one thing to the next. They end every day knowing that they were incredibly busy. But if they take a look back, they're not totally sure what they got done. But an effective CSM has a success plan that they built with the client that shows, this is what the next three months and six months look like." Forming that plan with the client requires the CSM to be assertive, but also inversely, having a possible plan in mind helps the CSM persuade the client of the right next steps to get them to an outcome. A planful mindset goes hand in hand with persuasive communication.

Grit → *Playbooks*

Every role has a "hustle" aspect to it. Learning and executing on playbooks is the hustle that's most common in the CSM role. To give a few examples, CSMs will need to learn their company's methodology for getting clients to value, the process for handling an escalation, and the best practice for ensuring a renewal closes (whether they're doing it themselves or working with Sales). Executing playbooks consistently requires self-discipline, a high degree of organization, and respect for the thought leaders within the company who created the playbooks. Even while CSMs are following the playbooks, it's equally important for them to give feedback on those to their manager or the CS Operations team that maintains them. They should be attuned to the results that these playbooks generate and in the mindset of learning what works and what doesn't and suggesting improvements that can optimize the playbooks. That kind of rigorous learning is also a form of hustle.

For the Director or Manager of CSMs

IQ → *Situational Problem-Solving*

When an escalation or unique scenario comes up, the situation sometimes falls outside the set that the playbooks were intended to address, so the CSM will usually go to their manager for help. As a result, a director needs to be skilled in helping the CSM think through the problem. The ideal director will ask the CSM questions to probe deeply into the situation, leveraging a series of *why* questions to get to the root of the problem—not in an accusatory way, but in a way that conveys intellectual interest and a desire to coach the team member.

- "Why do you think this result occurred?"
- "Ah, I see, so X is the reason. If you think even deeper about it, what's the reason why X happened?"

- "Got it. It sounds like Y is causing X. Do you think there's a deeper factor Z that resulted in Y?"

Once the director and CSM have together arrived at the root causes of the problem, they can begin to brainstorm solutions. This requires creativity on the director's part. They may throw out ideas with the CSM and see what sticks, and also encourage the CSM to think outside the box about the right solution.

Vinje from Glide Consulting encourages directors to coach their CSMs to think through these questions in advance of bringing the situation to their managers. He explains, "This trains the CSM to think critically about the situation first so that they can come to the table with ideas. Ultimately, I have found this to be an effective way to reduce the amount of time that a manager needs to handle escalations and teach the CSM to think strategically. The added bonus is that there are many situations where the CSM comes up with a great solution after thinking critically about the situation, runs it by the manager, and the manager replies simply with 'I agree.'" In summary, directors need to be highly skilled in situational problem-solving as well as skilled in coaching their CSMs on that same behavior.

EQ → *Emotional Regulation*

Because the director is often a beacon for discussions of challenging, emotionally charged situations, they will need to help their team members cope with their own emotions. This involves recognizing their team members' emotions in the first place as well as expressing empathy for them. This in turn requires the director to regulate their own emotions. If the director is stressed out by all the escalations that are coming their way, they may react impulsively to the team member, perhaps with frustration or anger. Especially since CSMs may not have the same ability to regulate their own emotions (depending on their level of seniority), the director needs to carry that burden of managing the group's emotions. This can make the management role challenging, but also highly fulfilling, since the director's success in helping the group can make the CSMs feel understood and appreciated. The CSMs also learn by watching the director role-model this emotional self-regulation.

Grit → *Achievement*

Directors should have a thirst for translating day-to-day actions—the execution of playbooks and other activity—into the achievement of goals. They may not yet have developed a deep intellectual understanding of that link between activities and results (see the capabilities required for VPs ahead), but they're not satisfied if the team's hustle doesn't result in the achievement of goals. They'll drive conversations with their teams about what it takes to make the number and whether it's a target for Gross Retention, Net Retention, or another metric. If they don't make their number at the end of the quarter, they're disappointed and want to do better next quarter.

For the VP of CS

IQ → Long-Term Planning

Once that director becomes a VP, they'll need to have a deep understanding of how customers contribute to revenue. This requires "immersing themselves in the numbers," according to Andrea Lagan, the former COO at the professional services automation company FinancialForce and current chief customer officer at HR software company BetterWorks. Lagan notes that CS executives "need to be able to have a deep conversation with a CFO and the board about the metrics that explain how Customer Success contributes to the go-to-market framework." Specifically, we think that VPs should be able to analyze the linkages along the following chain:

- Activities
- Leading indicators
- Lagging outcomes (financial metrics)

Here are some common questions that a VP should be able to answer about the linkages between these:

- **Activities → Leading Indicators:**
  - How exactly will what CSMs are focused on today lead to improvements in the Customer Health Score(s)?
  - Why does that happen?

- Will that always happen in the future?
- How will our change in company strategy affect the linkage?
- How long is the delay from the completion of an activity to an improvement in the Score?
- Will CSMs have time to execute on activities A and B if we're now also giving them responsibility C, and how will that affect our ability to achieve a certain improvement in Customer Health Score?

- **Leading Indicators → Lagging Outcomes:**
  - How do improvements in the Customer Health Score(s) result in improvements in Gross Retention Rate and Net Retention Rate?
  - Why does that happen?
  - What's the exact correlation between the two? In other words, if we improve the Customer Health Score by X points, how many incremental points of Gross Retention Rate or Net Retention Rate does that generate?
  - Will that always happen in the future?
  - How will our change in company strategy affect the linkage?
  - How soon before the renewal does a customer have to be in a Green Health Score in order to make the renewal highly likely?

The VP may work with an analyst on their CS Operations team to answer these questions, but they'll need to own the knowledge of these linkages themselves. These are the types of questions that a capable CCO, CEO, and CFO will ask them during an executive meeting or when preparing for a board of directors meeting.

EQ → Executive Sponsorship

The VP should be able to substitute for the CCO or CEO in an important meeting with senior people at the most strategic clients, whether it's a meeting to address an escalation or a regularly occurring review of the partnership. (*Note:* We do believe that the CEO and CCO should be meeting with many clients, especially the more strategic ones. At the same time, the CEO and CCO can't be in all of those meetings. They need to be able to rely on their VP.) This means the ideal VP can help the internal team set a vision for the meeting in advance and prepare an agenda and content that will likely achieve that vision; create the right tone during the meeting;

listen carefully and read between the lines, surfacing topics that need to be elevated; orchestrate the interactions of client and internal stakeholders during the conversation; and drive the meeting to the right next steps.

Grit → Accountability

Even though a culture of accountability should exist at all levels of the organization, the VP demonstrates through their actions what accountability means. They should be thoughtful about communicating what happens when a CSM does or doesn't make their target for leading indicators or lagging outcomes, and likewise when the team does or doesn't make their targets. They should be clear about the importance of following playbooks. The VP answers to the CCO and CEO for achieving the Gross or Net Retention number, which means they take responsibility when the target is and isn't met and they are disciplined in learning the root causes of that achievement.

For the Chief Customer Officer

IQ → Cross-functional Orchestration

A company that's customer-centric will resemble a symphony, where every function is playing a different instrument but everyone is playing according to the same sheet music. While it's not the CCO's job to run the company, the CEO should be deeply familiar with the sheet music, design a significant section of it (for the functions that report to the CCO), and recommend improvements to the rest of it. This requires an ability to see a company's engagement with its clients as a system, as opposed to a loose collection of unique situations that aren't related to each other. Systems thinking involves detecting patterns and also imagining how alterations to those patterns could result in a system that generates better results for clients and for the company.

EQ → Inspiration

In our high-grit CS organization, everyone is hustling to execute their playbooks and improve them, achieve goals, and ensure accountability. But even people with unusually high grit need inspiration to fuel their hustle. They're not always inspired by the numbers, by operational initiatives, or by short-term wins. They want to feel they are contributing to a broader purpose. It's the job of the CCO to illuminate that purpose.

Here's how Allison thought about it in her former role as CCO at Gainsight.

> There's a particularly strong purpose in Customer Success. How humans interact with technology is a fundamental question of our time. Software is eating the world, robots are more capable than ever, and AI can replicate at least some human capabilities. Interestingly, Customer Success Managers are at the forefront of human-machine interaction in the business world. When software has bad UI, when it's imposed top-down, or when it's not natural to adopt, the CSM is on the front lines, empathizing with the poor human being who's struggling to use the software. It's the CSM's job to break down the barrier between human and machine, in a way that's human-first. To me, serving that purpose is among the most valuable causes we can contribute to in our lifetimes.

Team members don't just want a purpose to follow; they also want to see that their leaders are motivated by a broader purpose. We've spent a lot of time thinking about our purpose in our work, particularly since we each spend a lot of time (too much time?) reflecting on more existential questions. Last year, Prakash Raman, an executive coach, joined an offsite that Allison was hosting for her extended leadership team. He posed a question: "When you're on your deathbed, what do you want your legacy to be?" For Allison, it's pretty simple:

- I want to have built meaningful relationships with my family and others who I am close with.
- I want to have followed the ethical precepts that I hold dear, every step of the way. (The means matter, not just the end.)
- I want to have built communities that inspire others to create a more ethical world.

If we as leaders can be open in sharing with our teams what we hope our legacy will be, and helping them define their own desired legacies, our teams will feel a whole new level of inspiration in their work.

Grit → Mobilize Peers

For some CCOs, helping teams see the purpose in their work is the fun part of the role. But like everyone else on their team, CCOs need to hustle. Their hustle is in mobilizing their peers—the head of Sales, Marketing, Product Management, Engineering, Finance, and others—to factor customer-centric thinking into their decisions. It's the job of the CEO to manage the leadership team, but CCOs can provide an irreplicable source of information to those other executives about the Experiences and Outcomes that clients have. The ideal CCO doesn't merely share that information. Over the course of likely many conversations—with steps forward and steps back—they discuss, debate, and negotiate with other functions about how they might act on that information.

Obviously, we'd all love to have a world where every function was customer-centric in the ways we described in Part II of this book. But the CS movement hasn't fulfilled its mission yet, which means the CCO needs to act as a torchbearer for customer-centricity in the company. Evangelizing on behalf of clients is hard work. We've seen CCOs experience disillusionment, frustration, despair, and burnout. This is why our events for CCOs often turn into group therapy sessions. We highly recommend that CCOs demonstrate self-compassion, a willingness to express vulnerability to others who may be going through the same thing, and support for others who are struggling along the journey.

How Do I Train My Team on These Skills?

Many of us are familiar with the tactics for developing team members. Those may include enrolling them in internal training sessions on the product, bringing in an instructor to train on communication skills, paying for them to attend conferences, offering them online courses on a subject of interest, or delivering management training. So we won't beat the drum on those here, but we will suggest a few training mechanisms that you may not have thought of.

Sales Training

We discussed earlier the importance of prescriptive communication—listening deeply to the clients' needs and then being assertive in recommending a course of action that's in their best interest. Interestingly, this type of communication has been taught for many years—not to CSMs, but to salespeople. Sales training often helps people learn to fine-tune their awareness of clients' deeper pain points, challenge clients to reframe assumptions that are holding them back, and navigate the power structures of a client organization—skills that CSMs should have, too. Therefore, methodologies like the Challenger Sale, Corporate Visions, Sandler, and ProActive Selling are relevant for CSMs as well.

Networking

Trading notes with other people in the field is arguably more important in the CS profession than in any other one, because that profession is evolving so quickly. "We're still settling in on best practices," says Gleeson at KeepTruckin. "So it's important to have a large network, to keep up to speed on the latest trends. You need to make it one of your personal KPIs to get out of the office, even if it's just 30 minutes a week, to meet another person in Customer Success. Ask them all sorts of questions about their business and learn why they did the things that they did. That's the best way to educate yourself." Managers can encourage their team members to do this by making it culturally acceptable to leave the office for networking meetings, by proactively connecting their team members with others in their community, and by assigning networking KPIs to their team members. You might worry about losing your team members if they get recruited by one of those contacts—but honestly, the job market is so hot right now, they're probably already getting contacted by those hiring managers on LinkedIn. The benefits outweigh the costs when your team members are taking charge of their own professional development by learning from others.

Executive Coach

As we've discussed, CS leadership roles are emotionally challenging. You're often receiving emotions from your board, CEO, and peers (as other leadership roles do) but also your clients, and your team is often more stressed than other teams, since they're inheriting your clients' emotions, too. CS leaders can benefit from having a thought partner to work through situations that are not only intellectually challenging but emotionally challenging as well. An executive coach can serve this role. Sometimes they're expensive, but the better results you'll get from your CS leader will more than cover the cost.

Coach through Questioning

CEOs don't typically have much time to invest in coaching their CCOs. But they do have time to ask thoughtful questions—during executive team meetings, in one-on-one meetings, and in preparation for board meetings—that help the CCO focus on the right objectives and think more deeply about the initiatives that will help them achieve those objectives. Consequently, those questions can be an effective tool for coaching. We'll turn to a specific list of questions you can ask your CCO in the next section.

Ten Questions CEOs Should Ask Their CCOs

If you're a CEO, you know that your entire company is looking to you for answers. You probably spend a good part of your day responding to emails asking, "What should I do next?" or "What's the plan here?" As important as it is to have those answers, good leaders know that it's just as vital, if not more so, to ask the right questions. Nick's whole team knows that when they meet with him, they'd better be ready to answer some difficult questions. If you're an experienced CEO:

- You've been through enough bruising quarters to know how to interrogate your head of sales about the forecast, the pipeline, rep performance, and that shockingly large expense report.
- You've seen enough empty tradeshow booths and "PR campaigns" covered by no one but "PRNewswire" to know how to scrutinize proposals from your VP Marketing.
- You've seen enough slipped releases to know how to sanity-check your engineering leader's estimates to see if he or she is smoking something or just sandbagging.

But how do you helpfully question your chief customer officer or VP of Customer Success? Because Customer Success is such a relatively new discipline, a number of CEOs have asked me, "What questions should I be asking my CCO or VP Customer Success on a regular basis?" So Nick put together this top-10 list. If your leader can't answer these questions with conviction, they might not be right for the role.

1. What does success mean for our clients?

Many Customer Success leaders transitioned out of Customer Support or Services roles. In those positions, success equals "case closed" or success equals "project launched." But if you're a CSM, success isn't so much about what you accomplish, but what your client accomplishes. Your success depends on their success. And for a client, success is based upon a business outcome (more revenue, happier employees, etc.) and your product is just a tool for achieving that outcome. Their endgame isn't to renew or expand, though ideally both of those things are functions of it. Your CSM leader's job is to ensure they are. To do that, he or she needs to know the core goals of your clients.

2. What are early indicators of risk?

In many companies, part of the CSM role is to be Smokey the Bear—prevent fires before they happen. To do that, your Customer Success leader needs a clear vision of the drivers of risk for every account. These are things like sponsor change, support issues, technical issues, low adoption, long onboarding, and so forth. The best CSM leaders have a strong framework of risk so you can talk about risk in a consistent and quantitative way.

3. How can we tell if a client is sticky?

Orthogonal to risk, a CSM leader should have a view on what makes a client sticky so that they are likely to stay long-term. In the subscription economy, a six-month or one-year client is quite potentially a net loss for you when you factor in all the costs of acquiring it and onboarding it. Lifetime Value is the definitive measurement of a client's worth to your company. That being the case, your CSM team needs to be on top of the factors that increase your clients' LTV. How intrinsic is your product to the success of your client? Measuring that stickiness could involve assessing deep workflow usage, API integration, levels of data integration, or other factors.

4. How should we segment our clients?

This sounds like an easy question. Segment your clients by revenue, right? It's not so simple. Sophisticated leaders think hard about the unique needs of clusters of clients and their short-term/long-term economic value. We talked about lifetime value. Your CSM leader needs to project which low-revenue clients have high-growth potential and segment accordingly. And what about new verticals? Let's say all your clients are US-based B2B tech companies and you're looking to expand overseas or into B2C or healthcare. Your first clients in those verticals need a higher level of touch to set the tone for your entire expansion. They may have lower revenue right now, but they still belong in a higher tier. Does your CCO or VP Customer Success think in terms of big-picture strategy?

5. What segments should we not serve?

Once you have a segmentation, you need to be strategic about whom we choose to serve, but equally important is whom we choose not to serve. No company has unlimited resources. Every company has a spectrum of capabilities with hard limits at both ends. Past that limit at the top end of the spectrum are high-value clients who, unfortunately, need more than you can offer, at least right now. Under the limit at the low end are clients who will take up way too much of your resources without returning enough value to justify the costs. Obviously there are always exceptions, and it's your CCO's job to recognize where the limits and exceptions are. Great leaders can tell you where you're not delivering on your promise and where the economics don't work out.

6. How do you decide on how many accounts your team members manage?

Great leaders also know how to play to the strengths of their team. A big part of your CSM leader's job will be strategizing how to vary CSM workloads by segment, revenue, and account-based loading. It's all about using the right tool for the job—and tools become essential for organizing your CSM touch levels. Your CCO or VP Marketing will definitely be incorporating pure or partial automation for many clients. They will need to make the call on which clients get which level of touch.

7. **What's our cost model?**

When you talk to your head of Sales, you don't just ask about revenues, you ask about costs. Just like you make sure to have a target gross margin, CSM leaders should have a perspective on target Customer Retention Cost, both today and long-term. The best Customer Success executives have thought through an overall model of the total annual cost to retain a given amount of revenue. Customer Success is rightfully concerned with the total LTV of customers, but the immediate day-to-day costs need to factor into your equations.

8. **What's your economic value—how should I measure you?**

When your Sales team consistently misses goals, it's a pretty cut-and-dried situation. A VP Sales knows that his or her value is intrinsically tied to revenues. But how is your VP Customer or CCO measured? Churn? Renewals? Upsells? All of those events are heavily influenced by every other customer-facing department. However they do it, top leaders put a dollar value on their work. Get your CSM leader to turn health scores, renewal rates, Net Promoter surveys, and other data points into an ROI for their team and their job—then hold him or her to those standards.

9. **What do you need from the rest of the company to drive success for our clients?**

As we said, every interaction a customer has with your company and your product is a potential hinge-point for their success. Their overall health is going to depend on your CSM team, yes, but also on your Product team, your Sales team, Services and Support, and others. World-class VPs of Customer Success build processes to feed customer input to Product teams and qualification criteria and messaging to Sales teams. As a CEO, it's your job to make sure that your whole company is aligned on Customer Success. In the subscription economy, it quite literally is your bottom line.

10. **What should I do and *not do* to culturally support Customer Success?**

You don't become a CEO by being insular to the culture of your company. When you read stories about failed startups and burned-out executives, they always have a huge cultural component. The only way to lead in this area is to constantly be in touch with your executive team and your employees. Specifically to Customer Success, you want a CSM leader who is pushing you to put the customer at the center of your strategy. When you make a decision, your VP Customer or CCO had better be convinced it has the best interest of your client base at heart. The strongest executives challenge their CEO on his or her calendar, messaging, and priorities to always keep customers' success top of mind.

Of course, this is all a moot point if you don't have a CCO or VP Customer Success. We know there are some companies out there that are still waiting to hire an executive. If that's you, you're behind the curve. If you've already hired an executive, continue to challenge them with questions like these to make them the best they can be.

Summary

We discussed in this chapter the importance of IQ, EQ, and grit to the CS profession and how CS folks can improve their skills in each area as they progress in their career. We also discussed how CEOs can ensure they're cultivating the right behaviors in their CCO by asking them questions that matter. Now that we've defined what "amazing skills" look like in this chapter, in the next chapter we'll turn to the best practices for creating an inclusive environment that encourages every team member to bring their "A Game."

28 | Inclusion: How Can I Create a Diverse Team?

"My job is to hire great people, put them in the right seats, and get out of the way." How often have we heard leaders share this statement? Unfortunately, this belief of what leadership entails is fundamentally flawed for many reasons. Although we never got law degrees, we're putting on our deductive reasoning hats!

We'll point to two flawed assumptions in the statement above:

(A) That each "seat" is a slot that can be filled by a person who is "strong" by some measure that is independent from the rest of the team
(B) That the people in those seats don't need to be actively managed

Regarding premise A, you've probably seen throughout this book that we believe that a company—together with its clients and community—is an organism with inextricably linked organs. No "seat" on a team is siloed from the others. As a result, we think a leader should manage their team like a *team* and not as a collection of unconnected individuals. As a result, a leader should fill a slot with the person that creates the best-performing *team*.

Despite the lists of skills that we believe strong CS professionals will exhibit (described in the previous chapter), at the end of the day your team won't be high performing if you hire a seemingly "top-notch" CS professional that doesn't contribute to a strong team dynamic.

We think premise B is also misguided because leaders need to actively foster a productive team dynamic. Even if we don't believe in strongly hierarchical organizations, we do believe that leaders exist for a reason: to make life better for everyone else.

In contrast with the beliefs above, we think that effective leaders:

- See their teams, together with their clients, as a complex ecosystem as opposed to a collection of siloed individuals.
- Optimize for the maximum performance of the team as a whole when filling open roles.
- Actively solve for a strong team dynamic on a day-to-day basis.

You might wonder, what does this analysis have to do with *inclusion*, the title of this chapter? As it turns out, we think it has everything to do with it. Specifically, effective leaders:

- Recognize that diversity, inclusion, and belonging are attributes of the most successful teams (as described in the abundance of literature on this topic, which we won't attempt to replicate here).
- Consider the diversity of the team as an important attribute to solve for when hiring for an open slot.
- Actively implement, on a day-to-day basis, best practices for making team members feel included and feel a strong sense of belonging.

That said, we're not experts on inclusion, and we're not looking to discuss inclusion as a broader topic here. What we do want to cover is the connection between inclusion and Customer Success. So let's turn to the experts to understand that topic more deeply.

Why Inclusion Is Specifically Important in Customer Success

Let's bring back Coco Brown, the CEO of Athena Alliance who spoke about purpose-driven organizations in Chapter 6. She says, "Our clients may be diverse on many dimensions—whether race, religion, place of origin, sexual orientation, or other attribute." And when our clients are diverse, they'll want to see that our teams are diverse, too. That's true even if you don't subscribe to the philosophy (and we don't) that you should pair "like" with "like" (i.e. match the CSM to the individual client with similar characteristics). The real point here is that diverse client organizations want to see diverse *vendor* organizations, because it makes them feel included in your ecosystem in the same way that your employees want to feel included in your organization.

Moreover, Brown points out that a CSM team that recognizes the diversity within its clients will likely also notice that "people experience products differently and need adjustments in those products and associated services to make them more accessible to a wider range of diverse people." A diverse CSM team can help give the feedback to other teams at the company to help make the product and services more inclusive.

Customer Success May Help Increase Diversity

For the reasons above (and for many others as well), we believe it's important that Customer Success teams should continue to improve their diversity and their team members' feelings of inclusion and belonging. Even though we have a lot more work to do, we as a community can point to some victories. We found through a LinkedIn data analysis in 2018 that 48% of CS professionals were female. And, the gender diversity that has already appeared within the Customer Success industry has been a driver of increased diversity at the senior levels of companies.

Alexis Hennessey, the executive recruiter at Heidrick & Struggles, observes,

> When I'm placing CS executives, they might be the only female member of the entire executive leadership team. Because this role wasn't at the executive level a few years ago, that opportunity didn't exist. Now that this role has been elevated and is oftentimes a direct report to the CEO, we're able to shift the makeup of executive teams, which is a great feeling. We're able to change the landscape of what executive teams look like by bringing in diverse talent in Customer Success.

In fact, the relatively strong presence of women in Customer Success (compared with many other functions within a company) and the rise of that function's importance has resulted in more women being evaluated for board positions. Brown observes,

> Boards are finally realizing that the boardroom needs to be far more dynamic than simply a set of former and current sitting CEOs and financial experts. Their combined capabilities are not sufficient to handle the kinds of issues that boards are faced with in today's world. Specifically, boards repeatedly fall down on the human elements that are actually all about Customer Success, for example, the crises that Boeing or United Airlines have faced recently. Today, crises like these have to be handled not just by the CEO but by the board, and with a great deal of care, because our lives are at stake sometimes, as well as the stock price and market share. So people who know how to build a deep connection to the customer, gauge their sentiment, engage with them, and feed customer sentiment back into the main engine of the organization—these people are extremely valuable as board members.

Who could be a better candidate to fill this gap in typical board capabilities than a CCO? And when a significant percentage of CCOs are women that means we'll end up with more women in the boardroom.

When there isn't someone knowledgeable about Customer Success in the boardroom, the board may not understand some of the key concepts their executive team is presenting to them. Brown notes, "If you're a growth-stage, SaaS, venture-backed company, every board meeting is likely to cover Churn, Net Promoter Score, and Expansion, and the CS leader has to be very strategic about how to address those metrics. The discussion goes beyond a salesperson's numbers and toward how to strategically engage customers." She adds, "Also, there are quite a few large public companies that we've talked to that realize that they have to embrace new ways of engaging with their customer, and that's not just about a marketing function. It's about how they listen to customers, how they onboard them, the innovation roadmap." A CS leader serving on a board can offer a unique vantage point to advise the executive team during those discussions.

Brown adds,

The boardroom used to be a place where you would go to share your wisdom in your retiring years. You'd fade off into the sunset through board service. But the problem is that business models are changing so rapidly. The Customer Success function didn't really exist ten years ago. So retirees may not be familiar with it. Modern boards are thinking more intently about hiring folks who are still in operating roles, which allow them to tap into more recently gained knowledge. That includes current CS leaders.

And many of them are women.

Summary

The rising tide of Customer Success presents a unique opportunity to create more gender-diverse companies, executive teams, and boards. Even though the CS movement may be a tailwind for more gender-diverse teams, CS leaders need to invest in ensuring greater diversity on other dimensions such as race, sexual orientation, and others, and to ensure that team members feel a sense of inclusion and belonging once they're on the team.

Now that you've studied the playbook for how to launch CS in an established business, what's next? In the next chapter, we'll send you on your way with a few action items in hand.

29 | Next Steps to Take

It's been a highlight of our careers to see so many people benefiting from Customer Success—from people pursuing their career dreams, to clients benefiting from more customer-centric vendors, to investors generating greater returns from shareholders due to stronger client retention and advocacy. Customer Success is truly one of those movements that has generated "Success for All."

Take this story from Jane Graham, the VP Customer Success and Renewals at Kronos, Inc.

Less than six years ago, I was a senior manager of a $700 million publicly traded company, managing a team of 15 people. Fast forward six years, I am the vice president of a global team of 200 people managing $1 billion in recurring revenue across thousands of customers. And that happened because I started focusing my career on recurring revenue and Customer Success precisely at the time that I did, and I embedded myself in that discipline. When I think about my career trajectory, if I hadn't focused on that specific area in the technology sector, I don't think I would have had that kind of amplified growth and amplified career opportunity.

Graham isn't alone. This is a space that tens of thousands of people are betting their careers on and they've grown tremendously because of it.

Consider also the impact on the investment community. Mark Roberge, the former CRO at HubSpot, began investing in startups with the intention of betting on companies with higher retention even more than higher growth.

> We think very differently from traditional investors. I believe as entrepreneurs and investors we suffer from a premature obsession over top-line revenue growth. One of the first questions that investors ask an entrepreneur is, "How fast are you growing revenue?" There's this belief that you need to "triple, triple, double, double" over four years. I am not against rapid scale. We simply need to understand the pre-requirements that need to be in place before rapid scale is pursued. The most important of these prerequisites is consistent customer value creation. That is why I look at Customer Success and retention first when I'm considering an investment.

Roberge points out that Customer Success can lead to a higher success rate among entrepreneurs, helping more people change their lives and their industries and generating higher returns among investors.

And of course, the CS movement has revolutionized the client experience. Customer-centric vendors help employees at their clients cope with the overwhelming intervention of technology into their working lives. Here's how Catherine Blackmore, the GVP of Customer Success at Oracle, explains it.

> The thing that I love about this profession is that we've gone well beyond the trainings, the tutorials, the pushing buttons, the launching of campaigns. We've now gone to changing individuals' lives and changing the way we even think about developing technology. I tell my team that you are here to change lives, to change the industry, to change the future of software. We are here to ultimately change the face of professions and of how we see the future of humanity using technology. But it has to start somewhere. It has to start with these little things that we do every day to help people use technology.

Beyond just benefiting individual stakeholders, we truly believe that the Customer Success movement is one of the primary forces that will shape human-machine interaction in the twenty-first century. We hope we've convinced you that the Customer Success movement is a win-win-win for your team members, your investors, and your clients. So what should you do next?

If You're a CEO

1. **Work with a recruiter to hire a great CS leader:** As we've discussed in this book, hiring in CS has dramatically evolved since the early days of the movement. Look for a CS leader with strong interdepartmental leadership skills, orientation toward revenue growth, and a systems thinker. Headhunters can be helpful in finding this candidate, but you'll need to help close them by demonstrating during the recruiting process that you'll set them up for success by being customer-centric yourself!

2. **Start including CS metrics in your board deck:** Think of your Customer Success metrics across three broader categories: Topline Financials (Gross and Net Retention), Cost Metrics (CSM Cost as % of Revenue, and ARR per CSM), and Leading Indicators (e.g. a Customer Health Score).

3. **Talk to more clients:** Chances are you're under-budgeting your time spent with customers. As a CEO, the most valuable thing you can do with any given hour is spend it talking—or more importantly, listening—to your customers. As we discussed, the average CEO spends 5.6% of their time with customers according to the *Harvard Business Review*. We think a good starting point for most CEOs would be to at least double that.

4. **Figure out how to "industrialize Customer Success":** Using the phrase from a CEO earlier in the book, we challenge you to figure out how to take the cultural values of customer-centricity that are likely on your walls and in your peoples' hearts and turn them into results in the eyes of your clients. Just like you brought data, process, and systems to sales, marketing, finance, HR, and other areas, it's time to do the same for your clients and for your long-term revenue.

5. **Assess and benchmark your customer success maturity and capabilities.** Research has proven that more your customer-facing teams unite around better processes and technology, the faster your revenue will grow. So how close are you to taking that step? Gainsight has created a helpful online assessment to help you find out by evaluating: 1) How you compare to companies your size across the 14 core Elements of Customer Success; 2) Where your company's strengths and weaknesses lie in terms of Customer Success; and 3) How to improve your sophistication in each Customer Success Element. You can take the free, personalized assessment at https://www.gainsight.com/maturity-model/.

If You're a CS Leader

1. **Conduct an offsite with your team about what customers expect of you (not what you expect of them):** The core of becoming a truly customer-centric company is a fundamental mindset and culture shift away from "inside-out" thinking and toward "outside-in" thinking. That means everything needs to start with the customer: who they are, what they expect, and how they define success.

2. **Hire a consulting firm to design your customer journey:** Your customer journey is going to define everything you do, not just in CSM, but in every touchpoint from every department. As the most important strategic exercise your company will do, it's critical you get it right.

3. **Training for your team around new skills for CS:** The amount of resources available has increased dramatically, and best practices have begun to standardize. An education and certification platform like Pulse+ will give you prescriptive best practices for both career and departmental development.

4. **Participate in events:** Pulse is the largest annual Customer Success conference in the world. It's hosted by Gainsight, but it's not a client conference—it's truly for the industry and it's not a product pitch. Attending industry events like Pulse plugs you into the latest research and networking opportunities, and above all, lets you know you're not alone.

5. **Join the CS community on LinkedIn:** The Customer Success Community on LinkedIn is one of the most vibrant communities for

leaders not just in CSM but in many post-sales roles at customer-centric companies.

6. **Assess and benchmark your customer success maturity and capabilities.** Research has proven that more your customer-facing teams unite around better processes and technology, the faster your revenue will grow. So how close are you to taking that step? Gainsight has created a helpful online assessment to help you find out by evaluating: 1) How you compare to companies your size across the 14 core Elements of Customer Success; 2) Where your company's strengths and weaknesses lie in terms of Customer Success; and 3) How to improve your sophistication in each Customer Success Element. You can take the free, personalized assessment at https://www.gainsight.com/maturity-model/.

If You're a CS Practitioner, or if You Want to Become One

1. **Enroll in Pulse+ training:** Pulse+ was designed and built by some of the longest-tenured CS practitioners in the world and is the largest repository of educational materials in the CS universe.
2. **Read the CS Handbook:** *The Customer Success Handbook* (also published by Wiley—available in bookstores everywhere) is indispensable for CS practitioners. It's the only tactical, day-to-day guide for the CSM job and was written with incredible detail and academic rigor.
3. **Join the Customer Success community on LinkedIn:** Your next career opportunity is likely to come from the connections you make in this community. Be active and involved and watch your career blossom!
4. **Participate in Events:** As valuable as events like Pulse are for CS leaders, they can be even more valuable for connecting and training the CS leaders of tomorrow.
5. **Assess and benchmark your customer success maturity and capabilities.** Research has proven that more your customer-facing teams unite around better processes and technology, the faster your revenue will grow. So how close are you to taking that step? Gainsight has created a helpful online assessment to help you find out by evaluating: 1) How you compare to companies your size across the 14 core Elements of Customer Success; 2) Where your company's strengths and weaknesses lie in terms of Customer Success; and 3) How to improve

your sophistication in each Customer Success Element. You can take the free, personalized assessment at https://www.gainsight.com/maturity-model/.

And if you've made it this far, you are on to the path for driving more results for your clients, for your team, and for your business. Here's to your success!

Notes

1. Michael Porter and James Heppelmann, "How Smart, Connected Products Are Transforming Companies," *Harvard Business Review, Harvard Business Publishing,* October 2015, https://hbr.org/2015/10/how-smart-connected-products-are-transforming-companies.

2. Marc Andreessen, "Why Software Is Eating the World," *Wall Street Journal, Dow Jones Publications*, August 20, 2011, https://www.wsj.com/articles/SB10001424053111903480904576512250915629460.

3. Laura Ramon, "Advocate Marketing Creates B2B Customer Relationships That Last a Lifetime" (Cambridge, MA: Forrester Research Inc., September 28, 2015), https://static1.squarespace.com/static/5006b364e4b09ef2252d3129/t/5911fa46d2b857d98bac89cb/1494350409563/forrester-advocate-marketing.pdf.

4. "Referrals Fuel Highest B2B Conversion Rates," *eMarketer, eMarketer Inc.*, February 10, 2015, https://www.emarketer.com/Article/Referrals-Fuel-Highest-B2B-Conversion-Rates/1012000.

5. Allyson White, "The Tortoise Wins the Race: The Value of Retention," *Insight Partners (blog)*, July 27, 2016, https://www.insightpartners.com/blog/the-tortoise-wins-the-race-the-value-of-retention/.

6. Oriana Bandiera, Stephen Hansen, Andrea Prat, and Raffaella Sadun, "CEO Behavior and Firm Performance," Harvard Business School Working Paper, No. 17–083 (March 2017), https://dash.harvard.edu/bitstream/handle/1/30838134/17-083.pdf?sequence=1&isAllowed=y.

7. "The BVP Nasdaq Emerging Cloud Index," Bessemer Venture Partners, updated January 2020, https://www.bvp.com/bvp-nasdaq-emerging-cloud-index.

8. Tim Urban, "If You Could Design Your Child, How Would You Dole Out IQ, EQ, and Grit?" *Wait But Why*, https://waitbutwhy.com/table/iq-eq-grit.

Acknowledgments

There are countless people whom we'd like to thank for their role in bringing this book to fruition. You may be a client who inspired us during a meeting, a participant at a Pulse conference who asked a thoughtful question, an organizer of a local Customer Success meet-up who shared an observation, or a community member who messaged one of us on LinkedIn. These interactions, no matter how brief, helped shape our perspectives on the Customer Success profession and on how our industry can transform client relationships. Thank you for sharing your voice with us.

We're indebted to the dozens of insightful leaders who shared the many perspectives, stories, and case studies of Customer Success that are spread throughout this book. You're thought leaders in your own right, and we're grateful that you took the time to be interviewed by us and lend your perspectives. This book is much closer to being a true guide to navigating the CS economy because you were a part of it.

We'd like to thank several people who were instrumental in the writing of this book. Robin Garcia-Amaya, Gainsight's VP Communications and Chief of Staff to Nick, led and managed this journey from inception to delivery and then launch; her insight on the narrative and ability to corral executives across the Customer Success industry and our team of editors was invaluable. Natalie Alderete, Allison's all-star executive assistant, went above and beyond her role to conduct dozens of interviews and coordinate the process of many revisions. Our designer Hayley Cromwell created all the beautiful images in this book and delivered on a tight timeframe. Saphiya Hindeyeh, our Public Relations Manager, helpfully stepped in to project-manage the last mile of submitting the manuscript.

We'd like to thank several Gainsight team members for their contributions and for the content of the original blog posts that informed parts of this book (in alphabetical order by last name): Carissa Aiello Berube, Saphiya Hindeyeh, Matt Klassen, Barr Moses, Ruben Rabago, Will Robins, Saood Shah, Priyanka Srinivasan, and Seth Wylie. Along with other CS executives at Gainsight, our CCO Ashvin Vaidyanathan has been a major contributor to the development and implementation of many of the best practices described in this book over the last five years. Gainsight's VP Finance Alka Tandan and CFO Igor Beckerman offered their financial expertise to inform several chapters.

The Wiley team have been partners to us in our book writing for years. We're grateful to Richard Narramore, our executive editor at Wiley, for believing in the audience for books about Customer Success and making this sequel to the first CS book possible. We're also grateful to Victoria Anllo and Vicki Adang from Wiley for guiding us through this process and generously giving us as much flexibility as they could in the timeline for editing.

Finally, we'd like to thank the people in our lives who were supportive during the writing of this book. Allison would like to thank her husband, Scott, for being an incredibly thoughtful sounding board, even when her ideas are half-baked. She is also grateful to Scott, her brother Andy, her parents Estee and Peter, and her close friends for their consistent encouragement during the long, wondrous, exciting, and challenging journey that is building a company and community. The start of that journey was sparked by Ajay Agarwal and Roger Lee, partners at Bain Capital Ventures and Battery Ventures, respectively, who connected Allison and Nick in 2013. The journey was made all the richer by Allison's team, who have given her fond memories of painting on blank canvases that seemed too big, all while questioning what art means to begin with. Finally, it wouldn't be right for Allison not to thank Nick for his partnership through thick and thin all these years, made even more enjoyable by a shared appreciation for philosophy, Salt & Straw ice cream, and Taylor Swift's music.

Nick would like to thank his partner of nearly 20 years, Monica Gupta Mehta, for being the source of confidence, strength, and dynamism in his life. Thanks to Asha, Amar, and Anjali for defining child-like joy for Nick every day. Thanks to Nick's parents, Ramesh and Meena Mehta, and brother, Samir Mehta, for giving him so much love every day. On the work front, thanks to Roger Lee from Battery Ventures, who got Nick started on the journey with Gainsight. Thanks to Gainsight's founders, Jim Eberlin and Sreedhar Peddineni, for bringing Nick into Gainsight in 2013. Thanks to the rest of the Gainsight board and investors: Ajay Agarwal from Bain Capital Ventures, Byron Deeter from Bessemer Venture Partners, Jeff Lieberman from Insight Venture Partners, Nakul Mandan from Lightspeed Venture Partners, Kirk Bowman, Kristen Helvey, Sue Barsamian, Pegah Ebrahimi from Cisco, Greg Goldfarb from Summit Partners, and Ben Johnston from TPG Sixth Street Partners. Thanks to the almost 700 Gainsters who live our values every day, and to the families that support us. And Nick would like to close by thanking Allison for six years of business friendship—from Pulse to PX, from career growth to karaoke, from Mountain View to Hyderabad, from hedgehogs to foxes, with ice cream throughout.

And special thanks from both of us to the massive and growing Customer Success community. To quote *Hamilton*, "Scratch that, this is not a moment, it's a movement!"

About the Authors

Nick Mehta is CEO of Gainsight, *The Customer Success Company*. He works with a team of nearly 700 people who together have created the customer success category that's currently taking over the SaaS business model worldwide. Nick has been named one of the Top SaaS CEOs by the Software Report three years in a row, one of the Top CEOs of 2018 by Comparably and was a finalist for EY's Entrepreneur of the Year. On top of all that, he was recently rated the #1 CEO in the world (the award committee was just his mom, but the details are irrelevant). He also co-authored *Customer Success: How Innovative Companies Are Reducing Churn and Growing Recurring Revenue*, the authoritative book on the field.

He is passionate about family, football, philosophy, physics, fashion, feminism, and SaaS customer success. People told him it's impossible to combine all of those interests, but Nick has made it his life's mission to try.

Allison Pickens is one of the world's top experts on the business transformation that accompanies the shift to the cloud, having coached thousands of executives at public companies and startups alike. She is part of the Fortune Most Powerful Women community and was named one of the Top Women in SaaS and Top 50 People in Sales and Business Development. She has served as chief operating officer at Gainsight, an independent board director, an investor at Bain Capital and an angel investor, and a strategy consultant at BCG. Allison's passion for moral philosophy has made her an advocate  for technology that puts humans first. She has a degree in Ethics, Politics, and Economics from Yale and an MBA from Stanford.

Allison and her husband love to spend time hiking in the woods, deep in conversation about climate change, the gut biome, affordable housing, or a recent podcast they listened to.

Index